BARNUM

This Large Print Book carries the Seal of Approval of N.A.V.H.

BARNUM

AN AMERICAN LIFE

ROBERT WILSON

THORNDIKE PRESS
A part of Gale, a Cengage Company

Farmington Hills, Mich • San Francisco • New York • Waterville, Maine
Meriden, Conn • Mason, Ohio • Chicago

LIBRARY OF CONGRESS CIP DATA ON FILE.
CATALOGUING IN PUBLICATION FOR THIS BOOK
IS AVAILABLE FROM THE LIBRARY OF CONGRESS

ISBN-13: 978-1-4328-6425-5 (hardcover alk. paper)

Published in 2019 by arrangement with Simon & Schuster, Inc.

Printed in the United States of America
1 2 3 4 5 6 7 23 22 21 20 19

For Martha
and for
Leyli Thea Wilson
and
Lawrence Ritchie Wilson

In Memory of
Mario Pellicciaro

CONTENTS

INTRODUCTION:
"DO YOU KNOW BARNUM?"

Adopting Mr. Emerson's idea, I should say that Barnum is a representative man. He represents the enterprise and energy of his countrymen in the nineteenth century, as Washington represented their resistance to oppression in the century preceding.

— John Delaware Lewis,
Across the Atlantic, 1851

In 1842, the man who would become America's greatest showman received a visit from a museum owner in Boston who needed his help. Moses Kimball had made his way to P. T. Barnum's office in New York City with a box that, he baldly claimed, contained the remains of a mermaid. When the box was opened and the object was unwrapped, what Barnum saw was a shrunken, blackish thing about three feet long that seemed pretty obviously to be the head and torso of a

9

monkey joined to the lower portion of a large fish. Kimball had a story to go with this desiccated corpse, something about its being discovered by sailors in the South Seas, but he had no idea what to do with it. Although the two men had not previously met, their establishments had collaborated on several acts and exhibitions. Barnum had recently acquired a dusty old museum on lower Broadway, dubbed it the American Museum, and dedicated it to natural history, art and artifacts, performances, and an exuberant miscellany of anything that caught his eye. The growing renown of the new museum, along with Barnum's already established reputation as an impresario with a knack for publicity, made him a logical person for Kimball to go to for advice.[1]

While Kimball wondered what could be done with this grotesque specimen — so different from the beautiful mythological beings that people had imagined for centuries — Barnum didn't hesitate. He offered to lease the object from Kimball and present it to the public himself. After giving the creature an exotic name — the Fejee Mermaid — he created a bold strategy to conjure up a storm of interest in it.

Within days Barnum was executing a complicated plan to acquire free publicity from the press. He sent letters to friends in cities in the South, all telling a made-up story about a British naturalist who had acquired the mermaid in the Fiji Islands and was stopping in New York on his way to London, where it would be put on display. This naturalist was supposedly passing through the South, and every few days a friend from a different southern city would mail one of Barnum's letters, which were written as news reports of local happenings, to a different New York newspaper. While he was whetting the appetite of the press, Barnum had posters made of beautiful, bare-breasted mermaids with long blond curls, implying that this was what the Fejee Mermaid had once looked like. By the time the supposed naturalist reached New York, the press was in a frenzy, and Barnum gave three different newspapers an unsigned report that he had written defending the existence of mermaids, along with an idealized image in woodcut, suitable for printing. Each of the newspapers was promised an exclusive, and it was only when all three published the story on the same Sunday morning that they knew they had been hoodwinked. If the editors were miffed, they didn't show it by withholding coverage of the exhibit. After all, Barnum was a steady advertiser, and this new exhibit would mean new ads each day in their newspapers.

It's safe to say that most people who came to see the Fejee Mermaid and hear the ersatz naturalist talk about it were not taken in. But Barnum's early publicity drew huge crowds to the display, and even if they doubted that this shriveled specimen had ever been the lovely, storied creature in the posters, still it was a thing worth seeing and judging for themselves. Whatever the skepticism of his patrons, the showman didn't let up in the weeks that followed. With a steady stream of ads, often warning that the display would soon be leaving for London, augmented by a barrage of pamphlets and posters, he kept the customers coming. When the flow of visitors finally slowed, he sent the Fejee Mermaid out on the road. His plan, which had come to him in an instant when he first saw the specimen, had worked to perfection.

Later in life, Barnum would confess that he was not proud of this exhibit, but even then he could not resist exulting in the success of his publicity scheme. The Fejee Mermaid was characteristic of Barnum's exhibitions during his early years; even as a young man he had an unfailing sense of what the public wanted, yet he could be brazenly manipulative and unafraid of controversy. These qualities made him successful as a showman, but they also made it possible for him to push too far. When, for instance, he had put on tour an elderly slave woman who claimed to be the 161-year-old former nursemaid to George Washington, the newspapers and other guardians of public virtue howled, condemning him for exploiting her. At other times, Barnum drew criticism less for his actions than for his attitude. When he published the first version of his autobiography, in 1855, detailing his many humbugs and the riches they had afforded him, some reviewers were disgusted not so much by the original sins but by his seeming pride in admitting to them. He was often seen as a man who would do anything for a buck, and by the time he was middle-aged, the quip "Where's Barnum?" was applied to any novelty, discovery, or invention of the day, under the assumption that he would soon show up to add it to his museum collection.

The missteps of Barnum's early career would ultimately damage his reputation in a lasting way. Well after his death in 1891, his image in the public mind congealed around another phrase, this one attributed to Barnum himself: "There's a sucker born every minute." The cynical saying implies that he was no better than a huckster, whose chief goal was using fast talk to trick people out of their money while giving them nothing in return. Even to this day, these words serve as shorthand for Barnum's philosophy as a showman, but no evidence exists that he ever spoke or wrote them. What's worse, they utterly misrepresent the man as he really was.

The actual arc of Barnum's life is much more interesting, and much more consequential, than his present-day reputation suggests. He may have begun his career as a promoter of sketchy acts in a business that was often considered less than respectable, but he changed both himself and the business over the decades, earning the respect of Americans of every station. Because he had so determinedly placed himself in the public eye, people knew all about his early missteps as well as his successes — his "struggles and triumphs," as the title of a later version of his autobiography puts it. He didn't hesitate to show his flaws, but he would also reveal in time that he was that rare thing, a man who was steered by his ideals, becoming a better person as he navigated a long lifetime. Over many years, Barnum became a steady, civic-minded, fun-loving man who cultivated a close relationship with his audience and embodied many of the best aspects of the American character. He eventually won over the public with his unflagging energy, his wit and buoyant good humor, his patriotic zeal for the Union side in the Civil War, and his commitment to charitable causes, good government, and his Universalist faith.

He is known today primarily for his connection to the circus, but that came only in the last quarter of his long life. His principal occupations before that were running the American Museum and being the impresario behind the witty and talented dwarf Tom Thumb, the angelic Swedish soprano Jenny Lind — who created a sensation in America in the early 1850s — and dozens of other acts and traveling shows. Less well known today is that he was also a bestselling author, an inspirational lecturer on temperance and on success in business and in life, a real-estate developer, a builder, a banker, a state legislator, and the mayor of the city of Bridgeport, Connecticut, near or in which he lived for most of his adult life. He was even a candidate for Congress, losing a bare-knuckle contest to a cousin also named Barnum. In all of these endeavors he was a promoter and self-promoter without peer, a relentless advertiser and an unfailingly imaginative concoctor of events or exhibits to draw the interest, often the feverish interest, of potential patrons.

Throughout his life, Barnum worked steadily to transform the image of public entertainment in America. In the long middle of his career, his American Museum included what he called a Lecture Room, where, in addition to lectures, both dramas and melodramas were presented. At the time, theaters were not considered morally or even physically safe places for children and families. Prostitutes often plied their trade in the balconies, and sobriety was not much in evidence even in the orchestra seats. But Barnum enforced an environment in both the museum and the Lecture Room that was free of drunkenness, improper behavior, and anything else that could give offense to people whose scruples might otherwise keep them away. He emphasized the moral quality of his dramas and the safety of his exhibit spaces, ensuring that customers of all ages could enjoy them. Later he and his partner James A. Bailey brought this same commitment to the rough-and-tumble world of the traveling circus, presenting entertainment that even Barnum's many preacher friends could defend, in a setting that was appropriate for families and children.

By the end of his life, he was admired and respected not only in the United States but also across much of the globe. When the Barnum & Bailey Circus, immodestly but accurately called The Greatest Show on Earth, traveled through the American heartland in the 1880s, Barnum would often go out to meet the show and thereby boost its attendance numbers. Rural circus-goers took special trains put on to carry them to the cities where the traveling extravaganza typically stopped. The reason for these excursions, on what were known as "Barnum days," was often to see the showman as much as the show. He had become as close to a global celebrity as a person could be at the time. After Ulysses S. Grant's second term as president, the great general made a two-year tour of the world, promoting the United States. Upon his return, Barnum said to him, "General, I think you are the best known American living," to which Grant replied, "By no means. You beat me sky-high, for wherever I went . . . the constant inquiry was, 'Do you know Barnum?' "[2]

Central to Barnum's philosophy and success was the relationship to his audience that he developed during his decades as a showman. That relationship centered on the single word most associated with Barnum in his lifetime: *humbug.* As he himself wrote in his 1865 book, *The Humbugs of the World,* Webster's definition is "to deceive; to impose on." Definitions today include the words *hoax, fraud, impostor, nonsense, trick.* Barnum's book is a survey of such practices, intended, he said, to save the rising generation from being bamboozled by the unscrupulous, whether in religion, business, politics, medicine, or science. But for Barnum, not all forms of humbug were hurtful; sometimes humbuggery could be harmless, even joyous. He claimed that, for him, the "generally accepted definition" of *humbug* focused on this benign variety, what he defined as "putting on glittering appearances . . . novel expedients, by which to suddenly arrest public attention, and attract the public eye and ear." In other words, what he did. The crux of the matter was that a person who attracted patrons in this way but then "foolishly fails to give them a full equivalent for their money," would not get a second chance from customers who would "properly denounce him as a swindler, a cheat, an impostor."[3]

So for Barnum, who sometimes called himself the "Prince of Humbugs," humbuggery was a mildly deceitful way to get people in the door, but its harmlessness depended entirely on how satisfied they were once inside. "I don't believe in 'duping the public,' " he wrote in a letter in 1860, "but I believe in first *attracting* & then pleasing them." For many years, he charged only a quarter, half that for children, to visit his museum and see his shows there, while he tirelessly searched the globe for more and better acts, exhibits, and curiosities, and spent freely on them to reward that small investment by his patrons. People might be drawn in to see the human curiosities he exhibited, the giants and little people of both sexes, the bearded ladies, fat children, and stick-like men, the albinos, American Indians, Chinese princesses, Siamese twins, and the What Is It? — an exhibit presented as the possible missing link between beast and man suggested by Darwin's recent book about evolution. But once inside his museum, they would be exposed to what he advertised as a million objects. In a period when public education, photography, the telegraph, the railroad, and the newspaper were all making the world a smaller and more knowable place, people flocked to

Barnum's museum, and when he took displays to other cities, he rarely failed to draw big crowds.[4]

As a businessman, Barnum never apologized for making vast amounts of money, but he did believe that his museum offered his patrons the chance to learn. And if a little trickery — such as turning a hideous, shrunken thing into an alluring mermaid from the South Pacific — was needed to get people to view the serious exhibits, then, he came to believe, they should be in on the trick. He would often hint at the dubiousness of his latest sensation, even promoting his skeptics' views, and then challenge his audience to judge for themselves. This strategy was good for business if people were moved to go back for a second look, paying a second quarter, but it also recognized the need his customers felt to exercise their own critical skills. He generally approached them with a knowing wink so they could be part of the fun. "Good old Barnum," they would say with affection upon figuring out what they were seeing. He entertained but also stimulated them, making them feel excited about their growing understanding of the world beyond the rural homestead, the isolated village, or the crowded urban neighborhood.

The nineteenth century was a time of rapid democratization in both the United States and Europe, as the old monarchical and aristocratic structures and the barriers of class came tumbling down. Barnum, who was born ten years into the century and died nine years before its end, embodied the period's great narrative of breaking social boundaries. Americans often saw him as an exemplar of what it meant to be one of them, and the Europeans he encountered on his many trips abroad also saw him as a representative of the American character. He was born into a family that had to hustle in its small Connecticut village to stay solvent. Through hard work, a lot of brass, and a genius for exploiting the new technologies related to communication and transportation, he became world famous and wealthy beyond his dreams. And he did it all by appealing to popular tastes and interests. He understood what ordinary Americans wanted, as they sought forms of entertainment beyond staring into the fire of an evening or listening to readings from the Bible after the family supper.[5]

We live in an ahistorical age, one that is quick to condemn historical figures using the standards of the present. We too easily dismiss them for their worst qualities even if they are counterbalanced or even heavily outweighed by their best qualities. Barnum's reputation today has fallen so far that his name often evokes comparisons to scoundrels, to politicians who lie shamelessly to the public, to deceptive advertisers, or to sleight-of-hand businessmen. But this doesn't do justice to the full story of who he was. Barnum embodied some of America's worst impulses, but also many of its best. He came to represent much of what was most admirable about his young country, and he did so with a sense of humor and a joy in living that is rare in today's public figures. He led a rich, event-filled, exhilarating life, one indeed characterized by both struggles and triumphs. His is a life well worth knowing and celebrating.

ONE:
THE RICHEST CHILD IN TOWN

"I was born and reared in an atmosphere of merriment," P. T. Barnum recalled in his autobiography, which he wrote at the ripe old age of forty-four. He entered the world on July 5, 1810, in the small village of Bethel, Connecticut, where "the associations of [his] youth" filled him with the ebullience and zest for living that stayed with him for more than eight decades. During all that time — as Barnum made his name in New York and London, in the capitals of Europe, and across the American continent — his birthplace never lost its grip on him. The people and peculiarities of life in small-town Connecticut, he wrote, were integral to any clear understanding of what "made me what I am." After traveling the world, he would die just seventeen miles from his birthplace, in the city of Bridgeport.[1]

The single most remarkable characteristic

of life in Bethel, in Barnum's telling, was his neighbors' propensity for practical jokes. Concocting pranks, setting them in motion, turning one another into victims, and then gossiping about the aftermath — this amounted to a chief form of entertainment in the village. The defining attribute of Barnum's neighbors and family was a concentrated dose of a widespread regional trait often labeled "Yankee cuteness." *Cute,* at the time, was not a word used to describe someone's looks but a shortened form of the word *acute,* meaning clever or shrewd. It suggested a competitive sort of sharpness, an eagerness to outdo or flummox another person.

Yankee cuteness was often displayed in the business dealings of the region's rural economy, which depended less on cash and more on barter. The value of goods offered was not fixed but determined by the interaction of buyer and seller. In this sense, *cute* was a term of approval when applied to oneself, and of disapproval when applied to others, just as the joy in a practical joke depends on which end of the transaction one is on.

Anyone in the village who wanted to stand out — or simply to find excitement amid the humdrum routines of village life —

24

relied heavily on this form of wit. Cuteness, tall tales, and the well-planned joke were the place's stock-in-trade, and even the victims of the more outlandish schemes easily overlooked the tinge of cruelty often attached to them. Given the small size of the village, the chances were good that everyone would have ample opportunity to be on one side of a practical joke or the other. So the pressure was always on to be a good sport — and to bide one's time.

The man for whom Barnum was named, his maternal grandfather, Phineas Taylor, was a paragon of these qualities. Young Phineas Taylor Barnum, who went by Taylor, or more intimately by Tale, was often called a "chip of the old block," referring in this case to his grandfather rather than his father. Phineas, known affectionately as "Uncle Phin" in the village, was well known for his ebullience and because he "would go farther, wait longer, work harder and contrive deeper, to carry out a practical joke, than for anything else under heaven." One of his most famous and long-unfolding jokes, involving the value of a gift of property, would have his grandson Taylor on the receiving end — and its outcome would continue to affect Barnum throughout his life.[2]

Even so, Taylor adored his grandfather. The older man was the first person he could remember seeing. "I was his pet, and spent probably the larger half of my waking hours in his arms, during the first six years of my life," often sucking on a lump of sugar that Phineas had given to him. Uncle Phin adored his namesake and demonstrated his affection not just with sweets but with showers of pennies, along with the admonition to always get the "lowest cash price" when spending them in a shop.[3]

Uncle Phin did have his serious side to balance out his mischievousness. He had been a soldier for four years during the Revolution, before acquiring a large amount of property in Bethel and its vicinity. He had represented Danbury (of which Bethel was a part) in the Connecticut legislature, and, closer to home, he ran lotteries, took the census, and, until his retirement at age seventy, served as a justice of the peace. Taylor's mother, Irena, was one of four children born to Phineas and his first wife, Molly. Only one of the four children fully shared their father's aptitude for joking, with Irena having the smallest measure of this quality, according to her son. "But what is lacking in all the children," Barnum would later write, "is fully made up with compound interest in the eldest grandson" — meaning himself. Taylor's paternal grandfather, Ephraim, a member of the fourth generation of Barnums in America, had been a militia captain in the Revolutionary War. His son Philo, Taylor's father, was one of fourteen children. Philo himself had ten children by two wives, Irena being the second. So young Taylor grew up in a place filled with grandparents, aunts, uncles, and numberless cousins. In time he would also have four younger siblings.[4]

In Taylor's childhood, newspapers came to Bethel only once a week, and it took at least two days to get to the growing metropolis of New York, or "York," as it was called. Bethel was still primarily a farming community, where hogs were let out to wander the streets, but the area had also become a center for the manufacture of hats and combs. Even so, just to get by in the village, let alone to prosper, required a willingness to hustle and to master a multiplicity of skills. Philo Barnum made his living, just barely, by farming, tailoring, running a store, keeping a tavern, and operating a freight delivery wagon and a livery stable. Taylor would remember that his mother and the other hardworking women in Bethel supported their families by "hetcheling their flax, carding their tow and wool, spinning, reeling, and weaving it into fabrics . . . knitting, darning, mending, washing, ironing, cooking, soap and candle making." They also "picked the geese, milked the cows, made butter and cheese, and did many other things" to keep the household running. Few people in the village had carriages or even wagons, and horses were the way people transported grain to the mill or got to church on Sundays.[5]

The church itself was a modest building, which Taylor would later recall as "the old village meeting-house, without steeple or bell, where in its square family pew I sweltered in summer and shivered through my Sunday-school lessons in winter." He also remembered "the old school-house, where the ferule, the birchen rod and rattan did active duty, and which I deserved and received a liberal share." He began attending school at about age six and was "accounted a pretty apt scholar," "unusually quick" at arithmetic. He remembered being called out of bed by his schoolmaster one night to calculate the number of feet in a load of wood. His teacher had bet a neighbor that Taylor could solve the problem in five minutes. When the neighbor gave him the dimensions of the load, the boy went to work, writing his calculations on the stove-pipe, and beat the deadline by three minutes. His teacher and proud mother showed their "great delight," and the neighbor was "incredulous." Taylor's later success in business would depend not just on this quickness in figuring. His linguistic abilities also turned out to be formidable and must have been innate, given how soon his schooling ended and how far they took him. His skill as a speaker and a writer would draw the world's attention, and hold it.[6]

Taylor would write in his autobiography, "Head-work I was excessively fond of [as a boy, but] hand-work was decidedly not in my line." He hated the drudgery of farm chores and apparently succeeded at doing them so reluctantly that he soon developed the reputation of being "the laziest boy in town." His father "insisted that I could hoe and plough and dig in the garden as well as anyone else, but I generally contrived to shirk the work altogether."[7]

But the problem was not laziness so much as lack of interest. What did interest him from an early age were money and its accumulation. "My organ of acquisitiveness must be large," he would write, "or else my parents commenced its cultivation at an early period."[8]

The pennies his grandfather gave Taylor began to add up, until Phineas took him at the age of six to the village tavern to exchange them for a silver dollar. The shiny disc seemed enormous in Taylor's small hands, making him feel richer than he would ever feel again and also giving him the sense of being "absolutely independent of all the world." He liked that feeling and wanted more. In time his grandfather began to pay him ten cents a day to ride the plow horse leading a team of oxen on his farm, but even that did not add up fast enough to satisfy young Taylor. The boy decided that for extra money he could start making sweets and selling them to soldiers on the days when the militia trained. Within a few years he could afford to buy sheep, a cow, and other property that "made me feel, at twelve years of age, that I was quite a man of substance." All that kept him from being as rich as Croesus, he believed, was his father's decision to make him buy his own clothing.

In January 1822, when Taylor was not quite twelve, a friend of his family's passed through Bethel on the way to New York to sell "a drove of fat cattle." The man mentioned that he was looking for a boy to help with the droving, and Taylor got the job.

Thus came about his first chance to "go to York" and see the great city. For spending money on the adventure, his mother gave him a dollar. Once the man and boy arrived in the city, Taylor had a week on his own while the farmer was busy disposing of the cattle. Again, Taylor felt that a single dollar in his pocket made him immensely rich, but what followed was the usual lesson: that the excitement of a great city does not come cheap. He spent much of his time in a toy store, buying things, exchanging them at a loss, and buying other things until, over a period of several days, not only was his money gone, but he had, in his frenzy of acquisitiveness, bartered away his handker-chiefs and a pair of socks. When he returned home with no presents for his siblings and his mother noticed the missing articles of clothing, he was "whipped and sent to bed." Still, for Taylor, the painful lesson was mitigated by the mere fact that he had "been to York," which made him "for a long time quite a lion among the school boys."[9]

Eventually, out of "sheer despair of making any thing better of me," Philo Barnum put his son to work at a general store that he and a partner had built and stocked in Bethel. Taylor's connection with his father was not as easy as that with his grandfather, but Philo had come to understand his son's nature. The saving of pennies, the boyish acts of entrepreneurialism in the village, and the schooling on his trip to New York had prepared him well for work in the shop, even bringing out the boy's natural theatricality. In this new setting, he was utterly transformed:

> I strutted behind the counter with a pen back of my ear, was wonderfully polite to ladies, assumed a wise look when entering charges upon the day-book, was astonishingly active in waiting upon customers, whether in weighing tenpenny nails, starch, indigo, or saleratus, or drawing New-England rum or West India molasses.[10]

As his enthusiastic creation of a clerking persona suggests, Taylor thrived in the give-and-take of the country store, where, as was often the case in the young Republic, prices were negotiable and barter was encouraged. Yankee cuteness reigned, and the faster talker on either side of a transaction tended to be the more successful. "I drove many a sharp trade with old women who paid for their purchases in butter, eggs, beeswax, feathers, and rags," Taylor would remember, "and with men who exchanged for our commodities, hats, axe-helves, oats, corn, buckwheat, hickory-nuts, and other commodities." His own sharpness was often matched by that of his customers, who would pack stones in bundles of rags to make them heavier or vow that a load of grain was several more bushels than it actually was. When he got older, Barnum would call these acts by his neighbors exceptions to the general rule of honesty, but they made him wary. This lesson and the one learned on the New York trip were the beginnings of his education as a businessman.[11]

Many of these memories of the grown-up Barnum are varnished with self-deprecatory amusement at his younger self. He reports, for example, that his sense of his own importance in his clerk's role caused him to resent his other duties in the shop, such as sweeping, keeping the fire, and taking the shutters off the windows. Still, his father allowed him to augment his modest store salary by running a separate business, in the same store, of buying and selling candy for children, which he did with an even sharper focus than he gave to his general clerking. He also began to create private lotteries, something Uncle Phin had adopted as a sideline. Taylor's grandfather had once concocted a wildly popular scheme in which every ticket resulted in a prize, an unheard-of offer, but in the end he had made his money by deducting 15 percent from each prize awarded. This was widely considered, with some admiration, to be "the meanest scheme ever invented," resulting in his reputation as "a regular old cheat" and "the cutest man in those parts." In Taylor's lotteries, the top prize would be $5 or perhaps $10, and most tickets, as is usual in lotteries, would result in no prize at all. He found that he could easily sell tickets to the workers in the hat and comb factories, and if he sold them all, he could earn as much as 25 percent above his outlay.

His elder self speculates, then, that young Taylor's eagerness to make money was both a born trait and one nurtured by his parents and his surroundings. Because people all around him, those in his family and more generally in Bethel, were scrambling to get by, their collective influence on him was enormous. Barnum's outsized eagerness to enrich himself also seems to have had a unique psychological source. To see it, one need look only to Uncle Phin and his most protracted practical joke. The story goes that Taylor's grandfather was so pleased to have a namesake that he immediately went out and bought a rich and beautiful farm and put it in his grandson's name. By the time he was four, Taylor began to hear not only from his grandfather but also from his parents and others in the village of his "precious patrimony . . . the most valuable farm in Connecticut," making him "the richest child in town." Not a week went by without his grandfather mentioning the farm, and his father even asked Taylor if he would support the family after he came into his fortune. The boy would often assure his father "in the most perfect good faith" that he would "see that all the family wants were bountifully supplied." In his dreams about the future source of his wealth, Taylor "not only felt that it must be a land flowing with milk and honey, but caverns of emeralds, diamonds, and other precious stones, as well as mines of silver and gold."

This fantasy went on until the boy turned twelve and had an opportunity to visit his inheritance, on what was known as Ivy Island, which was not far from Bethel but was inaccessibly located in the middle of what is now known as East Swamp. Before the big day arrived, his mother solemnly warned him not to become overexcited when he saw his farm, nor to "feel above speaking to your brothers and sisters when you return."

On the appointed day, his father took him out with a group of workers to hay a field near Ivy Island, and at the noon rest a hired man named Edward led Taylor to his enchanted spot. They had to cross the swamp to reach the island, and after he floundered through a long expanse of bogs, certain he would drown — and after he had fended off an attack by hornets and been painfully bitten — he finally reached his little piece of paradise, only to see a muddy flat landscape of "stunted ivies and a few straggling trees." No flowing honey, no precious stones or metals. "The truth rushed upon me. I had been made a fool of by all our neighborhood for more than half a dozen years." The land, he realized, was "not worth a farthing." To add insult to injury, at that moment a "monstrous black snake" came menacingly their way, and Taylor and Edward hastily abandoned Ivy Island. When they got back to the hayfield, all the other workers burst into laughter, having been clued in on this strangely cruel and astonishingly drawn-out joke.

Still, when Taylor returned to Bethel late that afternoon, now just another young man without immediate prospects of wealth, his mother, grandfather, and neighbors would not let the pretense go and continued to act as if Ivy Island were a rich inheritance, not five useless acres. It was Yankee cuteness at its fullest, and meanest. These dashed expectations must have created in Barnum the drive to fill his pockets with silver and gold for the rest of his days.[12]

At the time of Taylor's birth, Bethel was a Congregationalist village in a state where this was the official religion. He received his religious instruction under the stern influence of the Saybrook Platform, which for a century had consigned non-Congregationalists, including even children, to the conflagrations of Hell and considered the pope in Rome to be the Antichrist. Sour as these doctrines were, they were intensified by the Second Great Awakening, the post-Revolution revivalist movement that rejected the eighteenth century's rationalism and deism. As a boy, Taylor attended the revival meetings that were ubiquitous during the awakening, often returning home "almost smelling, feeling and tasting those everlasting waves of boiling sulphur, and hearing the agonizing shrieks and useless prayers of myriads of never ending sufferers . . . my eyes streaming with tears and every fibre of my body trembling with fear."[13]

But within the boundaries of Taylor's own family, religious faith was based more on love than fear. When he was fifteen, his maternal grandmother, while walking in her garden one day, stepped on a rusty nail, and her foot soon grew dangerously infected. Realizing she was at death's door, she called her grandchildren around her and told them of the joy her religious belief had brought to her and how it made her unafraid of dying. She told them that the best way they could show their love of God was to love their fellow human beings. "I was affected to tears," Barnum wrote, "and promised to remember her counsel." Many years later, he still vividly recalled that deathbed scene and believed that his own life had been affected by his grandmother's sincere faith and exemplary way of living and dying.

In 1826, a year after his grandmother's death, Barnum's father died of a lingering illness, leaving his family with debts in spite of the several businesses he had been running and the parcels of land he owned in and around Bethel. Now the eldest of five children, with the youngest only seven, Taylor remembered the family returning from the cemetery "to our desolate home, feeling that we were forsaken by the world, and that but little hope existed for us this side of the grave." He was given the chance to pick his own guardian and chose his mother's younger brother, Alanson Taylor, who was only about eight years older than he himself. Among Philo's debts was one he owed to his own son, which was ruled ineligible even for the fifty-one cents on the dollar that the other creditors received. Taylor's mother went to work in the inn that Philo had run, and "being industrious, economical, and persevering, she succeeded in a few years in redeeming the homestead."[14]

The boy continued to work for a short time in his father's store, but he soon went up the road a mile to the village of Grassy Plain to clerk at a different general store. His interest in conducting lotteries had grown, and in the new store he had the opportunity to create a lottery reminiscent of Uncle Phin's famously outrageous one. He would offer a large number of prizes, but many of them would have a value less than the price of a ticket. The store had a quantity of blackened tinware that it could not sell, and Taylor himself bargained with a peddler to trade other slow-moving store items for a wagonload of green glass bottles, which he would use as rewards. In one of his first forays into advertising, he hand-wrote the headings on the flyers for the lottery in "glaring capitals," claiming "MAGNIFICENT LOTTERY!" and "OVER 550 PRIZES!!!" Workers from a local hat factory streamed into the store to buy tickets, without paying too much attention to what the noncash prizes were. When the drawing occurred and the prizes were distributed, a good many of the "winners" went away with armfuls of green bottles and worthless tinware. "My grandfather enjoyed my lottery speculation very much," Taylor later wrote with understated satisfaction. He was, indeed, a chip off the old block.[15]

At the Grassy Plain store, the competition between clerks and customers was even fiercer than in Bethel: "It was 'dog eat dog' — 'tit for tat.'" Because "each party expected to be cheated, if it was possible," Taylor had to develop a new level of skepticism, allowing himself, with his fellow clerks, to believe "little that we saw, and less that we heard." He also became practiced in the art of cheating. "Our ground coffee was as good as burned peas, beans and corn could make, and our ginger was tolerable, considering the price of corn meal." That his "conscience, morals, and integrity" were not utterly destroyed, he said, could be attributed only to his not working there longer than he did.[16]

In old age Barnum recalled his youth in Bethel fondly and expressed surprise at how many memories of the village, going back to his fourth year on earth, remained at his disposal. But however much the village shaped his personality, he, like many people, lived his life in reaction to his childhood. The Calvinist strictures of his early religion, the banter and gamesmanship of work in the shop, the lengths to which his family members would go for a prank — all created themes that stayed with him throughout the decades. In a speech he gave in 1881 upon returning to the village, Barnum lovingly unspools these memories and the names of dozens of relatives, friends, and neighbors who had inhabited Bethel a half century and more earlier. But by then he had long since left it far behind, choosing the chaotic bustle of New York and London and striving for many years to make his adopted home of Bridgeport — "the Park City," as it is now ruefully known — into what would become the most populous, if not the most thriving, city in the state today.[17]

Early in 1827 the Grassy Plain store closed, and Taylor went to work in far-off York, at a Brooklyn grocery owned by another Taylor, a relation from Danbury who also owned a comb factory and store. Before long, the kindly Oliver Taylor developed enough confidence in young Barnum, not yet seventeen, to send him out to purchase wholesale groceries, allowing him to pay cash at auctions or markets, buy in quantity along with other grocers to reduce the price, and in general refine the talent for trade that had begun in his father's store. Buoyed by his aptitude and the enthusiasm of youth, Barnum soon decided to start a business of his own. "My disposition is, and ever was," he wrote in his memoirs, "of a speculative character," and he knew even then that he would only be happy working for himself. At about the time he decided to leave Oliver Taylor, though, he developed smallpox and had to spend several months in bed, after which he went back to Bethel to recover in his mother's care, enjoying her "unremitting . . . exertions to make me comfortable" and catching up with old friends. When he returned to Brooklyn after a month at home, he gave Oliver notice and managed to pull together the money to buy a porterhouse for sale near the grocery. A porterhouse was a bar and steakhouse, which took its name from the brown beer offered there alongside other beverages.

Despite his resolution to run his own business, in only a few months Barnum had the opportunity to sell the place at a profit, and he took it. He then got an offer to move across the river to work at a more established porterhouse on Peck Slip, near what is today the Manhattan side of the Brooklyn Bridge and was then the terminus for the Fulton ferry.[18]

This establishment, owned by David Thorp, had two advantages, in Barnum's telling. First, it was a favorite of travelers from Danbury and Bethel, giving Barnum ample opportunity to see people from home. Second, Thorp allowed him time off when young friends came to town so Barnum could take them to the theater. "I had much taste for the drama," he remembered, and soon "became, in my own opinion, a close critic, and did not fail to exhibit my powers in this respect to all the juveniles from Connecticut who accompanied me." Here he began to develop his eye for theater and showmanship, and in time he would combine it with his already sound entrepreneurial instincts.[19]

But soon his fondness for home and the chance to run his own business drew him away from this happy period as a dashing young fellow in the big city. Uncle Phin seemed to miss his grandson as much as his grandson missed home, and he wrote to say that if Taylor would return to Bethel and open a business, he would make available at no cost half a carriage house he owned on Bethel's main street. Taylor was happy to accept the offer, and so skedaddled home with the idea of opening a fruit and sweets store, augmented by a barrel of ale. The store debuted on May 5, 1828, and the first day's take was a more than satisfactory $63. Soon Taylor expanded his offerings to include stewed oysters, toys, and inexpensive personal items such as combs, pocketknives, and pocketbooks. By the following spring, he had bought the building but not the land under it from his grandfather for $50.[20]

Uncle Phin was not the only person pulling Barnum back to Bethel in those days. Barnum also heard a siren call from a young woman named Charity Hallett, who worked in a tailor shop and whom he had met while clerking at Grassy Plain a year and a half before. On one auspicious Saturday night back then, after a fierce thunderstorm, Barnum was asked to accompany to Bethel a "fair, rosy-cheeked, buxom-looking girl, with beautiful white teeth." This was Charity, known as "Chairy." As they rode on horseback the mile from Grassy Plain to Bethel, Barnum was so charmed by her that, despite the storm, he wished the distance had been even farther, especially when a stroke of lightning gave him a clear look at her. After getting her safely home, he wrote, "that girl's face haunted me in my dreams that night." Barnum saw her in church the next morning and on subsequent Sundays until he left the job at Grassy Plain. When he had returned home from Brooklyn to his mother's care in Bethel, he had managed to see the "attractive tailoress" several times, which did not "lessen the regard which I felt for the young lady, nor did they serve to render my sleep any sounder."[21]

Now, in the summer of 1828, having opened his store in Bethel, he again sought Charity out, and it soon seemed that "my suit was prospering." She was nearly two years older than he and came from a large family in Fairfield, Connecticut, that was not well off, a situation that got worse when her father decamped, perhaps across the sound to Long Island. But Charity and Taylor were a nicely matched couple: in addition to being from large Connecticut families and sharing a churchgoing habit, both were modestly educated but clever. Both had dark hair and dark eyes and strong, pleasing faces — his having escaped un-scarred from smallpox — with hints of the fleshiness to come.

Over the next year, their affection for each other grew. Barnum's mother felt that Charity was not a socially desirable match for her son ("The girl had not got money enough to suit her ideas," she said), but those who knew Charity believed just the opposite, that "she was altogether too good for Taylor Barnum." Barnum wittily asserted that he "perfectly agreed with them in their conclusions and . . . proved it by asking her hand in marriage." She consented, and in October 1829 they were married at her uncle's house in New York, with members of her family present, but not of his. The newlyweds returned to Bethel, moving in with the family with whom Charity had been living. Taylor's mother pretended that she knew nothing of the marriage, apparently upset that it had taken place in secret. But he went to visit her every day, and within a month she asked him to bring his wife to visit on a Sunday, and a reconciliation occurred.[22]

In June 1830 Barnum purchased three acres "a few rods south of the village," and there he had a house constructed for Charity and him to live in. The house, two and a half stories tall, cost just over $1,000 to build. By the next spring, at about the same time they moved in, Barnum had another structure built in Bethel, this one intended to accommodate a country store on its first floor and a family on the floors above. The Yellow Store, as it was known, opened in the summer of 1831, selling dry goods, groceries, and hardware — "everything from Bibles to brandy." Barnum started the business with his uncle and guardian Alanson Taylor, but within a few months Barnum bought out his uncle, explaining diplomatically, "Like most persons who engage in a business which they do not understand, we were unsuccessful in the enterprise." Barnum alone didn't fare much better. He had trouble collecting what was owed him, and even advertised in the newspaper a warning that he was prepared to sue in order to collect. By the spring of 1832 he was looking for a buyer for the business; it took a year to find one.[23]

While the dry goods store stumbled, Barnum's other interests found footing. Since his return to Bethel, he had become ever more avidly involved in the lottery business. After starting with his own small-scale, local offerings, he began working with large

47

statewide lotteries, from whom he would buy tickets in bulk, and employing agents, among them his Uncle Alanson, who also became his partner in this new venture, to sell them across the land. By early 1830 he had lottery offices in Bethel, Danville, Norwalk, Stamford, and Middletown. For the first time, he made widespread use of "printer's ink" to publicize his lottery sales, and soon newspapers "throughout the region teemed with unique advertisements." He also had tens of thousands of handbills and circulars printed "with striking prefixes, affixes, staring capitals, marks of wonder, pictures, etc.," and his main lottery office, which he called the Temple of Fortune, was plastered with gold signs and colorful placards. The purpose of this publicity maelstrom was not just to draw attention but also to emphasize that his customers were luckier than those who bought from other agents. At one point the business became so successful that his agents were bringing in as much as $2,000 a day in sales.

His lottery work did not just teach him about the efficacy of advertising. It also began to develop his insight into the complicated nature of his customers, a realization that outwardly respectable people might have interests that were not entirely respectable. Buying a lottery ticket was, after all, a form of gambling, something that the powerful churches looked down upon. Yet lotteries were popular not only among many churchgoers but also, as Barnum reported, with "a number of clergymen and deacons," whom he counted among his "private customers." In his autobiography, he told the story of a pious husband, "a frequent exhorter at prayer meetings," and his wife, who would each buy a ticket from him secretly on the condition that he not tell the other spouse, who was presumed to be "opposed to such things." The peaceful coexistence of piety and the pie-in-the-sky nature of lotteries might say more about human nature than about any particular historical period, but it also suggests a change in the social order of the day, in which ordinary New Englanders were yearning for something more from their lives than what was being offered from the Sunday pulpit.[24]

Barnum's own reaction to the role of religion in public life was becoming more pronounced. He was growing skeptical of the fervor of the revival era. Beyond the hypocrisy related to gambling habits was the incongruous coexistence in Bethel and elsewhere of strong religious views and strong drinking habits. He'd long seen that "even at funerals the clergy, mourners and friends drank liquor," at the same time that alcohol was denounced from the pulpits. Barnum would never be shy about pressing his opinions on others, but even as he had barely reached voting age, he grew publicly concerned about the "religious frenzy" spreading through the land, featuring large numbers of people, especially young people, converting to the churches where revival meetings took place. He was equally troubled by talk among "certain overzealous sectarian partisans" of the creation of a Christian political party advocating that only believers should get the vote, which suggested that the boundary between church and state might disappear.

Connecticut had disestablished the Congregational Church in 1818, but the church still held sway in matters of politics and governing. Like his grandfathers on both sides and his father, Barnum was a Universalist and a Democrat and firmly held to the Jeffersonian ideal of separation of church and state. He decided to spread his views in letters to a weekly paper in Danbury — a paper that soon would be associated with his Uncle Alanson. When his writing was refused, Barnum "became exceedingly indignant" and took his rejections as evidence that the religious influence had already become "so powerful as to muzzle the press." With that, ever eager to take the initiative, he decided to publish his own newspaper to promote his views.[25]

Just after he turned twenty-one, on July 5, 1831, Barnum bought a printing press and type sets, and by October 19 of that year he had published in Bethel the first number of his *Herald of Freedom,* a weekly four-page broadsheet. Thanks to cheap postage, improvements in technology, and an increasingly literate populace with a growing interest in the world, starting a small newspaper, especially one that had a particular audience in mind, was not an expensive proposition. By 1828 the city of New York itself supported 161 papers, their readers drawn not only to news from the neighborhood and the larger world but also to particular political, ethnic, or religious perspectives.[26]

If the lottery business had acquainted Barnum with the power of publicity, he now discovered the power of publishing his own paper. Just below the masthead on the front page of the *Herald of Freedom* were the words "P. T. BARNUM . . . PUBLISHER." Suddenly he had acquired a whole new level of visibility in his community and beyond. (He later said the paper was circulated nationally.) However, Barnum soon turned visibility into notoriety. Eight months after that first edition appeared, he managed to attract a libel suit from none other than his Uncle Alanson, who had in the meantime purchased the Danbury paper that had rejected Barnum and become its editor, renaming it the *Connecticut Repository*. In his own paper, Barnum slammed his uncle regularly and with real ardor, accusing him of advocating for the church-state merger and of telling lies about those with whom he disagreed. In response to Barnum's accusations, Alanson sued. The case never went to trial "on account of the absence of witnesses," as Barnum wrote in a letter to a fellow newspaper editor, but a second libel action, "brought by a butcher in Danbury, a zealous politician, whom I accused of being a spy in the caucus of the Democratic Party," eventually cost Barnum several hundred dollars in damages.[27]

It was a third case, however, that turned Barnum into a regional hero, at least to those who agreed with him. This third libel prosecution was brought on behalf of a Congregationalist neighbor and fellow merchant named Seth Seelye, whom Barnum accused in the *Herald of Freedom* of "taking usury of an orphan boy." A conservative judge named David Daggett, who was also a Yale law professor and an avowed Federalist, heard the case. Judge Daggett (whom Barnum referred to in a letter as a "lump of superstition") took an active part in the prosecution. In one outrageous example of the overreach of a state religion, Barnum was not permitted to mount the stand because of his Universalist beliefs. At the recommendation of the judge, he was convicted by a jury and sentenced to forfeit a bond of $100 and pay court costs, or serve sixty days in jail.

"I chose to go to prison," Barnum wrote to Gideon Welles, editor of the *Hartford Times,* "thinking that such a step would be the means of opening many eyes." Indeed, he continued, because of the trial, "the excitement in this and the neighboring towns is very great, and it will have a grand effect." His purpose in writing Welles was to tell him that another newspaper editor would be covering the matter at length, as would the *Herald of Freedom,* of course, and to ask Welles to "make such remarks as justice demands." His ability to marshal not just his own paper but also the goodwill of others was a harbinger of things to come. It was the first clear example of his flair for drawing attention to his beliefs, his enterprises, and himself.[28]

In his memoirs, he writes that he was allowed to have his cell in the Danbury Common Jail fitted out with wallpaper and carpet, which is surely a rarity in the annals of imprisonment. While in jail he was allowed to continue editing his newspaper, to write numbers of letters, and to receive so many friends that he found their ceaseless visits burdensome. These communications with the world beyond the cell also allowed him not only to stir up local newspaper coverage but also to engineer what can only be called a local holiday to celebrate his release. A group called the Committee on Arrangements was formed. They met him at the jail on the morning of his last day there, December 5, 1832, and strolled with him across the village green to the very room in the courthouse where he had been tried. The crowd was so large — Barnum's paper reckoned it at fifteen hundred souls, and even at half that size it would have been immense — that those who could not fit in the building formed a parting sea for him to pass through. Once settled in there, he was honored with an ode composed for the occasion and a speech defending freedom of the press called "The Nation's Bulwark," written and declaimed by a prominent lecturer, the Rev. Theophilus Fisk, himself the editor of the *New Haven Examiner.* There followed the hymn "Strike the Cymbal" ("Crime & sadness, yield to gladness, Peace! the heav'nly powrs pro-claim"), after which a crowd of "several hundred gentlemen," Barnum recalled, retreated to the nearby hotel of one G. Nichols and enjoyed "a sumptuous dinner . . . toasts and speeches." The twelfth toast, we are told, described Barnum as "a terror to Bigots and Tyrants — a young man just on the threshold of active life whom neither bolts, nor bars, nor prison walls, can intimidate."[29]

As if all of this were not enough to fete an incautious twenty-two-year-old who had not exactly suffered at the hands of the law, Barnum stepped from the Danbury hotel into a coach drawn by a six-horse team. Seated with him in the coach was a small band of musicians playing patriotic tunes, and a parade in his honor had formed to take him the three miles home to Bethel. A marshal carrying the Stars and Stripes led the parade, followed by forty people on horseback, and behind Barnum's coach was a carriage carrying Reverend Fisk and the president of the day's proceedings, followed by sixty more carriages filled with local people. As this impressive retinue got under way, cannon boomed on the village green and several hundred more people who were gathered there gave Barnum three cheers. When the carriage reached Bethel, the band played "Home Sweet Home," and three more cheers went up as Barnum alighted. Thus a day begun in jail ended in well-orchestrated and raucous triumph.[30]

Neither Barnum nor anyone else said for certain who organized the many events of this day, or who chose the members of the Committee of Arrangements and its president. Barnum carefully did not give or take credit when he later described the celebration in detail in his memoirs, and without doubt it was in Barnum's interest to imply that the day unfolded almost spontaneously, propelled by the enthusiasm of his neighbors for his cause and, indeed, for himself. After all, he had grown up in the village and had many, many relatives there and nearby. He had gone to church in the village, had clerked in its stores, still owned a store there, heavily advertised his lotteries, and now ran a newspaper from there. Democrats, Universalists, and others who thought as he did would naturally have wanted to support him. But odes and formal speeches do not occur on the spur of the moment, nor do bands and coaches arrive by chance, and even if the celebratory luncheon involved only dozens rather than hundreds of trenchermen, a provincial hotel would need fair warning to feed so many. Of the various tactics that Barnum would master as he became a successful showman, one was to know when to stand in the wings and when to step to the footlights to take a bow. It seems likely that in this case he was in both places at once.

Others might have thought to sponsor an ode *or* an oration, engage a chorus *or* a band, plan a banquet *or* a parade, envision three cheers rather than three cheers twice, and might have forgotten the cannon salute altogether. But not Barnum. Beginning on December 5, 1832, more would always be more, keeping sympathetic newspaper editors close would always be useful, commissioning songs and poems and speeches would ever enhance an occasion, mixing serious intentions with entertainment sure to draw a crowd would continue to be a good strategy for engaging the public, and his own notoriety would never fail to be a calling card ready at hand. Seemingly small but consequential details — like returning to the courtroom where he was convicted or overlaying it all with patriotic zeal —

would never elude him. This day had all the earmarks of a Barnum production. It was the day when his career as a showman began.

Two:
The Nursemaid

The life that Barnum and Charity made for themselves in Bethel went well over the next two years. His lottery business continued to be profitable, and although the Yellow Store was less so, given his customers' unreliability in paying up on their accounts, he managed to sell his share in it in early 1833. Soon after, in May, their first child, Caroline, was born. Barnum's notoriety as a freedom-loving newspaper publisher was such that on the Fourth of July, the day before his twenty-third birthday, a large gathering of Democrats praised him at a dinner in nearby Newtown as one who had been "bitterly persecuted by the enemies of civil and religious freedom." Even more flattering, perhaps, were toasts made in absentia at Federalist events on the same day, as his enemies decried Barnum for his newspaper's homilies by calling him "reverend" and a "self-made priest." These arrows apparently did not wound, and he used them to burnish his reputation, reporting them in the *Herald of Freedom and Gospel Witness,* as he was now calling his paper.

However, in late May 1834, the state legislature banned lotteries in Connecticut, and without this source of income, Barnum had to change course. He decided he could not afford to keep publishing the paper, and in November, having brought out 160 issues in three years, he stepped away. Given the large profits from the lottery business, he ought to have been in sound financial shape, but the lottery customers had also been less than honorable in paying their debts, so he now had "no pecuniary resources" other than attempting to make good on what he was owed. He blamed himself for his situation, writing that "the old proverb, 'Easy come, easy go,' was too true in my case." Still, he was confident in his ability to earn money and believed he could start saving "at *some future time.*" For the present, he decided to move his young family from Bethel to a rented house on Hudson Street in lower Manhattan, entering "that great city to 'seek my fortune.' " But it would take many months, and an unlikely encounter, before he would find the way to his life's work and the fortune that he sought.[1]

At first, things went so badly in New York that Barnum feared for the health of Charity and Caroline as he searched the want ads for an appropriate job. One ad he saw came from Scudder's American Museum, suggesting that for a small investment the person who applied could be part of an "IMMENSE SPECULATION." Barnum was intrigued because, as he wrote in his autobiography, "I had long fancied that I could succeed if I could only get hold of a public exhibition." He had made a successful public spectacle of himself on the day he had been released from jail, but this was the first hint that he might want to make his living by promotion, exhibition, and showmanship. However, the speculation in question, a "hydro-oxygen microscope," required an investment well beyond his means. Nothing else turned up in the want ads during the whole winter of 1835, and Barnum's prospects in the city looked dim.

Finally, in the spring, several hundred dollars came his way from a debt collector in Bethel, who had succeeded in hounding some of Barnum's long overdue accounts. With that small influx of cash, on May 1, 1835, Barnum opened a boardinghouse on nearby Frankfort Street catering to people he knew from Connecticut who were visiting the city. Business was steady enough that he could soon buy into a grocery store with a partner named John Moody on South Street, near the porterhouse where he'd worked during his earlier sojourn in Manhattan.[2]

Once the immediate need to feed his family was satisfied, Barnum had the freedom to think more about what he really wanted to do to make his way in the world. While he was thinking, the world made its way to him. "The business finally came," he wrote. "I fell into the occupation, and far beyond any of my predecessors on this continent, I have succeeded." This boast, which refers to his career as a showman, has the value of being true, and is somewhat softened, at least in a later edition of his autobiography, by Barnum's admission that the event that would set his life on its course "was the least deserving of all my efforts in the show line." By this he meant in part that the elements for its success were already in place and required little creative showmanship on his part — beyond a willing suspension of disbelief. But it also became the episode in his life of which he was the least proud, one that spurred him to begin to be the better sort of showman he would eventually become.[3]

In late July 1835, a man named Coley Bartram walked into the store that Barnum and Moody ran. Bartram was from Reading (now Redding), Connecticut, just a few miles south of Bethel, and knew both Moody and Barnum. As Bartram talked, it came out that he had recently sold an investment in a traveling act featuring an emaciated, incredibly ancient, black slave woman. What made her of interest to the public was the claim that she had been present more than a century before at the birth of George Washington in Westmoreland County, Virginia, and had been his nursemaid there when he was growing up. Her name was Joice Heth, and her act consisted of singing hymns and telling stories about the great man she had helped to raise.

Even as they stood chatting in the store, Bartram said, Heth was performing under the direction of Bartram's former partner in Philadelphia. He produced an advertisement from the *Pennsylvania Inquirer* dated July 15, 1835, describing Heth as "one of the greatest natural curiosities ever witnessed," not least because she was, the article claimed, 161 years old. The life expectancy in 1835 for a white woman hovered at around forty years, and it was less still for the average enslaved black woman. But Barnum does not remark in his autobiography or elsewhere on the implausibility of this claim of Heth's longevity.

If nothing else, as a person already becoming adept at newspaper publicity, he must have marveled at the brashness of the clipping he had been handed. He had already been aware of Heth's existence from articles in New York newspapers praising her as a "wonderful personage," so when he heard from Bartram that his former partner was himself eager to "sell out" because "he had very little tact as a showman," Barnum's only thought was that he must go to Philadelphia at once. Perhaps Heth's act would be the sort of public exhibition he had been looking for. "Considerably excited" at this prospect, off he went to meet Bartram's former partner, a Kentuckian named R. W. Lindsay, and to see this marvel.[4]

Barnum's impulse to exhibit a fellow human being who could arouse the interest of the public may seem shocking to a modern onlooker. Such traveling exhibitions, however, were common in nineteenth-century America. In a country that was still largely rural and at a time before railroads vastly improved the convenience of transportation, any impulse to entertain, educate, or bamboozle required extensive travel from town to town. Since colonial times in America, people far from cities could expect a stream of people passing through their villages — "strolling peddlers, preachers, lawyers, doctors, players and others," as the subtitle of Richardson Wright's *Hawkers and Walkers in Early America* has it. The Victorian era, in both England and America, would be a time of special enthusiasm on the part of audiences for traveling exhibitions, not least the exhibition of "curiosities." For this was an era of increasing awareness of the wider world. The full abundance of the earth's flora, fauna, and human culture was still only becoming apparent to the average American. Elephants, birds of paradise, orchids, species previously known only in myth were now touring the countryside.[5]

This same trend ushered in a heightened fascination with human exhibits as well. Leslie A. Fiedler explored in *Freaks* (1978) how societies throughout history have often imputed mythic status to people who are born looking vastly different from those around them — treating them as monsters or as omens for good or ill. In the nineteenth century, driven by this same impulse as well as a heightened worldliness, crowds flocked to see anyone who was unusually large or small, unexpectedly pigmented or lacking all pigment, or who was in any way out of the ordinary. Barnum's era was a heyday for human exhibitions, and he was happy to play his part, slaking his audience's desires to be impressed or confounded, to gawk and chatter, especially if he could present so-called curiosities that also knew how to perform a winning act. If the blind and aged Heth had indeed exceeded the normal female lifespan by a factor of four and been central to the national mythos, she would fit the bill.

When Barnum reached Philadelphia and met Heth, he was deeply impressed with her. It was not because she looked robust and vibrant — in Barnum's eye, this would have made her story less plausible — but the opposite: "so far as outward indications were concerned," Barnum recalled, "she might almost as well have been called a thousand years old as any other age." She was "totally blind, and her eyes were so deeply sunken in their sockets that the eyeballs seemed to have disappeared al-together. She had no teeth, but possessed a head of thick, bushy gray hair. Her left arm lay across her breast, and she had no power to remove it." Still, she seemed healthy despite outward appearances, and she talked up a storm, especially on the subject of religion. She sang "a variety of ancient hymns" and referred often to "dear little George," telling good stories about him and declaring she had "raised him" during her time as a slave owned by George's father, Augustine.[6]

Barnum asked Lindsay for some proof of who she was, and Lindsay produced a document that Barnum described much later as "a *forged bill of sale*"; it claimed that Augustine Washington had in 1727 sold Heth, then age fifty-four, to a neighbor for thirty-three pounds. When he first saw the purported document, Barnum noticed only that it had "the appearance of antiquity," being yellowed and worn through at its folds. That, and Lindsay's explanation that the long-ago sale had taken place to reunite "Aunt Joice" with her husband, who was one of the neighbor's slaves, "seemed plausible," Barnum wrote. Far more plausible is the idea that Barnum was so eager to take on the challenge of exhibiting her — despite the comparable eagerness of first Bartram and then Lindsay to be rid of her — that he was willing to be duped. Lindsay wanted $3,000 to transfer his rights to Heth but agreed to $1,000 if Barnum could produce the money within ten days. Barnum hustled back to New York, where he had $500 on hand. He managed to persuade a friend to lend him an equal amount based on the "golden harvest which I was sure the exhibition must produce." Barnum also sold his share in the grocery to his partner Moody, presumably to acquire the means to begin promoting his exhibit.[7]

Barnum hurried back to Philadelphia with the $1,000, but just what did he purchase with it? Lindsay had entered into an agreement with Heth's owner, John S. Bowling, also from Kentucky, to join him in taking Heth from city to city for a year, sharing in the profits or losses from exhibiting her. That agreement had been signed on June 10, 1835, but only five days later Bowling, who was not in good health, sold his rights to exhibit her to Coley Bartram, who, only a few days before he approached Barnum, sold them to Lindsay. Thus Lindsay then had the sole right to exhibit her. Barnum reproduces in his autobiography the text of the contract between himself and Lindsay, but different biographers have interpreted it in different ways. Some have argued that the contract suggests Barnum, a future abolitionist, now owned Heth, while others suggest that he was in effect "renting" her. In either case, it was a tangled and morally specious engagement; in his eagerness, Barnum was embarking on one of the most objectionable moneymaking schemes of his career, one that he would never quite live down.[8]

What is clear is that Barnum's agreement gave him the legal right to show Joice Heth for the remainder of Lindsay's year. If exhibiting Heth was Barnum's first experience as a showman, it was not his first as a salesman, and he reckoned that promoting her act was not so different from selling lottery tickets or bargaining across a countertop over dry goods. Besides being a newspaperman himself, he had realized and exploited the power of advertising and press coverage to create public enthusiasm for his lotteries. With Heth, he wasted no time, and his instincts proved sound. On August 7, 1835, the day after he signed the contract with Lindsay, an article appeared in the *New York Evening Star* announcing that she would be arriving for exhibition at Niblo's Garden, an attraction located on Broadway between Prince and Houston. Well-off New Yorkers went there to eat ice cream, drink coffee, lemonade, or something stronger, and listen to music or watch traveling entertainments amid the greenery, escaping the noise and squalor of the more densely urban streets to the south. The article puffed her as "a greater star than any other performer of the present day." Barnum and William Niblo — an Irish immigrant known as Billy who had been a waiter in a pub before marrying the owner's widow and acquiring the resources to start his own place — had agreed to split the profits from the exhibition, with the latter providing the venue and paying for the advertising. For his part, Barnum hired Levi Lyman, a "shrewd, sociable, and somewhat indolent Yankee" lawyer from the distant Finger Lakes town of Penn Yan, New York, to assist him in promoting and displaying Heth.[9]

Barnum and Lyman arranged for a private press showing at Niblo's once Heth arrived from Philadelphia, inviting a number of local newspaper editors "to get the first peep at the new wonder of the world," as Lyman described it later in a story for the *New York Herald.* For this later story, which appeared well after the episode was over, Lyman also provided the *Herald* with a list of how much he and Barnum paid that newspaper's competitors to become "firm believers" in the claims they were making for her, the payments inducing "sudden conversions" in the editors. The incentives ranged, if Lyman is to be believed, from a high of $49.50 for the *New York Courier and Enquirer* to $5.67 for the more persuadable *New-York Gazette & General Advertiser,* and totaled more than $200. It was a good investment, apparently, because the papers outdid each other in trumpeting their lack of skepticism and journalistic integrity, and the crowds eagerly made the trip up to Niblo's, where the gross amounted to about $3,000 for the two weeks she was on display.[10]

Barnum also attributed their early success to a short biographical sketch that Lyman wrote, relying largely on his imagination, which was published in a pamphlet Lyman sold for six cents, pocketing the profits. It featured a woodcut engraving of Heth in a neat bonnet and calico dress, her hands prominently displaying long, clawlike fingers and nails. Her hands were in reality twisted and arthritic, and one did have nails four inches long, but the woodcut portrayal was grotesque in a way meant to heighten public curiosity. The pamphlet included several of the early newspaper blurbs Barnum and Lyman had purchased, as well as "certificates" from people who had supposedly known her for a long time and testified to her piety and reliability. Barnum also had many posters and handbills printed, advertising "the nurse of Washington," displaying the wood-cut image, and featuring copy similar to that the newspapers used — quite likely because Barnum had written it for them. He also created "two ingenious, back-lit, out-of-doors Joice Heth transparencies two by three feet in size," showing her name and the claim of "161 Years Old," which would be displayed wherever she was appearing. In those days before electricity, the back-lighting would have come from candles or oil lamps, which caused the thin paper of the printed posters to glow.[11]

In his autobiography, Barnum describes what a showing of Heth entailed:

Our exhibition usually opened with a statement of the manner in which the age of Joice Heth was discovered, as well as the account of her antecedents in Virginia, and a reading of the bill of sale. We would then question her in relation to the birth and youth of General Washington, and she always gave satisfactory answers in every particular. Individuals among the audiences would also frequently ask her questions, and put her to the severest cross-examinations, without ever finding her to deviate from what had every evidence of being a plain unvarnished statement of the facts.[12]

While on exhibit, Heth often smoked a pipe as she lounged on a bed in a house on Niblo's grounds, as visitors passed through, shaking her hand and sometimes even taking her pulse, as if to test whether she were clockwork or flesh and blood. Heth was by all reports a convincing, charismatic performer. She laughed often at her own stories or at things her visitors said, and regularly broke into obscure, old-fashioned hymns that seemed to prove her advanced age. Barnum made the most of her religious streak, at times inviting ministers to hold public conversations with her, which appealed to the devout and added credibility to the proceedings. Much patriotic fuss was made in the advertising about her connection to the Father of Our Country, and Heth was prepared with anecdotes that, in truth, seemed less personal than derived from the widespread myths that had attached themselves to the first president. The generation of the Founders had now passed from the scene, and people were patriotically eager to be in the presence of this vestige of their greatness.

But it was her looks that seemed to draw

the public most, a fascination with her physical attributes and how old she appeared to be. One article in the *New York Evening Star* described her as resembling "an Egyptian mummy just escaped from its sarcophagus." Barnum claimed in the advertisements that she weighed only forty-six pounds, and observers often compared her immobile arms and long fingers, with those fingernails curving out several inches, to claws or paws. To say that the reactions of those who saw her were influenced by their racial views would be an understatement, and even the widespread acceptance of the preposterous claims about her age was connected to her race. Her longevity was thought to be at least partly attributable to having lived in the Africa-like warmth of the American South. Later, when she died in Connecticut during the winter, commentators used the circumstances to reinforce theories that black people were ill-adapted to survive northern climates.[13]

After her Niblo's run in New York, Barnum and Lyman took Heth on to Providence and Boston. An article in the *Providence Daily Journal* on August 30 picked up a fictitious theme from Lyman's pamphlet about Heth, in which he claimed that she had given birth to fifteen children and had an unspecified number of grandchildren, all now either freed or dead, but that five great-grandchildren remained enslaved in Kentucky. Their master, the pamphlet claimed, had agreed to free the five if he could receive two-thirds of the amount he had paid for them. "This work" — meaning the pamphlet itself — "together with what may be collected from exhibition, after deducting expenses, is expressly for that purpose, and will be immediately done whenever there can be realized the sum to do it." The whole story was made up, which is despicable enough, and we know from Barnum that Lyman was pocketing the proceeds from the pamphlet. Because Providence and Boston were cities where abolitionist feelings were growing stronger, it is likely that Barnum planted the article in the *Journal* in order to deflect any questions about Heth's own status as slave or free woman. The disingenuous story about freeing the great-grandchildren also implied that Heth herself was free, while Barnum avoided mentioning the subject directly in his advertising or newspaper promotions.

Barnum was in a sense testing his limits in this early endeavor, seeing how far he could push the truth to promote Heth. He was attentive to the flow of customers, keeping it going as long as possible and then moving on when it slowed; he was also learning that depriving the public of an exhibit could increase interest in a return engagement. Presumably this is why Barnum moved Heth from Niblo's after only two weeks, despite the energetic campaign to promote her there, since he would soon bring her back to New York for another run. The false manumission article in Providence made it profitable to extend Heth's time there for a week, and he would soon add an even more extreme — and dehumanizing, viewed from our own time — ploy to increase the patronage in Boston.

Barnum and Lyman's preparations for the Boston showing were as assiduous as those for New York and Providence. One newspaper editor, Joseph Buckingham, wrote, "JOICE HETH. These are the words, which, printed in large capitals, and posted at every corner in the city, announce an exhibition at Concert Hall." Buckingham's *Boston Courier* had accepted paid advertisements for the exhibit, and as Barnum tells it, "the newspapers had heralded her anticipated arrival in such a multiplicity of styles, that the public curiosity was on tip-toe." Not all of those styles were flattering, however. The editor of the conservative *Boston Atlas* complained, "We have been annoyed the last week by a score of puffs dropped in our communication box — in poetry and prose," promoting Heth. The editor went on to say that a "more indecent mode of raising money than by the exhibition of an old woman — black or white — we can hardly imagine." Regardless, the initial crowds were so large that the room in the Concert Hall proved inadequate, and a fellow exhibitor in the building's ballroom had to be "induced" to vacate.[14]

That exhibitor was Johann Nepomuk Maelzel, a Bavarian engineer and inventor who for nearly two decades had toured in Europe and then the United States with "the Turk," a life-size, chess-playing automaton dressed in a white turban and baggy Turkish pants. The automaton would match wits with and generally beat challengers from the audience, and years of speculation about how the hoax was done ended when a young writer named Edgar Allan Poe saw the act several times in Richmond, Virginia, and wrote a piece correctly speculating that a man hidden in a box onstage directed the automaton's moves.[15]

Barnum wrote about Maelzel in his autobiography, "I looked upon him as the great father of caterers for public amusement," and because of this he often spoke with the older man, who eventually invited Barnum to team up with him. Barnum declined but would soon draw inspiration from Maelzel's contraption. The crowds were big at the Concert Hall for several weeks, thanks to a drumbeat of "novel advertisements and unique notices" in the papers, but then the numbers started to fall off. Here Barnum came close to admitting one of his notorious humbugs, implying that he himself had placed a notice in a Boston newspaper calling out Heth as a hoax. The article said that she was not a 161-year-old slave, and "not a human being" *at all,* but "simply a curiously constructed automaton, made up of whalebone, India-rubber, and numberless springs ingeniously put together." Heth was a machine, induced to speak, laugh, and sing hymns by the work of a ventriloquist — a particularly cruel line of publicity in an era when black Americans were already roundly dehumanized, though it's unclear whether or not this ever crossed Barnum's mind. In his autobiography, he wrote that the Turk "prepared the way for this announcement" and that the result was hundreds of new visitors, as well as old visitors who wanted to see whether they had been duped on their original visit. "Our audiences," Barnum wrote, "again largely increased."[16]

Barnum, Lyman, and Heth bounced around New England for the next month, then returned to Niblo's Garden in late October at the same time a fair put on by the American Institute of the City of New York was under way there. Many of the upward of one hundred thousand visitors to the fair had come from out of town, and a healthy number of those, after examining the new products on display — ten thousand exhibits ranging from artificial flowers to threshing machines — crossed the garden to see Joice Heth as well. Barnum would accompany Heth on only one more trip, to Albany, and after that she was in Lyman's charge, beginning with an exhibit in the Bowery aimed at a more working-class New York audience than the one at Niblo's.

Around the time of his own departure, Barnum hired a woman to serve as Heth's nurse and attendant on the road. After her New York showing, and a return to New England, Heth's travels soon had to be suspended. She had not been able to get over a cold, and after an exhibition in New Haven in late January, Barnum had her moved, along with her nurse, to his half brother Philo's house in Bethel to try to recuperate. There, Barnum wrote, "she was provided with warm apartments and the best medical and other assistance." Nevertheless Heth's sickness intensified, and she died in Bethel on February 19, 1836.[17]

Philo Barnum had Joice Heth's body shipped to his brother in New York, and it arrived by horse-drawn sleigh at Barnum's boardinghouse on February 21. If Heth really did have relatives other than the ones Lyman had invented, nobody knew where they were, and if John Bowling, off in Kentucky, still technically owned her, he apparently did not offer to pay for her burial or ask that her body be returned to him. Barnum could have tried to seek out relatives himself, or he could have immediately given her a respectable burial. Instead he chose an entirely different approach, which would increase both his profits and his infamy.

Over the course of Barnum's promotion of Heth, he had courted demand for an autopsy upon her death to answer the question of her age (and humanity) once and for all. Upon the coffin's arrival in New York, he went to visit a well-regarded surgeon and anatomist he knew, who had looked Heth over during one of her showings at Niblo's and at the time expressed an interest in autopsying her should she die.

Barnum and the physician, David L. Rogers, agreed that the procedure would take place on February 25, and Rogers, who had undertaken some high-profile jobs of this sort in the past, had no objection to Barnum's selling tickets to those who would like to watch him at work.[18]

Ads with such sober headlines as "ANATOMICAL EXAMINATION" invited the public to join those with a somewhat legitimate medical interest in viewing the dissection, for which Barnum rented an amphitheater in the City Saloon on Broadway. It was a large enough space to accommodate the fifteen hundred people who paid Barnum fifty cents apiece to watch the procedure. Among those he invited were representatives of the clergy. Richard Adams Locke, a descendant of John Locke and the editor of the penny paper the New York *Sun,* was a pal of Dr. Rogers and thus was given an exclusive in covering the event.[19]

Rogers, who had been skeptical of the age claims for Heth when he first saw her, now found that she had not died from the effects of a cold or the cold weather but from tuberculosis, and that she had been, as Locke reported, no "more than *seventy-five* or, at the utmost, *eighty years of age*!" The relatively good condition of all her major organs other than her lungs had led Rogers to this confident determination. Locke's story, which appeared in the next day's *Sun,* ran under the headline "Precious Humbug Exposed" and did not spare the grisly details of the old woman's dissection. Locke let Barnum off the hook publicly, concluding that he had been duped alongside everyone else. This was the case that Barnum had made to Rogers and Locke immediately after the autopsy, and he would stick to this story in his autobiography.

The next morning, Barnum showed up at the offices of the *Sun* and told Locke that he was now persuaded that Heth had not been as old as claimed, and thus had had no direct connection to George Washington in his youth. In an article in the paper about Barnum's office visit, Locke wrote that the showman "took our exposure of the humbug with perfect good humor." While Barnum cozied up to the influential editor, his compatriot Levi Lyman was approaching a pricklier newspaperman, James Gordon Bennett, the Scottish-born editor of the *New York Herald.* In the most brazen twist to the whole story, Lyman persuaded Bennett that the autopsy itself had been a hoax, that Heth was still alive and even currently on display in Connecticut. The dead woman that Rogers had dissected was thus not Heth but a woman identified only as "Aunt Nelly" from Harlem. Barnum wrote that Bennett "proceeded to jot down the details as they were invented by Lyman's fertile brain." In the next day's *Herald,* Bennett, his good sense overwhelmed by his competitive fury, reprinted the story from the *Sun* and headlined it "Another Hoax!" He called the *Sun* story "rigmarole" and exclaimed — in italics yet — *"Joice Heth is not dead."* Locke and the *Sun* naturally defended their story, calling Bennett a "despicable and unprincipled scribbler" editing a "loathsome little sheet." Bennett was slow to realize that Lyman, probably with Barnum's encouragement, had made a fool of him, even proposing a large bet with Locke over whether Heth was still alive. Sales of both newspapers undoubtedly benefited from the dispute, as the public continued to wonder where the truth rested.[20]

But even this was not the end of the Heth affair. The following September, Barnum wrote, Bennett ran into Lyman on the street and "proceeded to 'blow him sky high' " for lying to him. Lyman laughed it off as a "harmless joke" and offered to make it up to the editor by telling him, once and for all, the whole story of the Heth affair from beginning to end — "the veritable history of the rise, progress, and termination of the Joice Heth humbug." In Barnum's account, Bennett not only forgave Lyman on the spot but led him back to the office and once again began taking notes for a series of four front-page stories (ending without explanation before the chronological narrative was finished) that amounted to "a ten times greater humbug" than Lyman's first offering. Bennett's long, successful newspaper career and his famously irascible nature would suggest that his forgiveness and this new failure of skepticism could not have come easily. But the prospect of having the last word with a newspaper-buying public still obsessed with Joice Heth must have proven irresistible.

Lyman's narrative had it that Barnum had found Heth on a Kentucky plantation, pulled her teeth, taught her the George Washington stories, and increased her purported age as he moved her from city to city. Many members of the public embraced this version of the affair, false though it was, which would have repercussions for Barnum throughout his career and up to the present day. But in his autobiography Barnum was willing to make the same sort of calculation that Bennett had, pointing out, "Newspaper and social controversy on the subject (and seldom have vastly more important matters been so largely discussed) served my purpose as 'a showman' by keeping my name before the public."[21]

In the two principal versions of Barnum's autobiography, he told this story of Heth in detail, showing an eagerness to persuade the reader at every turn that he honestly believed her to be what he said she was. Those who paid to see her, he wrote, were not simply amused by her novelty but decided for themselves that she was genuine. We undoubtedly live in a more skeptical age than the America of two centuries ago, but even factoring in both a more general naïveté and the racism of the era, the notion of a 161-year-old woman seems so unbelievable that it is hard to take Barnum at his word about his own gullibility.

As Barnum grew as a showman, he developed a more refined and humane view of his relationship to both his performers and his audience. He settled into an approach where the fakery was not a scam or an attempt to fool his customers into believing that something false was true, but in which they were drawn into the humbug by sharing the knowledge of the hoax. The deal he would make with his audiences in the future was that they would be entertained and that they would get their money's worth, either by enjoying the state of doubt in which one of his exhibits placed them or by sharing in the pleasure of distinguishing between what was false and what was true. Barnum's insistence throughout his life that he was not duping his customers with Joice Heth is the best evidence that, indeed, he was — that he had not yet understood what his relationship to his audience should be.

The far more complicated question, however, has to do with Barnum's connection to Heth herself. He is at best ambiguous about whether he bought the rights to exhibit Heth from Bowling or whether he actually purchased her. But is renting a slave really so different, morally, from owning one? At this time it was still legal to own a slave in the South, but not in New York or his native Connecticut, and it was not illegal to bring a slave to a free state for prescribed periods. Growing up in a modest Connecticut village and working in middle-class businesses in New York, the young Taylor had not in his first quarter-century had much exposure to slavery. At this time in his life, his attitudes toward race were typical of white Americans at the time, meaning deplorable, as his willingness to exploit the racially tinged curiosity of his audience suggests. But however racist most Americans both north and south were in the middle of the 1830s, a considerable number of them had long believed, especially after the American Revolution, that slavery was both immoral and intolerable. Barnum was not in this number, and if he was willing to look the other way about the claims he made for Heth, he was equally willing to avert his eyes from the human reality of "Aunt Joice," as he often called her. (The term feels patronizing today but was often used in his time for older women of any race.)

As Barnum aged, his attitudes toward race would become more enlightened. He shows respect for Heth in his autobiography, and nothing suggests that he treated her less than well while she was in his possession. His hiring a nurse for her when she became frail evinces a concern for her, although his motive was without doubt to protect his investment, and he clearly hoped that she would recover and go back on the road. Barnum wrote that he bought a mahogany coffin and saw to it that Heth was "buried respectably" in Bethel, but it can't be ignored that he shamelessly exploited her death before any such burial.[22]

From the perspective of our own time, its seems clear that Barnum crossed the line numerous times in his exhibition and promotion of Heth. Within his own lifetime, he seems to have realized this as well. If it was the most troubling venture Barnum ever undertook, it was also his first effort in the national spotlight, coming at a time in his life when his eagerness to establish himself seems to have overwhelmed any scruples he might otherwise have had. Barnum would grow in judgment, and even in virtue, throughout his career as a showman. But he was more than willing to court disapproval early on, and he would never be able to escape the cost to his reputation, despite later efforts to improve himself and his approach.

THREE:
ON BROADWAY

Although newspapers at the time estimated that Barnum cleared more than $10,000 on Joice Heth while she was alive and another $700 on her postmortem, he struggled to find further success in the years that followed, and he was forced to scramble both before and after the Panic of 1837. That nationwide crisis saw bubbles burst and banks fail, and a severe recession resulted that lasted into the mid-1840s in many places, and into the late 1840s in New York City. Barnum would spend much of the five years after the Heth affair on the road with various acts, ranging from dancers to a small circus. In the meantime, he moved Charity and Caroline back to Bethel, where they lived above the Yellow Store, and after a few years they were joined by a second daughter, Helen. During this period he would sometimes be away from home for a year or more, and each time he returned he would say that his life on the road was over, that he wished to stay home with his family. But then off he would go again. The tension most of us feel between home and away, the domestic and the exotic, existed deeply in him. He grappled with it in the late 1830s and early 1840s, before he would eventually have the means to pursue both aspects of living on a grand scale.

The first act Barnum promoted during this period was a juggler named Signor Antonio, whom he met in Albany while on tour with Heth. Antonio specialized in the "balancing and spinning of crockery" and other feats that were unfamiliar to Barnum, so he signed the fellow up on the spot. Barnum's first thought was to rename him Signor Vivalla, reasoning that the name Antonio was not "sufficiently 'foreign.' " He took Signor Vivalla on the road, and he was well received until they reached Philadelphia, where a portion of the audience hissed him. When Barnum discovered that the hecklers included another juggler and his friends, he managed to engage this competitor in a series of sham contests between the two men. Barnum whipped up enthusiasm with publicized claims of a thousand-dollar reward for the winner, while paying the two jugglers far, far less than that. When he confessed to this scheme years later, explaining how it was done and adding that the same sort of thing was often done by the managers of other entertainers, Barnum said he did not think revealing "tricks of the trade" would hurt business, "for the public appears disposed to be amused even when they are conscious of being deceived." This would become a keystone of his philosophy.[1]

Barnum next became a short-term partner in a small circus based in Danbury, Connecticut, run by a man named Aaron Turner. Soon they went out on the road, with Turner's two sons, who were trick riders, and a clown who did magic tricks rounding out a troupe that now included Signor Vivalla. After they had been touring for six months, traveling as far south as North Carolina, Barnum created his own small troupe. Grandiosely named "Barnum's Grand Scientific and Musical Theatre," it wandered through the Deep South until May 1837. He went home to Bethel for a few weeks and then was off again, traveling with his troupe as far as New Orleans and returning home only after another year had passed. Barnum wrote, "I was thoroughly disgusted with the life of an itinerant showman." He was determined to settle into something permanent in New York.[2]

Despite this protest, life on the road, while often hard and sometimes dangerous, had clearly engaged if not enriched him, and he came home with a suitcase full of stories. He had kept a diary of his journeys, and although it is now lost, it provided ample fodder for the 1855 version of his autobiography. The tales included his learning magic tricks, preaching in local churches of a Sunday, being forced to ride a rail, nearly getting lynched because of a practical joke, and ruining a magic trick when a squirrel that was part of the act "bit me severely" and "I shrieked with pain."[3]

The tale of the near lynching is vintage Barnum. It happened in Annapolis, Maryland, one Sunday morning when he was traveling with Turner's circus. He had bought a new black suit the night before and, "feeling proud" of it, perambulated through the town to show it off. Turner, who like so many people from back home had a fondness for practical jokes and Yankee cuteness, had decided that the black suit made Barnum look like a preacher. He thought it would be amusing to tell the townspeople that Barnum was a well-known and widely despised reverend from Rhode Island who had committed an infamous murder and escaped justice. Barnum wrote that he was "very innocently, though rather pompously, strutting down the side-walk" when a group of townspeople overtook him: "I believe I must have been uncommonly proud of that suit of clothes, for I was vain enough to believe that my *new suit* was what attracted such special attention." Even when he heard people call out "Let's tar and feather him," he professed to think that they were speaking of someone else. Finally, the light dawned through the comic fog of self-absorption, and Barnum managed to persuade what had now become a lynch mob to ask Turner for the truth about his identity.

Turner revealed the joke to the crowd, which "roared with laughter" in response, but not before Barnum's new suit had been nearly ripped to shreds and he himself had been dragged in the dirt. "I was exceedingly vexed," Barnum wrote. When he asked his friend why he'd done such a mean and frightening thing, Turner's response was, "My dear Barnum, it was all for our good. Remember, all we need to insure success is *notoriety.* . . . Our pavilion will be crammed tomorrow night." Barnum admitted that their show attracted "immense audiences during our stay." But he wouldn't forgive his partner easily, because "self interest was an after consideration in this case, the joke being prompted solely by a desire to see some fun, no matter at whose expense." Presumably it would have been more acceptable for Turner to risk Barnum's life if the goal had not been merriment but instead profit. Still, Barnum had the good humor, years later, to make an amusing story of it.

In his autobiography, Barnum did not often reveal his deepest personal feelings, but he let his emotions slip out when he wrote about splitting off from Turner's circus and setting out on his own. He had signed a six-month contract with Turner, and had made enough money, $1,200, to start his own traveling troupe. His company included Vivalla, a black singer and dancer named James Sandford, a few musicians, horses, wagons, and a tent. They had set out before him, and Turner had given Barnum a ride in his carriage in order to catch up with them. "We rode slowly, because reluctant to part, and twenty miles of road was beguiled by pleasing conversation before we overtook" the troupe. When they did say goodbye, Barnum referred to Turner as "my old friend," and then admitted to feelings of loneliness for "several days." It's safe to say that Barnum was so rarely alone in his life that his periods of loneliness stood out for him as they do for his readers. But he shut the door on these feelings midsentence, adding, "but my mind was so occupied by business, that I soon became reconciled to my new position." Once again Barnum's helpless love of commerce cured an ill.[4]

Upon his return to New York in June 1838, Barnum again tested his belief in the efficacy of advertising, creating an ad seeking a partner for a "permanent, respectable business," and mentioning that he had $2,500 to invest, along with his own energy and enthusiasm. In those recession days after the 1837 Panic, Barnum received ninety-three replies, a third of them from owners of porterhouses, which suggests how few people had the income to spend on beer and beef. Among the other responders were many confidence men, as well as those who were openly criminal: patent-medicine purveyors, a confessed counterfeiter, the inventor of a perpetual-motion machine run by a hidden spring. Barnum turned his nose up at one oddly prescient, if felonious opportunity when a failed merchant dressed as a Quaker proposed they go into the oats business. The merchant suggested that the good reputation of the Quakers would permit him to sell underweight bags of oats to middlemen, who would be less inclined to weigh out shipments from a trustworthy source, and thus would he make his profit. (Presumably this was not the basis on which the Quaker Oats Company would be founded in 1901.) Barnum's reaction to this leering fellow: "There were better men in the State prison."[5]

Among those who responded to the ad, Barnum chose for his partner "a German named Proler," who came with a recommendation from a city alderman, which in New York at that time might itself have been grounds for suspicion. Together, Proler and Barnum set up a small factory on Bowery Street, producing an unlikely assortment of products, from paste blacking and Cologne water to bear's grease. After about six months, Barnum sold out his share on credit to his partner, but the German made haste back to Europe, leaving Barnum with nothing but his unpaid note and the recipes for the products. Years later, in his autobiography, Barnum good-naturedly shared them, "gratis." Although the recipe for bear's grease — at the time believed to restore hair growth in men — called for the fat of hogs and sheep but no bear, a note to retailers advised, "To encourage the faith of your customers, exhibit a live Bear in front of the store, with the label, 'To be slaughtered next!' "[6]

In May 1840 Barnum returned to what he knew best, public entertainment, renting a stage space in Vauxhall Gardens at the top of the Bowery in Astor Place. The recession left the theater world in a particularly bad spot, and as *Gotham,* a history of New York City by Edwin G. Burrows and Mike Wallace, puts it, "the shabby but genial Vauxhall Gardens . . . still offered substantial food at reasonable prices, and its promenades, deserted by toffs, were thronged with toughs."[7]

Barnum's plan was to beat the bad times by offering "variety shows," which were inexpensive to produce and featured a changing mix of performers who were hired only by the night. Barnum had recently discovered a young man he believed was "really a genius in the dancing line." The boy, named John Diamond, was white, but Barnum put him in blackface and "he became justly celebrated as the best negro-dancer and representative of Ethiopian 'break-downs' in the land." Such was the racism of the day that "Negro dancing" was all the rage among white audiences, but only if it was not performed by an actual black person. At some point while Barnum was putting on shows at Vauxhall Gardens,

Diamond was unavailable, so Barnum searched the dance halls of the Five Points area for someone to replace him. He found another young man who, according to the contemporary journalist Thomas Low Nichols, danced even better. The problem for Barnum was that this person "was a genuine negro, and not a counterfeit one, and there was not an audience in America that would not have resented, in a very energetic fashion, the insult of being asked to look at the dancing of a real negro." Undeterred, Barnum rubbed the young man's face with grease, then blacked it with burnt cork, colored his lips red, and put him in a "woolly wig." His Vauxhall audience, assuming that the blackface disguised a white face, was roundly satisfied with the performance.[8]

Nevertheless the dancers, singers, street performers, and storytellers upon whom Barnum drew were not enough to make headway against the bad economy, and Barnum was forced to give up the Vauxhall business after only a few months. Afterward Barnum decided to take "Master Diamond," as he styled his young blackface dancer, "a lad of about sixteen years of age," back on the road. Once again he left Charity, Caroline, and now Helen behind to set off to Canada with a troupe consisting of

Diamond, a singer, and a fiddler. They then made their way south to Detroit, Chicago, St. Louis, and finally New Orleans. "With blackened face and hands," wrote a theater manager in New Orleans, Diamond continued to dance "to the no small delight of many who admired such exhibitions of suppleness. He could twist his feet and legs, while dancing, into more fantastic forms than I ever witnessed before or since in any human being."[9]

Barnum returned home eight months later, in April 1841, "re-resolved that I would never again be an itinerant showman." The sentiment was undoubtedly genuine, and his next move would underscore his determination to settle down. But itinerant he would always be, and he would never again be known as anything but a showman — even as he pursued secondary careers beyond the show line. Still, New York remained a hard place to get ahead. He set up an unprofitable Bible-selling business, made another run at putting on acts at Vauxhall Gardens, and even clerked for an equestrian show at the Bowery Amphitheatre, for which he also wrote advertisements at $4 a week. In his autobiography, he glided over an extended literary effort from this period, one that he had probably worked on in the first months of 1841, describing it only by saying, "I also wrote articles for the Sunday press" in order to "keep the pot boiling" at home. The work, appearing serially on Sundays in the *New York Atlas,* was a picaresque novella called *The Adventures of an Adventurer, Being Some Passages in the Life of Barnaby Diddledum.* The first four letters and final two letters of his antihero's name suggest that the sketches are autobiographical, but the name was also meant to be comic and uncomplimentary.[10]

Outwardly the adventures are the same ones Barnum himself had on his travels and are based on the journal that he would consult for his autobiography. But he turned his fictional self into a hard-bitten, cynical fellow who would do anything to make a buck — an approximation of what his reputation has become today. In the Joice (or "Joyce," as Barnum spelled it in his narrative) Heth affair, he portrayed Diddledum as the culprit Lyman had invented for James Gordon Bennett, the man who discovered her on a plantation, taught her the George Washington stories, and concocted the entire deception. Barnum called his alter ego the "King of Humbugs," using *humbug* in its most exploitative sense, meaning a bald-faced fraud, whereas when he would later refer to himself as merely the "prince of humbugs," the definition was softened considerably to mean an event put on to arouse public curiosity. *The Adventures of an Adventurer* is an odd effort, clearly true in some places and fictional in others, an attempt, perhaps, to expel the demons of actions he regretted and to remind himself of what he must never become.[11]

After a few months of barely getting by with these activities, months in which his family's health had turned from "excellent" to "poor," Barnum later wrote, "[I] began to realize, seriously, that I was at the very bottom round of fortune's ladder, and that I had now arrived at an age when it was necessary to make one grand effort to raise myself above want." He heard that Scudder's American Museum, where he had once turned down an opportunity to invest in a hydro-oxygen microscope, was looking for a buyer. This "collection of curiosities," located on Broadway across from St. Paul's Church, had its origins in 1791 in a museum room in City Hall created by the New York Tammany Society to "protect and preserve whatever relates to our country in art or nature." But offerings soon consisted mostly of "stuffed animals and doleful curiosities," as *Gotham* described them. Perhaps the low point in the Tammany Museum's early days came when, in a grotesque display of republican solidarity during the Reign of Terror in France, it exhibited a guillotine complete with a beheaded wax-figure counterrevolutionary.[12]

Like many such collections, the museum had passed from hand to hand, each owner adding attractions. John Scudder, an amateur taxidermist, began to manage it in 1802 and became its owner in 1810, specializing in natural history specimens until his death a decade later. New York City had given his New American Museum space in a building in City Hall Park in 1816 for the cost of one peppercorn in annual rent, an arrangement that lasted for nearly ten years after his death, when neighbors persuaded the city to make a change because of the noisy crowds the museum now drew with "vaudeville shows of magicians, freaks, ventriloquists, and tame Indians." A board of trustees ran the museum for the family after Scudder's death, intermittently asking Scudder's son to operate it. Although John Jr. soon "deteriorated into an unreliable and unpleasant alcoholic," he retained a showman's touch and briefly made the museum pay, "mainly by forsaking any remaining educational value it had." When in 1831 Alexis de Tocqueville visited the establishment, now housed in a building at Broadway and Ann Streets, expecting to see fine paintings, he "laughed like the blessed" at the disjunction between something called the American Museum and its dusty exhibits and magic-lantern show.[13]

One thing that had distinguished the museum throughout its earlier history was its educational appeal. Even when Scudder's had turned to vaudeville to keep the customers lining up, its educational content had helped to show which side of the vice/virtue street it inhabited. Whether or not the museum had been stripped of its educational value by the younger John Scudder depends to a large extent on where the line is drawn between education and entertainment. The collection in its various iterations reaching back to its eighteenth-century beginnings had never been purely educational, but with the senior Scudder's earnest interest in natural history, its educational value had been emphasized and recognized. As making a profit from a museum with unchanging exhibits became harder throughout the 1820s and 1830s, more and more emphasis was placed on amusements that would bring people in the door, and often those new visitors were not themselves very well educated. The response of Tocqueville and other members of the educated class was predictably one of alarm and condescension. But a historian of the American Museum gives a more democratic view of its contributions in the decades before Barnum acquired it:

This museum's presentations — of things animal, vegetable, aquatic and mineral; of paintings and panoramic views and waxworks; of machines and automatons and chemical and electrical experiments; of primitive implements and mummies and mastodon bones; of magicians, ventriloquists, minstrels and dramatists — had worked as a steady leaven of enlightenment. While traditional educators hesitated, the American Museum carried on as a combined kindergarten, academy, and college for America's culturally neglected Everyman.[14]

The museum went steadily downhill throughout the 1830s. Once valued at $25,000, it was now for sale for $15,000. But even this was far more money than Barnum had at his disposal, since "my recent enterprises had not indeed been productive, and my funds were decidedly low." In one of the more famous passages from his autobiography, Barnum told a friend that he was hoping to buy the American Museum. When the incredulous friend asked what with, Barnum replied, "*Brass,* for silver and gold I have none."[15]

It's a memorable line, and it's mostly true. In the convoluted series of events that led to Barnum's control of the museum, his brass was augmented primarily by his wits and personality. He decided to seek out a complete stranger, a retired merchant named Francis L. Olmsted, who owned the building in which the museum was housed, with the quixotic goal of persuading him to buy the collection for him on credit, arguing that he would be a more reliable tenant than the struggling Scudder family. This, against all odds, Barnum was able to do, partly because of the impression he made on Olmsted, partly because friends of Barnum, including William Niblo and Moses Yale Beach, who owned the New York *Sun,* were willing to go in person to speak up for him. When Barnum visited Olmsted the day after his friends had, the older man gruffly said, "I don't like your references, Mr. Barnum." After Barnum replied that he was sorry to hear it, Olmsted continued, now laughing, "They all speak too well of you."[16]

Olmsted said he was willing to make the deal with Barnum, but he wanted some collateral. Barnum owned only one mortgage-free piece of property, that five acres of utterly useless land on Ivy Island that his grandfather had given to him. He paused just a moment for moral qualms when offering the property to Olmsted as collateral, then absolved himself by remembering the land as he had imagined it as a boy, not as it was — and by assuring himself of what he could not yet know, that he was going to make a success of the museum and thereby not fail to pay Olmsted back.

Barnum then went to the Scudder family's representative and talked him down to a price of $12,000 for the collection, but before the deal was signed the directors of a rival museum swooped in and offered the original price, putting up $1,000 in earnest money. Barnum was "thunderstruck" to have lost his purchase, but he was undeterred. He suspected that his rivals, who were bankers and not showmen, had created what they called the New-York Museum Company in order to join the remnants of another collection with Scudder's,

106

selling stock in the enterprise with no real ambition to make a go of it. Barnum went to his newspaper friends and offered to expose what he portrayed as a swindle, and he "wrote a large number of squibs, cautioning the public against buying the Museum stock." Sure enough, soon "the stock was as 'dead as a herring.' " Barnum went back to the Scudder's administrator and elicited a secret deal that if the New-York Museum Company directors did not buy Scudder's on the day they promised, he could have it for the negotiated price.

In the meantime, his rivals contacted Barnum with an offer to run their operation, presumably so he would stop undermining their stock scheme. Barnum saw an opportunity to lull them into thinking he was no longer an antagonist or even a competitor, and so accepted their offer. The day for payment arrived, and the directors, feeling no urgency to pay, didn't act. Thus the museum slipped into Barnum's hands. Just to rub salt in their wounds, he wrote to the directors the next day, offering them free passes to the museum that was now *his*.

Olmsted's building was located just across Broadway from St. Paul's Church and the Astor House, which was the city's, and indeed the country's, premier hotel. When Barnum acquired the museum, Olmsted's many-windowed marble building presented a bland façade to the street, matching the reputation of its overly familiar exhibits. Barnum quickly moved to liven up its look. He mounted a collection of foreign flags along the roof on the Broadway side to accompany a huge American flag. He installed a large Drummond light on the roof, employing a powerful beam of limelight with reflecting lenses to, for the very first time, turn the Broadway night into day. But even this did not satisfy Barnum's need to attract attention to his new enterprise, so he had large, colorful, oval paintings of individual creatures — a Noah's ark of animal portraits — placed between the eighty windows in the upper floors of the building. He waited to have them installed until all the oils were completed, creating the maximum dramatic effect by hanging them all on a single night. He attributed an immediate hundred-dollar increase in his daily draw to the paintings' impact.[17]

The museum was auspiciously situated to suit Barnum's ambitions. St. Paul's, City Hall, and Astor House drew the city's fashionable residents, who would promenade along Broadway and in City Hall Park to see and be seen. But too few members of the upper crust existed to support a museum on the scale Barnum foresaw. The growing success of the Bowery as an entertainment center for the thousands of workers and seamen who lived in boardinghouses in lower Manhattan proved that hoi polloi would spend their money on amusements fairly priced. Between the Bowery and the museum, just northeast of City Hall Park, began the infamous Five Points, a swampy area where Irish, free blacks, and various immigrant communities lived tightly packed in uneasy proximity. "All that is loathsome, drooping, and decayed is here," Charles Dickens wrote about the Five Points after his 1842 visit to America. Its dens of gambling, drinking, and prostitution appealed not only to the working classes but also to better-off New York men and tens of thousands of visiting businessmen. But vice and virtue existed side by side throughout the teeming neighborhoods of lower Manhattan, and moral reform societies and temperance groups also had their energetic supporters in places like the Five Points. As the city began to climb its way out of the recession, about 30 percent of Manhattanites were middle class. Because of the fluidity of class status in a rapidly growing city vulnerable to booms and busts, achieving or maintaining respectability was a serious matter, demonstrated by one's possessions, taste, and manners, or by whether one boarded, rented, or owned a house.[18]

Barnum wanted to attract this rising middle class and the aspiring members of the surrounding neighborhoods. They had more money to spend than those in the boardinghouses and were more likely to spend it on wholesome activities, and with their higher rates of literacy, they were more susceptible to newspaper advertising. As Barnum began to add to the museum's collection, he continued the institution's long tradition of emphasizing exhibits that would both entertain and make his customers think. So many newcomers to and tourists in New York, then as now, were drawn to the city by its promise not just of excitement but also of connection to a wider world than the one on view back home. Barnum had an unachievably ambitious plan for satisfying this hunger to learn: he aimed to acquire at least one example of every single thing in existence, living or dead. In the 1820s a Scudder Museum advertisement had claimed 150,000 items in its collection, and by the 1860s Barnum would advertise that his museum contained a "million wonders."[19]

It was almost impossible to describe the breadth of what the museum held even before Barnum acquired it and began energetically adding to its exhibits. After he had been at it for a few years, the task became so hopeless as to be laughable. A humorist using the pen name Q. K. Philander Doesticks visited the museum in 1854 and wrote a piece that parodied the attempt, giving a good sense of how overwhelmed a visitor to the American Museum must have felt. What Doesticks claims to have seen included:

pictures, paddles, pumpkins, carriages, corals, lava, boats, breeches, boa constrictors, shells, oars, snakes, toads, butterflies, lizards, bears, reptiles, reprobates, bugs, bulls, bells, bats, birds, petrifactions, putrefactions, model railroads, model churns, model gridirons, model artists, model babies, cockneys, cockades, cockroaches, cocktails, scalps, Thomashawks, Noah's ark, Paganini's fiddle, Old Grimes's coat, autocrats, autobiographies, autographs, chickens, cheeses, codfish, Shanghais, mud-turtles, alligators, moose, mermaids, hay-scales, scale armor, monsters, curiosities from Rotterdam, Amsterdam, Beaverdam, Chow Sing, Tchinsing, Linsing, Lansing, Sing Sing, cubebs, cart wheels, mummies, heroes, poets, idiots, maniacs, benefactors, malefactors, pumps, porcupines and pill machines, all mingled, mixed, and conglomerated, like a Connecticut chowder.[20]

From the later vantage of the first edition of his autobiography, Barnum mused on the relative merits of entertainment and education in this chowder, and although there is no good reason to doubt him when he insisted that the entertainments existed to promote the educational elements, he undoubtedly worked at both sorts of exhibits with energetic glee.

If I have exhibited a questionable [humbug] in my Museum, it should not be overlooked that I have also exhibited cameleopards, a rhinoceros, grisly bears, orang-outangs, great serpents, etc., about which there could be no mistake because they were alive; and I should hope that a little "clap-trap" occasionally, in the way of transparencies, flags, exaggerated pictures, and puffing advertisements, might find "an offset" in a wilderness of wonderful, instructive, and amusing realities.[21]

He went so far as to suggest that in his experience the members of his public were not only not offended by the harmless laying on of claptrap but that they preferred their realities sweetened with some imaginatively presented foolery. His success in creating entertainment with a veneer of the worthwhile was soon apparent. Barnum reported that receipts for the museum in its last year with the Scudder family, 1841, were $10,862, a number that is specific enough to be credible, as is the number for the next year, his first of proprietorship, $27,912.62. With the frugal assistance of his beloved if often out-of-sight Charity, who helped him in the first year to keep expenses for the family below $600, he managed to absolve his $12,000 debt to Francis Olmsted in about a year and a half — "every cent having been paid out of the profits of the establishment."[22]

But Barnum knew that however cluttered with wonders the rooms of his museum were, he would need to keep generating profits to keep the museum expanding (and to allow his family to live less frugally). This would depend on return business, and to achieve that would require a regular schedule of new amusements, augmented by well-publicized amazements. Even if profit had not been a motive, Barnum saw by now that his talent and his enthusiasm made him a showman first and a curator second. How could he resist scheduling the Lecture Room in his building with shows of the sort he had been taking on the road for years and creating an occasional excitement in the exhibit rooms with marvels that would test his customers' credulity?

FOUR:
THE MERMAID

Within months of his gaining control of the museum, the thirty-two-year-old owner of the Boston Museum, Moses Kimball, arrived at Barnum's door with an unusual specimen. Nothing suggests that Kimball and Barnum, not quite thirty-two himself, were acquainted before this visit, but they were undoubtedly aware of each other. Kimball could not have missed the splash that Barnum had made in Boston with Joice Heth, and Kimball's Boston Museum had now been in operation for more than a year. Within days of its opening, the *New York Herald* published an article calling it "all the rage . . . the most splendid establishment of its kind in the Union." Barnum's pulse must have quickened when he read that this new museum of Kimball's had a theater capable of seating one thousand patrons, its confines described by the *Herald*'s Boston correspondent as "airy, perfectly comfortable in every respect, and hung with paintings of a high order." Even as Barnum had been scheming to acquire the Scudder family collection, in the autumn of 1841 such acts as "Winchell, the comic drollerist" were moving between the American Museum and the Boston Museum. With the entrepreneurial Barnum now in charge, Kimball must have seen the benefits of a more deliberate collaboration.[1]

What Kimball brought for Barnum's inspection toward the middle of June 1842 was far more exciting in name than in reality. He called it a mermaid, from a distant part of the ocean, embalmed and miraculously preserved. It appeared in fact to be the upper body of a small female monkey of some sort, attached to the lower half of a large fish. Barnum could see the ruse immediately and later admitted that the "mermaid" was "an ugly, dried-up, black-looking, and diminutive specimen, about three feet long," which displayed a permanent grimace, suggesting that it had "died in great agony." He did, however, admire the craftsmanship with which the two halves were joined. Such specimens had become fairly commonplace, as Barnum himself pointed out, generally having been concocted in Asia. He chose not to dwell upon the difficulties, however, but instead envisioned a "Fejee Mermaid" — invoking the paradise of the South Pacific — and realized that this was an exhibit the public could be induced to pay good money to see.[2]

Still, Barnum made a show of feigning ignorance about the creature's authenticity. He took it to his museum's longtime naturalist, Emile Guillaudeu, for an opinion of the *"genuineness"* (Barnum's italics) of this mash-up of fauna. The naturalist expressed surprise because he was unfamiliar with any monkey or fish that looked like those employed in the mermaid's "manufacture."

"Then why do you suppose it is manufactured?" Barnum asked.

"Because," the naturalist replied, "I don't believe in mermaids."[3]

Barnum professed not to accept his expert's opinion, but he knew as well as anyone that Guillaudeu had it right.

Kimball told Barnum how he came to possess the specimen. The story he had been told was that a sea captain from Boston, having made port in Calcutta in 1817, had been offered the mermaid for purchase, its seller attributing its provenance to Japanese sailors. The price was steep, a fact that undoubtedly contributed to a sort of delirium that developed in the captain, who leaped at the notion that this lump of matter could make his fortune. He was evidently a better ship's captain than he was a man, because even after he stole $6,000 from the ship's account to buy the mermaid and made off with his specimen to London, leaving the ship in Calcutta with its first mate, the owner did not prosecute him but eventually gave him another ship so he could work off his debt. At his death, the captain still had the object in his possession — his only son's only inheritance. The son had sold it cheap to Kimball, who had as little notion of what to do with it as the captain had. Thus Kimball had brought it to Barnum.

Kimball's story, or Barnum's retelling of it, might accurately recount the one that the captain's son had told, but the truth was somewhat different. In the early 1990s, a Swedish physician living in London named Jan Bondeson, whose pastime was researching medical curiosities, pieced together the real story through documents and periodicals at the British Museum, the Royal College of Surgeons, and elsewhere. The Boston ship captain, named Samuel Barrett Eades, was also a one-eighth owner of a merchant ship, the *Pickering,* whose principal owner was an Englishman named Stephen Ellery.

While in port in Batavia, now Jakarta, in what was then the Dutch East Indies, Eades was shown the purported mermaid by Dutch merchants, who, in line with Kimball's story, had purchased it from Japanese fishermen. So great became Eades's need to own the mermaid that in January 1822, without consulting Ellery, he sold the *Pickering* and all its cargo and set off with his prize for London. When he reached Cape Town on the journey home, he exhibited his specimen to make some money. Among those who flocked to see it was a respected churchman, who was so persuaded by what he saw that he wrote back to London, "I have to day seen a Mermaid, now exhibiting in this town. I have always treated the existence of this creature as fabulous; but my skepticism is now removed." The letter went on to describe the specimen in detail, in terms that match the object that Kimball would take to Barnum. The churchman's letter was widely reprinted in London newspapers and magazines, stirring up interest in the public and, as it would turn out, in British customs officials.

When Captain Eades arrived in London in September 1822, the mermaid was immediately confiscated and held at the East India baggage warehouse for some days.

After Eades was finally able to retrieve it from customs, he engaged the famous British illustrator George Cruikshank to draw it from the front and side and began to advertise his plan to exhibit it in a room at the Turf Coffeehouse in St. James Street in London. Cruikshank's drawings closely match one that Barnum would commission two decades later of Kimball's mermaid. As many as several hundred people a day paid a shilling to see it at the coffeehouse, and the matter of its authenticity was never seriously questioned. Finally in November, a naturalist named William Clift, who had been allowed to examine the specimen while it was being held by customs on the condition that he keep his findings in confidence, revealed in a newspaper article that it had been skillfully assembled from parts of an orangutan, a baboon, and a salmon. Her eyes were fake, her nails were made of horn or quill, and her pendulous breasts had been stuffed so that they hid the seam between ape and fish. Clift had been able to feel where the bones of the arms had been sawed to make the proportions closer to those of a human rather than an orangutan. The specimen was two feet, ten inches long. Clift's article was not good for business, but Eades continued to show his exhibit to smaller and smaller audiences at the coffeehouse and elsewhere in London. It then toured the countryside and appeared at fairs for the next few years, until it eventually disappeared from view, although there were reported sightings of it in France and elsewhere in subsequent years.[4]

Stephen Ellery tried to get Eades to pay him what he was owed for his seven-eighths share of the *Pickering* out of the proceeds from the exhibition, but Eades refused and threatened to leave the country. The ship owner went to court to prevent that from happening, and the ruling supported his suit. And there ends the trail of the relationship between Eades and Ellery. Somehow in the aftermath, the strange specimen made its way to America and into Kimball's hands.

In choosing Barnum to help him figure out what to do with the mermaid he had purchased, Kimball had come to the right man. They must have liked each other from the first, for a close relationship would quickly develop between them. Barnum would soon come to use his Boston brother as an almost daily sounding board. Kimball's presence seems to have had an immediate catalyzing effect on Barnum, helping him to realize how he could combine his new museum's solidity with his long-running instinct for amazement. He hatched a complicated plan for engaging the public's curiosity not only about the Fejee Mermaid itself but also about the alluring possibility that mermaids really did exist, a persistent myth in many cultures going back thousands of years.

First, Barnum signed a contract allowing him to exhibit the mermaid for up to three months, at $12.50 per week, after which Kimball would have it for the same period of time. Then they would jointly send it on the road for up to two years, splitting the costs and the receipts — a long-range commitment to collaborate that reflects trust between the two men. Barnum's scheme to "start the ball a-rolling" was to have friends in other cities forward letters to New York newspapers that Barnum himself had secretly written. The letters were constructed as a miscellany of local news, in which was included an item about the recent visit of a Dr. J. Griffin, who represented the (fictional) Lyceum of Natural History in London. The naturalist was reportedly on his way to New York and then to London with "a veritable mermaid taken among the Fejee Islands, and preserved in China, where the doctor had bought it at a high figure" for his London employer.[5]

Barnum's hoaxes were always certain to mention the great expense involved in the procurement of any exhibit, a detail meant to distinguish his offerings from run-of-the-mill claptrap, suggesting an element of respectability that would appeal to his targeted middle-class audience (or those who wished to be middle class). Throughout these letters, written from the confines of his muggy office at the museum, Barnum continued to call the specimen the "Fejee Mermaid," a name that must have added in incalculable ways to the allure the public would feel as it clamored to see her. He also tucked in the winning and irrelevant detail that the aptly named Dr. Griffin was "recently from Pernambuco," an exotic and mildly romantic name to an American ear, even if the possessor of that ear didn't know that it was a real place in Brazil. His careful attention to such seemingly small matters, similar to that he had shown in planning the celebration of his release from jail years before, undoubtedly distinguished him from others in his line of work, such as Kimball himself.

Barnum had the first letter mailed from Montgomery, Alabama, a second some days later from Charleston, South Carolina, and a third from the District of Columbia. A different New York newspaper fell for and thus published each of these letters, in which the non-mermaid news was plausible enough, and in the third letter the writer suggested that New York editors really ought to see the specimen for themselves. Before that would happen, a meeting was arranged with local reporters in Philadelphia, where they were introduced to the mermaid and to Dr. Griffin, who was in reality none other than Levi Lyman, Barnum's henchman in the Heth affair.

Barnum reports with evident satisfaction that "the plan worked admirably," and the columns in the Philadelphia papers served to further entice the New York press. By the time Lyman reached the foot of Greenwich Street in New York and signed himself in as Dr. Griffin at the Pacific Hotel, New York newspapermen were clamoring to see the mermaid. In the meantime, Barnum commissioned highly idealized woodcuts and engravings of beautiful, full-breasted, unclothed mermaids with flowing blond tresses, clearly meant to imply that this was what the Fejee Mermaid now, or at least once had, looked like. He added write-ups "proving" the authenticity of these formerly fictional creatures.

Barnum offered three different New York papers "exclusive" access to one of the images and a report, which he modestly acknowledged was "well-written." All three papers ran the exclusive on the same Sunday morning, July 17, 1842. Just one day short of a month from the date he had signed the contract with Kimball, Barnum had blown up a typhoon of interest.

At this point, Barnum released for sale on the streets, at a penny apiece, ten thousand copies of a pamphlet that contained all of the images and stories he had prepared. Then he rented the Concert Hall on Broadway and placed advertisements in the papers saying Dr. Griffin (again "recently arrived from Pernambuco") and the mermaid would be on exhibit *"positively for one week only!"* Although Barnum's connection with the mermaid must have been known to the newspaper editors to whom he was providing images, copy, and advertising, he deliberately kept his own name out of the ads and publicity, the better to suggest that the Fejee Mermaid was not a stunt but a legitimate discovery. For this reason, too, he did not at first display "her fish-ship" (his play on the honorific "her ladyship") at the American Museum, but instead sent her up

Broadway to the Concert Hall.[6]

The exhibit opened there on August 8, with Lyman, portraying the English Dr. Griffin, addressing the crowds and "learnedly descanting on the wonders of nature," in his boss's words. Barnum felt some concern that, despite his phony accent, Lyman would be recognized as a principal in the Heth affair, "but happily no such catastrophe occurred." The glaring discrepancy between the portrait of the beautiful mermaid that appeared on an eight-foot-tall transparency outside the hall and the shriveled, three-foot mummy on display within caused, Barnum declared, little consternation in the thousands of people who paid a quarter to see the exhibit. But Lyman's experience in coming face to face with these crowds was somewhat different from Barnum's rosy memory. Barnum did tell of seeing an old Dutchman ask Lyman if the blackened object on display was really the "*mare*-maid." When Lyman, "evidently ill at ease," said yes, the "Dutchman, with a look of scorn such as I have rarely seen equalled, turned to depart, exclaiming, 'Well, that is the poorest show I ever *did* see.' "[7]

When the Concert Hall week was up, Barnum was ready to advertise that he had acquired the mermaid (for a precious sum, of course) for his museum, where it would be displayed at no charge beyond the usual admittance fee of a quarter. He had made arrangements so that an eighteen-foot-long flag displaying an idealized mermaid "was streaming directly in front of the Museum." When Lyman saw the flag upon reporting to work on the Monday morning that the mermaid went on display, he hurried to Barnum's office, angrily insisting that it must come down. The difference between what was pictured on the flag and the mermaid itself was just too "preposterous," Lyman said. When Barnum defended the flag, arguing that it was "only to catch the eye" and that nobody would expect it to represent the real exhibit, Lyman tellingly replied, "I think I ought to know something of the public 'swallow' by this time, and I tell you the mermaid won't go down if that flag remains up." Barnum protested that he had spent $70 on the flag, but Lyman insisted that either the flag must go or he would.

Barnum portrayed the dispute as a friendly one, but Lyman was clearly quite serious, and the strength of his feeling could only have flowed from further unpleasant experiences with skeptical visitors at the Concert Hall. Because Barnum needed Dr.

Griffin to preserve some semblance of authenticity in the act, he took the flag down and never displayed it again. He good-naturedly told this story, chastening himself, but he couldn't resist adding in a footnote that Lyman eventually became a Mormon and moved to Nauvoo, Illinois, where Joseph Smith and his followers were ensconced and where Lyman became prominent in his new faith. We are left to presume that Lyman's budding religious beliefs engendered his sudden and otherwise inexplicable qualms about deceiving the public. For Barnum, this was a minor and ultimately transparent sort of deception. After all, those patrons who were actually surprised by the disjunction between the beautiful creature on the flag and the ugly reality inside would have a whole museum of wonders to recompense them for the quarter they had spent.[8]

Barnum understated the Fejee Mermaid's exhibit at the American Museum over the weeks it was on display as being an "attractive feature," yet he made a point of comparing the gate in the month before the mermaid arrived ($1,272) with the month it was on display ($3,341.93). Each time he wrote about the mermaid in his memoirs, he did so with less bravura. After the 1869 edition, he wrote that his purpose in displaying her had been "mainly to advertise the regular business of the Museum, and this effective indirect advertising is the only feature I can commend, in a special show of which, I confess, I am not proud." Still, even in this vein he is compelled to point out that as the exhibit subsequently traveled the country, "the fame of the Museum, as well as the mermaid, wafted from one end of the land to the other," and he knew that every dollar he sowed on advertising it "would return in tens, and perhaps hundreds, in a future harvest."[9]

The Fejee Mermaid was on tour by the following January, heading south. This represented a change in plans, but Barnum and Kimball evidently worked it out amicably, because by early 1843 a torrent of friendly letters found their way from Barnum to Kimball via No. 5 Wall Street, where the Adams Express pickup for Boston set out each afternoon at 4:30, on occasion bearing more than one letter for Kimball. Although Kimball's letters to Barnum are lost, Barnum's responses demonstrate that Kimball kept up his side of the correspondence. Barnum would sometimes ramble on for several pages in his hasty handwriting, liberally underlining words for emphasis. A twentieth-century fire at the Boston Athenaeum, where many of Barnum's letters to Kimball are still kept, charred their edges and sometimes obscured his words, but Barnum's energy for the business of acquiring acts for his museum is ever evident in them.[10]

At first, Barnum seemed satisfied with how the Fejee Mermaid was drawing crowds on the road as part of a traveling show similar to those he himself had often accompanied. The other acts included a magician, a ventriloquist, an automaton, a glass-blower, and an orangutan. Barnum's Uncle Alanson Taylor, long since forgiven for having sued Barnum for libel back in the Bethel days, had replaced Lyman, and on January 30, 1843, Barnum expressed what cannot have been a very serious fear that Taylor was sending the earnings to them too quickly and might not be holding back enough money to cover his expenses. By February 5 Barnum had received a letter from Taylor, who had appeared with the show in Charleston, South Carolina, from January 17 to 21. The letter, Barnum wrote to Kimball, "gives us occasion for more rejoicing. . . . Wasn't it lucky to get rid of slow-moving, lazy-boned Lyman?" Barnum burbled on, "[In] showing and scientifically explaining, Taylor not only equals Lyman, but far exceeds him in point of industry and perseverance. He is faithful as the sun." Barnum punctuated his optimism by informing Kimball that he had credited him $50 from Taylor's remittances.[11]

But the optimism barely outlasted the new week. On February 10, Barnum sent Kimball a newspaper clipping that suggested Taylor was under attack in Charleston and "may be obliged to come home — though I hope for better things." A Charleston minister and naturalist named John Bachman, two of whose daughters were married to sons of John James Audubon, had in January written a letter to a Charleston newspaper urging readers not to be deceived by the mermaid. Taylor counterattacked on January 21, offering $500 to anyone who could show him an example of a fake mermaid made of a monkey and a fish and insinuating that Bachman had once been on the wrong side of the law. On February 5 a group of local scientists and naturalists lent their authority to Bachman, calling the exhibit "an injury to natural science" designed to "extract money from the public under false pretenses." It was their duty, they wrote, to "expose this vile imposition." As Neil Harris writes in *Humbug,* his biography of Barnum, these scientists made the telling point that the Fejee Mermaid had been put together "with very little regard to anatomical accuracy, since there were present two chests and two abdomens."[12]

By February 13 Barnum's hopes for redeeming the tour were dashed. "The bubble has burst," he wrote, and poor Taylor "[has] gone through everything that a mortal could stand." The situation had gotten so bad so fast in Charleston, Barnum had been told, that "Fejee is on her way" by ship back to New York. "She will probably have to lie still a spell," Barnum warned Kimball, "— perhaps forever." Barnum and Kimball discussed whether Taylor should be cut loose while the mermaid made its slow return. It apparently arrived by February 21, Taylor having sent it to a third party in New York to prevent its detection. One day short of a month later, Barnum wrote to Kimball, "Some of our damned skunks have seen the Mermaid box stowed away on the top shelf of my office and that has been tattled out it seems. Now how the hell to keep anything from the damned traitors."[13]

Barnum raised the idea of suing John Bachman or — saving the expense of an attorney — simply to "pretend" that they had sued him, with a tip to the Charleston papers. Either approach might "breathe the breath of life into her nostrils again." Barnum did point out that, since the mermaid belonged to Kimball, Barnum's name would not be on the suit, although he pledged to "join in that speculation." Back and forth the correspondence went on the possibility of a suit, until Barnum concluded on April 8 that, "on reflection," he "would not try the Fejee again." At least from Barnum's perspective, the decision not to show her removed the need for the suit and its attendant publicity, and all discussion of the suit then disappeared from his side of the correspondence. A few days earlier he had written Kimball, "My wife and all the old maids in town think [showing the Fejee Mermaid again] would ruin me," but whether or not Charity's advice helped sway him to the safer course, we are left to speculate.[14]

More than fifty letters from Barnum to Kimball from 1843 alone found their way into the Boston Athenaeum collection. Even given his remarkable reserves of energy, Barnum could hardly have found time to write many more letters than that. He often apologized to Kimball that he was writing in haste, and the sheer number of subjects

133

on his mind on any given day reinforced the truth of this. By early 1843 Barnum had purchased what was known as Peale's Museum, which his rival, the New-York Museum Company, had owned. The directors of the company had bought it from Rubens Peale, the son of the painter and naturalist Charles Willson Peale, who had started the first great American natural history museum in Philadelphia soon after the Revolution. The New York Peale's, during its last days before Barnum acquired it, had created acts mocking Barnum's, such as one it called the "Fudge-ee Mermaid." At first, Barnum kept his ownership of Peale's quiet and hired the museum's last proprietor to stay on and keep up the mocking rivalry, which Barnum knew was good publicity for both of the museums. A month into his ownership, he shared with Kimball his weekly expenses for his new establishment ("lady doorkeeper at $3.50 . . . boy to sweep out $3.50 . . . advertisements $3.50 . . . fuel $1, Gas $8, Rent $25"). In all, he reported his expenses at $47 per week, whereas his weekly receipts were not lower than $56 and could be as high as $70.

Not only did Barnum go back and forth with Kimball about acts they could share ("I must have the fat boy or the other monster. . . . I think you had better come to New York and see these Indians and make a bargain") as well as exhibits ("Do you want a pretty good sized bald eagle skin? I bought two yesterday — shot on Long Island"), but he was also in regular contact with the Peale family museum in Philadelphia and one they owned in Baltimore about renting out acts or other exhibits.[15]

The level of affection and trust in his letters to Kimball suggests that a real friendship was developing, even if it was largely epistolary. Several letters from 1843 alluded to meetings or possible meetings in New York, since Barnum couldn't get to Boston: "If I ever see you it must be here — my leaving New York seems to be out of the question." But it is not clear that any of those proposed 1843 meetings happened. Barnum's greetings in letters from that year evolved from "Dear Moses" to "My Dear Moses" to "Friend Moses" to the mildly comic "Dearly beloved Moses" and back again. He generally signed off with "Thine," "As ever Thine," or "Thine as ever," or, more playfully, "Thine all over" and once even "Yours forever and a day," often followed by "Barnum" or just "B."

Barnum was more than willing to give advice and to receive it. On March 22,

1843, he wrote in characteristic good humor, "Your advice in your letter was very very good and thankfully received — but won't be strictly followed." Six months later, he wrote:

Drive ahead — don't share the steam — make all the noise possible — and by all means keep down the expenses!
Advice is cheap — ain't it?[16]

As might be expected of two men whose businesses were increasingly intertwined, their best-laid plans sometimes went astray. When Barnum crossed a line with Kimball at a time when things were not going well in Boston and Kimball was feeling, and expressing, his distress, Barnum didn't just apologize, he also sincerely sympathized with his friend and tried hard to josh him into a better mood. "Oh, Temperance! Oh Moses!!!" he began. "What a big oat you must [have] swallowed crossways when you wrote me. . . . Well, you are in rather bad luck just [now] and you have a right to be cross." Then Barnum lists all the things he knows are going wrong for his friend — "the armour was wrong, [the] Indian men were contrary . . . business was bad" — and he works into the middle of the list "Barnum w[as] greedy and was keeping [an act] longer south than he promised." Barnum calls his angry friend "a devilish clever fellow" and then begins to smooth things over with a vengeance:

And you may get cross once in a while, and [you] may write me cross letters, and I'll bear with [it like] a man; but you must permit me to laugh when I read your bitter effusions, for I know just how you feel, having felt exactly so a thousand times. But don't eat a fellow up now without giving him a chance for his life — pray don't! You may blow me up a little, and swear at me if you are a mind to . . . but don't — oh don't — tar [and] . . . feather me and draw me in quarters.[17]

It was quite a performance, all in all, and Kimball could only have been touched by the sincerity of the effort that his busy friend made to patch things up immediately rather than allow hard feelings to fester. Barnum's letters to Kimball from this era show a remarkable level of intimacy — not only the affection that Barnum openly expressed and also implied in his casual, humorous style, but also what is demonstrated by his willingness to share his best ideas and to admit his failures, such as when his daily intake was low or an act did not pan out.

His quickly formed trust of Kimball speaks to a need Barnum must have felt, perhaps without realizing it, for someone to confide in. Barnum said surprisingly little about Charity in his autobiographical writings, so we can only surmise that she did not fully satisfy this need in him for a confidante. Although he was building a circle of loyal friends in New York — think of the men who immediately stood up for him when he was purchasing the American Museum — he was a public figure now, someone about whom people gossiped to the newspapers (who were not above offering, for a price, to refrain from printing unflattering items about him, a practice Barnum rightly labeled "Black Mail"). Part of the attraction Barnum felt for Kimball could well have been Kimball's comforting distance from the stage Barnum trod.[18]

FIVE:
THE GENERAL

Barnum does not say how he first heard about young Charles S. Stratton, but he reports that he asked his older half brother, Philo Barnum, to set up a meeting with the child. Philo had moved in about 1838 to Bridgeport, then a small town only recently incorporated, and was now running a hotel there called the Franklin House.

Charley Stratton's ancestors had lived in coastal Connecticut for more than a hundred fifty years, and his grandparents had inhabited the village that became Bridgeport since early in the nineteenth century. His parents, who were first cousins, also settled there, occupying a saltbox house on Main Street. His father scraped by as a carpenter and his mother worked as a part-time maid in a nearby hotel. They had two daughters and then welcomed their son into the world at about the same time as Philo arrived in town. On January 4, 1838, the nine-and-a-half-pound baby was born, well-proportioned, healthy, unremarkable. When Charley reached the age of five months, however, now weighing fifteen pounds and less than two feet in length, he stopped growing. Otherwise his physical and mental development continued as would be expected in a child his age. People in town got used to seeing him accompany his mother to work or riding on the wagon of a local baker who drove through the streets selling his goods. Various townspeople would take credit for making Philo aware of this local sprite, but given the intimate size of the town, that would hardly seem to have been necessary. Barnum's reluctance to give Philo credit for bringing the child to his attention was likely due to Philo's later claim to a share in the considerable profits that would eventually grow out of the meeting.[1]

The fateful convergence of Barnum and the future General Tom Thumb occurred in the dining area of Philo's hotel in November 1842. Barnum had ridden a packet boat upriver from New York to Albany on a business matter, but while he was there the Hudson froze over, so he started back overland, via the Housatonic railroad, traveling on it as far as its terminal in Bridgeport, from which he would take a steamboat to

New York the next day. Always resourceful in the use of his time and ever on the lookout for a new act for his museum, Barnum made the most of this overnight stop. One local woman remembered that the Stratton boy wore a blue velvet suit to the meeting. In his autobiography, Barnum described Charley as the smallest child he had ever seen of walking age, "a bright-eyed little fellow, with light hair and ruddy cheeks," who was "perfectly healthy, and as symmetrical as an Apollo." The boy, not quite five years old, appeared at first to be what nobody would call him for the rest of his days, "bashful," in Barnum's description. But he soon opened up, persuading the showman that — as those bright eyes suggested — he was intelligent for his age. Still, Barnum detected no evidence yet of what would turn out to be Charley's extraordinary cleverness. Barnum claimed that the meeting left him doubtful about the boy's earning potential, and so he hired him to appear at his museum as a human oddity for only four weeks at $3 per week, plus his expenses and those of his mother, Cynthia.[2]

With his usual alacrity and willingness to fudge the truth, Barnum both detected and immediately solved the main problem in exhibiting Charley. If he revealed the young man's real age, how would people know that he was anything other than a smallish child rather than what was true, that he was a perfectly proportioned dwarf? "Some license might indeed be taken with the facts," Barnum ventured, and license was indeed taken in his promotion of the boy, beginning with simply changing Charley's age to eleven. While he was at it, Barnum claimed that his discovery was of a more exotic origin than a plain saltbox house in banal Bridgeport. This time he did not reach for Pernambuco but contented himself with saying that young Stratton was "just arrived from England." Barnum wrote that he did not intend to justify these deceptions, but then he went ahead and did it anyway. Changing the boy's age was acceptable in Barnum's mind because he had "reliable evidence" that Charley was *really a dwarf*; in that, at least, people would be getting what they paid to see. About the second deception he was more shameless:

I had observed (and sometimes, as in the case of Vivalla, had taken advantage of) the American fancy for European exotics; and if the deception, practised for a season in my dwarf experiment, has done any thing towards checking our disgraceful preference for foreigners, I may readily be pardoned for the offence I here acknowledge.[3]

Barnum makes this self-justification at least partly in jest. The American tendency in the first decades of the Republic to look to Europe in matters intellectual and cultural was under attack elsewhere, for example in Ralph Waldo Emerson's 1837 speech "The American Scholar," and as Barnum noted, he himself had observed the phenomenon before. But the idea that his "dwarf experiment" might actually school the public was played for comic effect, with more than a hint of self-mockery. After all, disparaging your audience even retrospectively is not a wise strategy for increasing its size. As if realizing this, in the later version of his autobiography, Barnum cut this passage and the rest of his justification for these deceptions.

To complete the promotional reinvention of Charley Stratton, Barnum gave him the name Tom Thumb, after the hero of an old English folk tale involving Merlin and King Arthur's court, where Sir Thomas, no bigger than a thumb, had been made a knight of the Round Table and sallied forth on a mouse. Perhaps the English origin of the name gave Barnum the idea of claiming England as Charley's homeland. In the Brothers Grimm version of the tale, Tom is purchased from his parents for the purpose of showing him. At least two dwarves dubbed Tom Thumb had already been exhibited in New York and regionally before Barnum discovered Charley Stratton. And one of them, whose real name was Joseph Stevens, was still appearing in the city when Barnum brought his new Tom Thumb to New York. Because Stevens was nearly four feet tall, more than twice Charley's size, and already established, Barnum sometimes referred to Charley as Tom Thumb Junior. Stevens also went by the name Major Stevens, and perhaps for this reason Barnum gave his Tom Thumb the higher rank of general.[4]

Barnum remembered that the boy and his mother arrived in New York on Thanksgiving Day, which in the year 1842 was celebrated across the state on December 8. According to a New York diarist, the weather was "very gloomy," featuring a "dark sky, rain, snow." Ads in the *Tribune* and the *Herald* announced that Tom Thumb would go on display at the American Museum on that very afternoon, and Barnum immediately began to introduce his miniature general to friendly journalists.[5]

James Watson Webb, the editor of the *Courier and Enquirer* (and known as Colonel Webb, a rank actually acquired in the army), wrote in his paper that "the distinguished *General Thomas Thumb*" and his unnamed companion had arrived at the door of his house unannounced just as he was preparing to carve the turkey for the family dinner. He described Tom frolicking on his dining-room table, kicking over a glass of water so as not to be drowned in it and avoiding the wineglasses for the same reason. The general greeted each of Webb's excited children and then took a seat and ate with gusto, stopping only to propose a toast, drinking from a glass of the sweet Madeira wine known as malmsey. After describing this scene, Webb then put in the plug for Barnum's new act that the showman clearly had been angling for. He wrote of Tom Thumb, "He is the greatest curiosity we have ever seen; and we are quite sure that all who omit to pay their respects to him, at the *American Museum,* will for ever regret it."[6]

Barnum introduced Tom Thumb to the city with the usual promotional blitz, making the rounds of editors and rewarding them with paid advertisements in their papers for favorable stories such as Webb's. He also had handbills posted around the city, which did not fail to mention the "extraordinary expense" of importing Tom from England. Tom and his mother lived on the museum's fifth floor, among such other human curiosities as two giants. Barnum and his family now lived next door in what had been a billiards parlor. Charity had given birth the previous spring to the couple's third daughter, Frances, joining Caroline, now nine, and Helen, now two. The five of them often made what little room was necessary at their hearth for their tiny new neighbor, as Barnum worked on the boy's theatrical education: "I took great pains to train my diminutive prodigy, devoting many hours to that purpose, by day and by night, and succeeded, because he had native talent and an intense love of the ludicrous."[7]

One of the woodcuts Barnum commissioned for his autobiography shows him sitting by the fire instructing Tom Thumb, who is dressed as Napoleon. This impersonation would be Tom's most famous, perhaps because it was both the most ludicrous and yet somehow appropriate, given the French emperor's reputed stature. The initial period of instruction must have begun before Tom reached New York, since a squib in the *Herald* on December 9 promised, "[Tom Thumb] is lively and full of fun, swings his cane with great nonchalance, talks of his unpleasant trip across the Atlantic in the steamship, and withal is quite a comic young gentleman." Cane swinging, knowing what to say about the fictional Atlantic crossing, and displaying a knack for comedy would all require preparation, and Tom was still a month from his fifth birthday. Perhaps the truest word in Barnum's comment about training Charley Stratton is *prodigy*, for how many five-year-olds can even speak at length, much less exhibit Tom Thumb's theatrical presence? In a very short time the boy would learn scripts, songs, and dance steps, take up mimicry, and contribute spontaneous witticisms to the puns and other wordplay that Barnum devised for him. No teacher, not even one as determined and experienced in theatricality as Barnum, could have taught so young a person so much so fast. But perhaps what Barnum was unwittingly doing was even more remarkable: revealing Charley's native ability to the young man himself. Both of them must have been excited by the transformation Charley was undergoing, making it easy to believe Barnum when he said that he and Charley quickly grew quite fond of each other.[8]

During Tom Thumb's first weeks at the museum, a tryout, in effect, as Barnum tested his initial doubts about how well the boy would attract patrons, no elaborate costumes or scripted remarks had yet been prepared. In his 2013 book, *Becoming Tom Thumb,* Eric D. Lehman says Tom at first appeared in the museum's Hall of Living Curiosities. He would spend most of his time (as Joice Heth had done when she was on display in various venues) interacting with the visitors to the museum as they passed by his station. This gave Barnum's customers a chance to see up close just how well proportioned Tom was and also how astonishingly small, small enough indeed to have emerged from a fairy story. Tom said later that once he and Barnum began to appear together on the stage in the museum's Lecture Room, Barnum would sometimes show up just as the performance was scheduled to begin, wearing an overcoat with flap pockets so deep that Tom could curl up in one of them to hide himself. When the audience members crowded around Barnum, asking where Tom Thumb was, Barnum would call out for him. Tom would push up through the flap and respond, "Here I am, sir."[9]

Tom's tryout period was cut short, a resounding success. Even during the boy's first month at the museum, Barnum had encouraged the public to visit immediately by advertising that his little man would appear only for "the rest of the week." The crowds clamored to see him. Just two weeks after Thanksgiving Day and three days before Christmas, Barnum signed a one-year contract with Tom's parents, raising the weekly payment to $7, $3 of which went directly to Tom's father, Sherwood Stratton, who had arrived on the scene and would put his carpentry skills to use as a museum handyman. Soon thereafter Barnum raised Tom's weekly rate further still, to $25. Barnum wrote, "He fairly earned it, for he speedily became a public favorite." As the act became more developed and more and more New Yorkers had seen him, Barnum began sending Tom out on the road, eventually exhibiting him in "numerous cities and towns in many of the States." By the beginning of 1843, Tom Thumb was traveling down the East Coast and into the South.[10]

In the weeks when Barnum and Tom Thumb were developing the act, the showman himself appeared on stage as both introducer and straight man. When he sent Tom and his parents on the road, Barnum would not entrust them to just anyone. An old friend from home, Fordyce Hitchcock, an ordained Universalist minister no less, filled the straight-man role and also protected Barnum's interest in the boy. For this, Barnum paid him $12 a week. When Tom went to Boston to appear at Moses Kimball's museum, Barnum urged "Friend Moses" to take on this added expense, or at the very least to find someone reliable to replace Hitchcock, someone who would not attempt to steal "Tommy" away from Barnum's employ.[11]

Evidently Barnum's confidence in Hitchcock was well placed. Not only did he keep the young star in the fold, but he later took the job of assistant manager of the American Museum and held it "for seven or eight years." Eventually, when Barnum was out of the country for an extended period, he left Hitchcock in control of the museum, which he ran, in his boss's estimation, "with consummate tact as well as the strictest fidelity." Barnum seems to have offered his friend a job when Hitchcock abruptly left the church and needed what he later called a "helping hand." Indeed one photograph of "the Parson" shows dark, haunted eyes set deep in his long, bewhiskered face. But whatever the cause of his leaving the clergy, Hitchcock's gratitude to Barnum for his loyalty as a friend lasted for the rest of his days.[12]

Barnum's letters to Kimball in 1843 gave a running commentary on how Tom Thumb was doing, both with Hitchcock on the road and during his interludes back at the American Museum. Kimball himself was eager to show Tom Thumb at his Boston Museum, and at one point grew annoyed at Barnum for holding him back. By late summer Barnum would accommodate Kimball, but he had reason to feel proprietary about what he had created in this act. Tom was, after all, Barnum's first great discovery and would be his most reliable moneymaker. Indeed, in the first of the following excerpts from letters to Kimball, Barnum explained his unwillingness to share Tom with another museum owner, one of the Peales who ran museums in Philadelphia and Baltimore:

February 5: "By the way Peale wrote me the other day to ask if I could not send him a Tom Thumb, [but] being now nearly new and without a rival, he was [very] valuable."

February 21: "At present, my museums

151

are neither of them making a penny, and all I spend is on Tommy."

March 6: "Tom Thumb is doing so well that I think of letting him go farther south and let you have him at cost three weeks. (If two won't do) say in May or June — perhaps sooner — certainly as soon as he returns from South after stopping with me a fortnight."

March 31: "I am only averaging $50 per night. Tom Thumb is only doing about the same. I fear his southern tour won't be as good as I anticipated."

April 15: "Tommy T. is doing but little more than paying expences."

May 15: "I expect Tom Thumb tomorrow. . . . I understand that the parents lately have . . . complained of my treating them ill in sending them south. . . . However I have no fears but I can straighten that out for First they can't leave me if they would. . . . [I will] blow the concern to hell before I'll allow anybody else [to take] up the fruit which I have shaken from the tree."

May 25: "The General is just bringing us up straight again. Yesterday we took $166 — I hope he will help you [earn] a couple of thousand dollars, and I am sure he will nearly do that if you push it right."

July 15: "I leave Sunday afternoon for Albany with Tommy and Co."

September 14: "I send herewith Tom Thumb's Boots, which I hope you will forward to him at Salem if convenient."

September 29: "Tom Thumb will be here some time next week and I shall keep him a spell."

October 12: "I have agreed to let John Sefton have the General one night next week at Niblo's for his benefit. I am to take General on the stage & show him off, & have him passed round, which I shall decline but express my regret at being obliged to do so, as he must return at once to the American Museum, but that they can see him, shake hands, & converse with him at the Museum any day during the week! Sefton gives me $50 and will not detain him 30 minutes."

October 24: "I only took $112 last night — lost some $30, probably by letting General go to [Niblo's]. Sefton had a jam and General killed 'em dead."

October 31: "Next week Tommy goes to Baltimore or Philadelphia."

November 15: "My business is shocking — last week took but $428 [in contrast to a $1,240.40 week when Tom Thumb was at the museum in October]. What about the Albino Lady?"[13]

But for all the attention Tom Thumb received in the private letters to Kimball as the year went by, Barnum summarized 1843 in a single sentence in both versions of his autobiography and skipped ahead to early 1844, when he set sail for England with the three Strattons. Leave it, then, to the *New York Herald,* which on December 1, 1843, summed up the success of Tom Thumb's first full year in Barnum's employ:

He has been visited by nearly half a million persons in America, and has been *feted* by many families of the first distinction. He is so graceful, so pert, so intelligent, and withal, so wonderfully diminutive, that all who see him are charmed with him at once, and his visits to all our cities, have necessarily been so many signal triumphs.[14]

The piece was so glowing that Barnum might have written it himself, even if it appeared in what was otherwise a news column under the heading "Theatrical." One column over in the same issue, an obvious

154

advertisement began, "☞ THE SPLENDID TRIUMPH OF THE AMERI-/can Museum, is owing entirely to the tact and talent displayed in the management." It went on to promise, "To-morrow will be a great holiday there, for ladies, families, schools, &c. General Tom Thumb will amuse thousands of little ones with his facetious songs, dances, jokes, &c." Another hint that the first item was either written by Barnum or in close collaboration with him was its expression of the showman's hopes and plans for the show's upcoming European trip: "[Tom Thumb] will undoubtedly visit Queen Victoria and be received with marked attention by all the nobility in Europe." The item then listed the cities Tom would visit and reiterated, "He will also call upon the Queen at Buckingham Palace." The repetition suggests that Barnum was making a resolution rather than announcing a firm engagement, for nobody at the palace had yet been informed of the visit.

Barnum eagerly made the most of Tom Thumb's imminent departure. He created an advertising campaign in the New York papers warning that the opportunity to see the little man before he slipped away was itself slipping away. Barnum would advertise a departure date and then come up with an excuse for why Tom Thumb was still around — his own variation on the going-out-of-business-sale stratagem. Early in January the date of his sailing was sometimes left vague but the ads made it sound alarmingly soon ("A FEW DAYS LONGER!"), but as the month wore on, the departure was fixed on January 16, when Tom would sail on the new packet ship *Yorkshire,* bound for Liverpool. Performances were promised up to the final hour. One advertisement in the *Tribune* said an appearance at 11 a.m. would be followed, "if the wind proves fair," by a noon sailing. As Barnum's commercial luck would have it, the wind did not prove fair, blowing as it was from the east, and so several more last-minute performances were made possible before the ship did finally sail on January 18. The New York correspondent for the *National Intelligencer* in Washington poked fun at Barnum's blitz, writing, "His Littleness sailed this morning for England — 'or so they say,' " and went on to speculate, "Possibly, MR. BARNUM has 'a contrary wind' in reserve, and he may be 'unavoidably detained' another week."[15]

But on that Wednesday a favorable fifteen-knot wind from the northwest blew in, and late in the morning Tom Thumb, dressed in military regalia, left the museum in an open carriage. He was preceded by the American Museum house band, which Barnum joked "kindly volunteered" to accompany him. Boys followed the carriage down Fulton Street, and ladies waved white handkerchiefs from the windows of buildings he passed, Tom all the while doffing his hat and taking bows. When the barouche arrived at the wharf, a thousand people were waiting. One reporter wrote, "The vessels in the neighborhood swarmed with these who had gathered for the purpose of seeing the General off."

Once he boarded the ship, Tom was placed atop its capstan, where he struck Napoleonic poses and waved to the crowd. Barnum, the Strattons, a servant, a tutor for Tom named George Ciprico, and the museum's naturalist, Emile Guillaudeu — along with a contingent of Barnum's friends and eight other passengers — all boarded the ship. At 11:30 a.m. two steamers towed it away from its moorings and through the harbor. The museum's City Brass Band, as Barnum had dubbed it, played aboard one of the towing vessels.[16]

A newspaper reported that some 3,200 people had seen Tom Thumb at the museum the day before, but in spite of this bonanza,

Barnum confessed to shipboard feelings that were not typical of him: "What with the depression of spirits I felt on leaving family, friends and home, and the dread of sea-sickness, I was in what we Yankees call 'a considerable of a stew.' " Still, he was engrossed by the action going on around him:

> The deck was covered with ropes, blocks, and cables; sailors were running in all directions; the pilot, a gruff looking chap with a high florid complexion, was giving orders in language that was Greek to me. . . . I became utterly confused. I was out of my element — I had got beyond my depth.[17]

It took the steamships two hours to tow the *Yorkshire* through the Narrows and out to Sandy Hook, at which time one of the vessels sounded a bell signaling Barnum's friends to board for the journey back to lower Manhattan. Barnum recalled, "That moment my usually high spirits fell below zero. As I successively grasped for the last time the hand of each friend as he passed to the steamboat, I could hardly restrain a tear." The band started to play from the deck of the steamer. When Barnum recognized the familiar notes of "Home, Sweet Home," "the tears then flowed thick and fast." His party stood on the quarterdeck, handkerchiefs swirling, and watched as the other steamer chugged off into the distance. "When the strains of 'Yankee Doodle' floated over the waters," Barnum wrote, "we all give three hearty cheers, and wave our hats, in which even the sailors join, and I care not to acknowledge that I wept freely, overpowered as I was with mingled feelings of joy and regret." Barnum concluded the scene by reporting that the gruff and florid harbor pilot boarded the second steamer at two o'clock, "and thus was broken the last visible living link that bound us to our country."[18]

Barnum described this scene three times, first in a letter written in England for the *New York Atlas,* then in the 1855 edition of his autobiography, and again in the 1869 edition. Each version is slightly different from the others, but in all of them his emotion seems genuine, and in all of them he contrasted his flowing tears with his deserved reputation for "high spirits," a "natural bias . . . to merriment." In the two versions of the autobiography, he protested that he was as given to "seasons of loneliness and even sadness" as the next person, but that his Christian faith pulled him through. He went so far as to say, "In all my journeys as 'a showman,' the Bible has been my companion, and I have repeatedly read it attentively, from beginning to end." The strong meaning he packed into this moment owes something to the growing importance that faith would have in his life as he grew older. However, even as he wrote the *Atlas* letter, which he began a half hour after docking in Liverpool, he saw the departure and the deep emotions it stirred up in him as a significant moment in his life.[19]

All those tears, that mixture of "joy and regret," suggest that he was honestly sorry to be leaving his wife, children, and members of his broader family, his many friends, and the comfortable home and work life he had built for himself in just two years. In telling this story of leaving America, he reported that he had now paid off all his debts for the Museum and that he had also bought out the rival Peale's Museum and created "a handsome surplus in the treasury." He now felt confident in his success and believed that his business "had long ceased to be an experiment" and was now in "perfect running order." The joy expressed in his tears reflected the side of Barnum's personality that contrasted with his need and love for domesticity — for all those things drifting away with the bleating brass band. He had realized his ambitions in an amazingly short period of time.[20]

But to his mind, a business in perfect running order no longer needed him. He was now, in effect, starting over. The challenge was not whether Tom Thumb would make him money in a new place; the challenge was the new place itself, a place that had no notion of who P. T. Barnum was. While he knew the language, everything else about the coming experience would be an experiment in whether what he had learned at home would work abroad, and if not, whether he had the wit to adapt. We know he set his sights on meeting the queen in Buckingham Palace, but he would also travel the length and width of the island in an attempt to win over Victoria's subjects. Whether or not he would succeed in the land of his forebears would be a test for Barnum of his own worth, of how far he had come and how far he might yet go.

Six:
The Queen

On a Monday morning, February 5, the snowy mountaintops of Wales came into view, and the *Yorkshire* slipped around the island of Anglesey and into the mouth of the Mersey. The ship docked in Liverpool, where a large crowd had gathered to see Tom Thumb disembark. But Barnum chose not to expose the little man to the public yet, and when Cynthia Stratton carried her son down the gangplank like a baby in her arms, as Barnum had asked her to do, the crowd did not notice them. Barnum's party and their luggage proceeded the few blocks to the domed, Greek-columned Customs House, where money was efficiently extracted from the sea-weary Yankees. Then it was on to the Georgian-style Royal Waterloo Hotel — "the best in the city," Barnum called it — where the porters showed more English efficiency by parting him from his half-crown coins. Feeling out of place and thoroughly fleeced, Barnum and company went to the hotel dining room, where "we washed down our indignation with a bottle of port" and dined on roast beef and "fried soles and shrimp sauce."[1]

That night, another bout of homesickness overtook him. Realizing that he was "a stranger in a strange land," he admitted to "a solitary hearty crying-spell." But his shore legs soon returned, and he was back to business. His intention had been to send letters of introduction to Buckingham Palace and go there with Tom Thumb immediately to set up "head-quarters." This plan went from highly improbable to impossible when Barnum learned that the royal family would "not permit the approach of entertainments" because it was officially mourning the death of Prince Albert's father, Ernest I, who had passed away in Germany on January 29.[2]

Undaunted, Barnum hired a hall in Liverpool and offered his Lilliputian prodigy to the Liverpudlian public for a short run. His advertisements in the city papers announced, "TOM THUMB ARRIVED!" and went on to make more profligate use of capital letters and exclamation points, including the noteworthy claim that "TOM THUMB, Jun., was visited in America by more than HALF A MILLION of Ladies and Gentlemen of the highest distinction."[3]

Barnum was about to get his first lesson in the challenges of conquering England. So strong was the prejudice against the former colonies that his assertions about his success in America didn't hold much sway. Dwarf acts were common in England, the prevalence of little people an environmental outcome of the country's rapid and incautious industrialization, and they were offered in venues even less respectable than the theaters, which were themselves not palaces of respectability. These acts did not have the polish or wit of Tom's performances, which is why Barnum's strategy was to present the general as a better form of entertainment than that offered at fairs in the countryside. Doing so would permit charging a great deal more for the privilege of seeing Tom at a venue like the one Barnum had hired, the Portico ("a small room, but neatly fitted up") in Liverpool's Bold Street. The public balked, however, as Barnum sought to charge a shilling, roughly a U.S. quarter, rather than the penny that people were used to paying at fairs.[4]

All was not lost, though, because the manager of the Princess's Theatre in London made the trip to Liverpool to see Tom

Thumb perform and offered Barnum a three-night spot on his stage. Barnum jumped at the chance. The little general made his London debut in Oxford Street on February 20 on a program with a farce called *Blasé* and a production of the new Donizetti opera, *Don Pasquale.* The next night he would again appear between the acts of an opera, this time Bellini's *I Puritani,* and for his final performance there, on February 27, he was again sandwiched in the Donizetti. Barnum had tried without much success to introduce Tom Thumb to the editors of London's newspapers, but only one paper wrote about the Princess's Theatre performances. The *Illustrated London News* deigned to devote a single sentence to Tom Thumb, and it was a doozy: "The production of this little monster affords another melancholy proof of the *low* state the legitimate drama has been reduced to!"[5]

But Barnum had not crossed the Atlantic to be deterred by a single bad newspaper notice. He saw Tom Thumb's reception differently, recasting it as a "decided . . . 'hit'" and a "visible guarantee of success in London." If his memory put a favorable spin on his situation, it was undoubtedly shaped by the success to come. Neither the poor showing in Liverpool nor the seeming indifference in London discouraged Barnum; instead, these stumbles seemed to invigorate him. He wrote that he was offered a second run at a "much higher figure" in London, but he chose a separate path altogether, making the decision that he would, henceforth, exhibit the general only on his own terms, and he busied himself to satisfy them.

Those terms still included, against all odds, the involvement of Queen Victoria. Barnum was in London less than two weeks before he managed to meet the American envoy to the Court of St. James, Edward Everett, thanks to letters of introduction from, among others, Horace Greeley, the editor of the *New-York Tribune,* with whom Barnum had an acquaintanceship that was growing into a friendship. The ambassador called on Barnum to meet Tom Thumb, and then invited the two of them to the midday meal at his house in Belgravia the next day, March 2, where Everett's family "loaded" the general with gifts. Everett was an American of real distinction. A brilliant professor of Greek literature at Harvard as a young man — his pupil Ralph Waldo Emerson considered him "his personal idol" — he had been a U.S. representative and then governor of Massachusetts, and he would become U.S. secretary of state and a U.S. senator in the 1850s.[6]

When Everett introduced Tom Thumb into his household in London's Grosvenor Place, he was undoubtedly acting less as a diplomat and more as a father and a husband. He, his wife, and their children were still mourning the death in October of their eldest child, Anne, and young Tom was an immediate source of joy. The delight his family took in the little man was perhaps the most compelling reason why Everett promised Barnum he would cross the street to Buckingham Palace and intercede in person with royal officials to have Tom presented to the queen.

Barnum's assault on London and the queen included renting a "magnificent mansion" in Mayfair, an area thick with aristocrats and the merely wealthy, and the employment of a "tinselled and powdered" servant to man the door. Out went invitations to editors and members of the nobility, who now came and were appropriately impressed with the young general. Soon "crested carriages" bearing uninvited visitors arrived at his Grafton Street address; Barnum had his servant politely turn them away, a matter of proper etiquette, Barnum averred, but also a way to increase the value of an invitation. Soon the beautiful, raven-haired Baroness Charlotte von Rothschild sent a carriage to take Barnum and Tom Thumb to her mansion at 148 Piccadilly, adjacent to the site of today's Palm Court at the Ritz. She was the wife and first cousin of Lionel de Rothschild, whose family in effect bankrolled the royal government and who, in Barnum's description, was "the most wealthy banker in the world." Barnum spent several paragraphs in his autobiography describing the splendor he saw at her house, the elegantly attired servants, impressive statues, marble stairs, and, in the drawing room, the "glare of magnificence" exuded by gold and gilt, huge chandeliers, and bijous wherever his glance fell. They spent two hours in the company of the baroness and a score of lords and ladies, and when they left, a "well-filled purse was quietly slipped into my hand, and I felt that the golden shower was beginning to fall!"[7]

After Barnum had another such payday from a banker (twenty guineas — about $125 — for a half hour of Tom Thumb's time), and now realizing that Everett's efforts at Buckingham Palace would not lead to an immediate audience with the queen, the showman rented a room in the Egyptian Hall in Piccadilly Street. The 1812 Georgian building, named for its façade, which was meant to evoke an Egyptian temple, had once housed, among much else, Napoleon's carriage from Waterloo, treasures James Cook collected on his travels, relics from the tomb of Seti I that inspired Shelley's poem "Ozymandias," and, thanks to the size of its main room, Géricault's massive painting *The Raft of the Medusa*. In recent years, such curiosities as "the Living Skeleton" and the Siamese Twins had been on exhibition there, leading the way to Tom Thumb.

Barnum engaged one of the two upstairs rooms at the hall, and in the great room downstairs was the American painter George Catlin's extensive collection of paintings of North American Indians — more than five hundred in all, hung from floor to ceiling — along with costumes, weapons, and other objects used by Native American tribes. At the center of the 106-foot-long room was a Crow teepee made of decorated buffalo skins. Twenty-five feet tall, it could hold eighty of Catlin's customers at once. Catlin had traveled through the western United States, Canada, and Mexico for seven years, painting portraits of the people he encountered and collecting artifacts of their vanishing cultures. His collection had toured in New York, Washington, Boston, Philadelphia, and elsewhere in America and had been on display at the Egyptian Hall for three years beginning in 1840. Despite a recent influx of customers over a short period when Catlin had brought nine Ojibwe Indians to the Hall to entertain crowds with ritualistic dance, his business had dropped off dramatically from its peak.[8]

Barnum asserted that a "rush of visitors" went to see Tom Thumb when he opened in March at the Egyptian Hall. The crowds would aid Catlin, as would Barnum's own connections, and in turn the artist would aid Barnum. As he became acquainted with Catlin, Barnum learned of the painter's growing concern that he was no longer making enough from his exhibit to cover his rent for the great room, so Barnum offered to switch rooms with him and take on the larger obligation if Catlin would leave his paintings on the walls downstairs, where Tom Thumb would now appear. Since exhibiting Indians was something Barnum had been doing at the American Museum, he also secured a new band of fourteen "Ioway" Indians, among them Chief White Cloud, who would board ship for England and demonstrate war dances in company with Catlin's lectures. In a letter to Moses Kimball at about that time, Barnum predicted of the Indians, "Catlin and self will make money on them. I think to a large amount," and by all reports they were well received in London.[9]

Tom Thumb had been on display at the Egyptian Hall for only a few days when Barnum's royal fantasies took a turn toward reality. The American envoy Everett had appealed to the master of the queen's household, Charles Murray, who also happened to be a long-standing friend of Catlin and had helped arrange for the Ojibwes to meet Queen Victoria and her court. Murray and Barnum had breakfast one morning at Everett's house, and within a few days a regally uniformed member of the Life Guards appeared at the Grafton Street house with an invitation for "General Tom Thumb and his guardian" for an evening audience with the queen at Buckingham Palace. Murray passed along Victoria's wishes that Tom not be schooled in the etiquette of addressing a royal personage, so that he might appear before her "naturally and without restraint."[10]

Late in the day of March 23, Barnum wrote out one of the most effective advertisements he would ever compose and affixed it to the front door of the Egyptian Hall. "Closed this evening," the notice read, "General Tom Thumb being at Buckingham Palace by command of Her Majesty." Barnum was determined, he explained in his autobiography, "to make the most of the occasion." He and the general presented themselves at the palace, Tom decked out as a court swell in formal evening attire and wielding a tiny cane. The lord in waiting met them and gave Barnum and Tom two rules of etiquette for dealing with the queen: never speak to her directly, and walk backward when leaving her presence.[11]

They were led along a corridor and up a wide marble staircase to the doors of the queen's long picture gallery. When the doors opened, the queen stood at the far end of the room, still attired in mourning for her father-in-law, wearing a black dress and no jewelry. Alongside her were Prince Albert; her mother, the Duchess of Kent; and "twenty or thirty" other members of court, the ladies "arrayed in the highest style of magnificence, their dresses sparkling with diamonds." Barnum reported that his tiny friend approached this forbidding group "with a firm step, and as he came within hailing distance made a very graceful bow, and exclaimed, *'Good evening, Ladies and*

Gentlemen!' " The gathering did not titter in aristocratic disapproval at this display of the little man's ebullience but greeted it with "a burst of laughter," a genuine expression of their delight. The queen, not quite twenty-five years old, whom Barnum would describe as "small of stature, and not of the most beautiful form or countenance," was "very sociable and amiable in her manners," putting one "immediately at ease in her presence." She took Tom's hand and led him around the gallery, showing him some of the hundreds of paintings on display and asking him many questions. Tom's answers kept the trailing retinue "in an uninterrupted strain of merriment," Barnum recalled, and soon Tom felt emboldened to compliment the queen on her art collection, which he called "first-rate." Tom then performed for her, singing, dancing, doing his imitations of famous figures, among them Napoleon, Frederick the Great, Cincinnatus, and Samson. Afterward he got in a long conversation with Prince Albert and others in the court, giving Barnum an opportunity to breach etiquette. He had been told that he could only converse with her using the lord in waiting as intermediary. The queen began to ask Barnum questions in this way, and Barnum answered in kind.

But soon he felt comfortable enough in her presence to address her directly, risking the disapproval of her henchman. She did not miss a beat, however, and began speaking directly back to him.

The audience lasted better than an hour, and then Barnum had the opportunity to display the lord in waiting's second piece of advice about etiquette, to retire from the queen walking backward. Barnum reminded us in his autobiography that it was an exceedingly long room to back out of, and he noted that because the lord in waiting was practiced in backward-walking, he kept "somewhat a-head (or rather a-back) of me." But with his tiny legs, Tom Thumb's reverse pace left him far behind (or rather, ahead), and so from time to time he would turn his back on the queen and run furiously to catch up with Barnum, and then begin once more to back decorously away until once again he needed to turn and sprint to catch up. Tom's antics continued to amuse the royal party, but one of the queen's "poodle-dogs" grew excited at the ruckus Tom was making and began to bark fiercely at him. Tom responded by threatening the dog with his diminutive cane, and a mock battle commenced, further amusing the queen and her party.[12]

The bedazzled showman made much of the audience at Buckingham Palace in one of his letters to the *New York Atlas* and included it in both versions of his autobiography. But he got a more immediate bounce from the visit by discovering, before he left the palace, that the man who wrote the "Court Journal" for the morning papers was in the building. Barnum asked to see the fellow and was pleased that he could persuade him that Tom Thumb's visit was newsworthy, and also that the reporter asked for an outline of the visit. Barnum provided on the spot a notice that then ran in the papers word for word. The evening had been a triumph in every conceivable way, not least because the queen promised Tom a second invitation so that the future king, three-year-old Albert Edward, could meet him (as their first audience had taken place after the Prince of Wales's bedtime).[13]

Barnum could not have known it, but A. H. Saxon points out in his biography of the showman that the one person who was not entirely swept away by the good feeling of the evening was the young Queen Victoria herself. In her journal for that day, she reported having seen "the greatest curiosity I, or indeed anybody, ever saw," but after describing Tom Thumb, she added, "One cannot help feeling very sorry for the poor little thing & wishing he could be properly cared for, for the people who show him off tease him a good deal, I should think." The queen's concern for Tom was based on her belief that he was twelve years old; how much more concerned would she have been if she had known that he was half that age and perhaps in need himself of the early after-supper bedtime enjoyed by the Prince of Wales? Barnum did convey to Everett, in a note of "ten thousand thousand thanks" written upon his return from the palace, that the queen "desired the lord-in-waiting request that I would be careful and never allow the General to be fatigued." As for the teasing, it seems likely that the queen simply misunderstood Barnum's jocular sense of humor, which was more American, perhaps, in its informality than anything she was used to. Even teasing, after all, suggests a level of equality and comfort between man and boy that might well have been unfamiliar in the formal royal household.[14]

Tom Thumb and Barnum returned to Buckingham Palace two weeks later, when the queen introduced the little general to Prince Edward and her other child, Princess Victoria. On this occasion the queen presented to Tom, "with her own hand," as the

Times of London reported the next day, "a superb souvenir of gold and mother-of-pearl, set with precious stones. On one side were the crown and the royal initials, 'V.R.,' and on the reverse a bouquet of flowers in rubies." She also gave Tom a gold pencil case with his initials. These and a gold watch presented to him in June by the Queen Dowager Adelaide at Marlborough House went on display at the Egyptian Hall, along with other baubles given Tom by members of the nobility. For some reason, probably having to do with their own need for favorable publicity, Buckingham Palace did not object to Barnum's exploitation of the royal family in this way. Barnum mentioned that after each visit to the palace he was sent a "handsome *douceur*" from the queen but admitted that this was "the smallest part of the advantage derived from these interviews." The biggest part was "the force of Court example in England." He played this advantage to the hilt, in newspaper ads and at the Egyptian Hall. But the nobility, whose members had adopted Tom as their special favorite, promoted him well enough themselves by going again and again to his performances. Barnum wrote that there were sometimes as many as "fifty and sixty carriages of the nobility" lined up on Piccadilly Street in front of the hall.[15]

Business, then, was good. Barnum averaged from all sources about 500 pounds, or $2,500, *per day* from March 20 until July 20, with Tom doing three shows a day and often giving two private showings in the evening. That adds up to $300,000 in four months, against expenses that Barnum estimated at about $6,000 for that time. His advertising strategy went beyond declaring Tom's connection to the royal family and eventually returned to the approach that had worked so well in the last days before they sailed from New York. This time Barnum warned of the general's imminent departure for Paris, and English crowds fell just as easily for this ploy, eager to get a last glimpse of Tom before the departure that seemingly never came.

One other publicity coup from this period had not been planned, or at least Barnum said it wasn't. Among the little general's regular patrons in England was the most famous general in the world, the Duke of Wellington, who had defeated Napoleon at Waterloo some three decades earlier. The first time the duke attended one of Tom's performances at the Egyptian Hall, Tom was doing his Napoleon bit, striding to and fro and seemingly lost in thought. When Barnum introduced the two, the duke asked Tom what he was so deeply contemplating, and Tom's sorrowful reply was instant: "I was thinking of the loss of the battle of Waterloo." Barnum gave credit for the witty response to young Tom, but the showman often deflected credit in this way — not as often as he claimed it, but still regularly. In any case, it was sold to the papers as an example of Tom's spontaneous wit, and the duke himself was so amused by it that he told the story wherever he went.[16]

The first six months in England could hardly have gone better for P. T. Barnum. As a businessman, and as a showman, he had had the instinct before ever leaving New York for how he would promote Tom Thumb. Before the plan took shape, the general was less than a success in Liverpool and the object of derision in London, but in a short time he became the toast of England and a means of enrichment for Barnum and, more modestly, for the Stratton family. Barnum's potent combination of naïveté, arrogance, persistence, and luck — very American qualities, even in the eyes of Americans themselves, but especially so to the British — somehow brought to fruition his far-fetched strategy of partnering with the queen herself. This ur-American successfully corralled not just the queen but also every ambulatory member of her court, despite a hearty British distaste for the former colonies and for the brash, uncouth, self-confident sort of American Barnum so utterly embodied. If Barnum went to England seeking a new Old World to conquer, then he inarguably accomplished that, perhaps even beyond his hopes.

SEVEN:
THE CONTINENT

By June 1844, Barnum had fully met the challenge of presenting Tom Thumb in London. Business was going so well that he turned the management of the general over to H. G. Sherman, a former singer Barnum had employed in the past, whom he now brought to England in part to be Tom's "moral instructor." Barnum intended to devote more time to writing his *Atlas* letters and to having experiences that could become the narrative center of these letters.

With that in mind, Barnum set off for Paris to visit the tenth national industrial exposition under way there. Among his goals was to acquire exhibits for the American Museum back home. The fair, located in a temporary structure built between the Seine and the Champs-Élysées (where the Grand Palais and Petit Palais now stand), held nearly four thousand exhibitions, ranging from steam engines to typefaces. Barnum snatched "a few thousands" from his coffers in London to purchase curiosities he found at the fair, and in three days of "calm examination" of the miles of displays, he gathered the cards of eighty-seven makers of automatons and other oddities he saw there, with the intention of visiting each of them while he was in Paris. Among those he met was the soon-to-be-famous magician Jean-Eugène Robert-Houdin, who was displaying his mechanical inventions in a prominent spot in what was called the Palace of Industry. One of his creations, an automaton he called the Writer, won first prize at the fair, and Barnum bought it or a copy of it "at a good round price" to display in London and eventually at the American Museum. The original mechanism featured a wax head carved by Robert-Houdin to resemble his own face and a carved wooden body, seated at a table, where it would write or draw responses to questions asked of it.[1]

A visit originally planned for several days lasted two weeks, as Barnum methodically followed up with each of the other mechanical craftsmen whose cards he had collected, purchasing other items to send back home. At the same time, he became neither the first nor the last American to fall hard for the charms of Paris, availing himself of touristic wonders ranging from the Louvre to Notre-Dame and Versailles. And like many an American in Paris, he wrote of his experiences in detail, even returning to the subject in letters written well after this visit.

Across the avenue from the fair was an elegant, sixteen-sided, equestrian-themed building in stone, known as the Cirque des Champs-Élysées, where the equestrian acts of the famous Franconi family gave their summer performances. Barnum went one evening and was almost as enamored of the three-year-old building itself — especially the steep arrangement of the seating around the circular ring — as of the riding feats on display. In the next year the Cirque would house a series of concerts by Hector Berlioz, featuring at great expense hundreds of musicians and singers, though the building proved to be better suited to horses than to music, its acoustics creating, in Berlioz's words, "deplorable harmonic confusion." But the design would stick in Barnum's mind for later use.[2]

When Barnum returned to London in the middle of the summer, he took advantage of the many doors that Tom Thumb's fame, and his own, were opening. "We had the free entrée to all the theatres, public gardens, and places of entertainment," he wrote, "and frequently met the principal artists, editors, poets, and authors of the country." Added to this social whirl were his many business enterprises; after listing them for Moses Kimball in a letter in August, he concluded, "I guess I have about enough on hand to keep one busy." Yet amid this jumble of activity, Barnum could not resist the temptations of sightseeing or of writing about his adventures for his audience in New York. As he put it, he always had an eye on his business, "but I also had two eyes for observation and these were busily employed in leisure hours."[3]

One of the writers with whom Barnum had become acquainted was Albert Richard Smith, a journalist, playwright, mountaineer, and performer. The two met in early September at Dee's Hotel in Temple Row in Birmingham, "a large clean town, with a pure country air blowing about its handsome streets," as Smith put it. On the morning of September 4, Smith noticed Barnum out the window of the coffee room of the hotel, "a tall, active person who was arranging the cortège, and cuffing the more intrusive boys into order." Barnum had just taken delivery of a tiny carriage, its deep blue body twenty inches high and eleven inches wide, which had been specially built for Tom Thumb in Soho. On its doors was an elaborate coat of arms including the words *Go-a-head.* Two Shetland ponies pulled the carriage, and boys in sky-blue livery coats and red breeches served as coachman and footman. As Smith watched, the miniature equipage was drawn into the street crowded with people eager to see it. The carriage would become a Barnum signature, one of his chief ways of advertising his scheduled shows of Tom Thumb — just as, in the future, a traveling circus would parade elephants through a new town when it arrived.[4]

Both Barnum and Smith chronicled a day of sightseeing that gave texture to the exhausting experience of spending time in the presence of a person with Barnum's energy and acquisitiveness. The day began at five the next morning with the eager showman rapping on Smith's door; by six they were aboard a mail coach "whirling" along on a thirty-mile journey to Stratford-upon-Avon to see sights associated with the birth and entombment of William Shakespeare. A soaking rain had left them chilled, so upon reaching the town they stopped at the Red Horse to warm by a fire and eat breakfast. They found a well-thumbed copy of Washington Irving's *Sketch-Book* in the inn's tiny parlor. A chapter of the book describing Irving's own experience in Stratford was "mended, and pencilled, and spliced," Smith wrote. The chapter opens with Irving seated in that very parlor of the Red Horse.[5]

The timbered house of Shakespeare's birth on Henley Street was "a humble-looking place enough," to Smith's eye, but Barnum apparently found it sufficiently interesting to someday secure first refusal to buy it. The idea would be to ship it "in sections to my Museum in New-York" for display, a possibility that aroused the British public to the point that several patriots pooled resources and purchased it, preserving it for the nation. Smith, who first published his account of the day in *Bentley's Miscellany* in 1847, was eager to ingratiate himself with the English audience of the literary and humor magazine. He reported that Barnum, noticing a portrait of Shakespeare on the wall, told the elderly proprietress of the house that he would send her a companion portrait of Tom Thumb, and then showered her with the general's cartes de visite and urged her to talk up the act with her visitors. After a short walk to Holy Trinity Church, where Shakespeare's funerary monument — which features a

sculpture of the Bard from the waist up —
had been in place for more than two hundred years, Smith purported to have caught
Barnum trying "to wafer one of the General's visiting cards on the monument, saying
it was for an advertisement."[6]

Then they were off to Warwick Castle,
where both men noted the presence of an
elaborate shakedown by a series of elderly
guides with hands extended. After one of
the guides went into elaborate detail about
relics belonging to the legendary Guy, Earl
of Warwick, Barnum wrote, "I told the old
porter he was entitled to great credit for
having concentrated more lies than I had
ever before heard in so small a compass. He
smiled, and evidently felt gratified by the
compliment." Both men remembered that
Barnum then nonetheless tried to purchase
the relics from the old man, but that the
porter was especially incensed by this
proposal. To which Barnum responded that
he would simply have them copied for his
museum so that Americans would not have
to cross an ocean to see them. This interaction was one example of a developing theme
for the outing. Smith wrote that Barnum
tried to acquire almost everything he saw in
the castle, including a Rubens painting of
St. Ignatius.[7]

Later in the day they visited Coventry, where Barnum came upon a traveling exhibit called the Happy Family, which featured two hundred animals and birds, many of them natural enemies, living peaceably together in a single cage. He bought it on the spot for the hefty price of $2,500 and engaged its owner to travel with it to New York, where, Barnum wrote, "it became an attractive feature in my Museum." Indeed it remained a staple at the museum for two decades.

From Coventry they took a train back to Birmingham, arriving at 10 p.m. Smith wrote that he saw more in that day than in any other of his life, and over supper Barnum told him that a person must "make thirty hours out of twenty-four in Merrekey" or he would "never go ahead." Part of Smith's comic portrayal of Barnum had him saying *Merrekey* for *America* and *trew* for *true,* and the whole concept of a "go-ahead day with Barnum," as Smith's title has it, is to poke fun at the American reputation for industriousness, a quality that often rankled the British. Barnum's avidity to acquire whatever he saw was always placed in the context of his wanting things for the museum, not for himself personally, and Smith made only a few hints at Barnum's Yankee "cuteness." But there was a bull-in-a-china-shop aspect to his sketch of Barnum, whose energy and self-confidence were portrayed as overwhelming to the point of rudeness at times. Smith seemed to mind especially when Barnum knew more about anything English — for instance the history of St. Michael's Church in Coventry — than he did. Whether or not Barnum was acting a part, his ebullience seems real enough, just one aspect of the general madness of his conquest of Britain.

His months in England with Tom Thumb changed Barnum's life in noticeable ways, but they would also expose aspects of his personality that were far from admirable. Tom Thumb's run at the Egyptian Hall, followed by successful touring elsewhere on the scepter'd isle, soon made Barnum a wealthy man. As he put it in an *Atlas* letter written at midsummer, he had "secured an independence." At the same time, the showman's letters to the *Atlas* were turning him into a celebrity back home. In these letters — perhaps a side effect of the ego-inflating wonder of his life in England — a callousness emerged in him that was not often evident in his other writings or in the view of those who knew him.

In June 1844, as he was laboring over one of his *Atlas* pieces in London, letters arrived from home conveying the terrible news that his youngest daughter, Frances, had died on April 11, not yet two years old. "But a few months ago," he wrote as an addendum to his piece, "I left her blithe and merry, blooming in health and happiness; and now, without a moment's warning, I learn that she is the tenant of the grave." He noted how much harder it was to receive such news at a distance, but he turned quickly, perhaps too quickly, to an acceptance of God's will in the matter. Nobody can doubt that his grief was heartfelt — he ended the letter abruptly, with the words, "I can write no more to-day" — and yet this is the only allusion to his daughter's death in his *Atlas* letters, and no mention of it at all appears in the autobiographies. It's possible, of course, that his grief was so palpable and personal that he did not find it appropriate to write more about it. Still, he made no acknowledgment of the grief of his wife and surviving daughters at home. If he considered the possibility of sailing back to New York to console them, he made no mention of this, either.[8]

He would not return to his family until October, and then without forewarning. He even saw fit on his arrival to play a practical joke on Charity. When he reached New York, he went to the museum and sent Parson Hitchcock with a message to her saying she must hurry with him back to the museum to meet a man who had just crossed the Atlantic bringing news. Under the circumstances, she could only have thought the news was of the grimmest sort. Barnum seemingly never considered the state he put her in, but only alluded to the questionable humor in the situation, writing in the *Atlas,* "I *guess* she was a little astonished." Thus he greeted his wife for the first time after the death of their daughter.[9]

He made plain in his *Atlas* articles that his visit home had to do principally not with shoring up his family but with work, which "rules 'men of business' with despotic sway." But when the business was done and he boarded the steamship *Great Western* on November 9 to return to England, he had Charity, Caroline, and Helen with him, presumably so the family could continue to grieve together over Frances and not suffer the loneliness of their long separations. Charity was not a good traveler, however, and in addition to suffering relentless and debilitating seasickness she often kept the others on board "in a half-suffocation of concealed laughter by her piteous moaning about the dangers of shipwreck." Disloyally reporting this to the *Atlas* audience, at the time of her greatest onboard discomfort Barnum entered into the fun by pretending with others to agree with her that the ship might well be about to sink. A. H. Saxon writes, about this and other times in the *Atlas* letters when Barnum poked fun at her, "One gathers that Charity herself was not amused by these indiscreet revelations, for her husband did not repeat them in his autobiography."[10]

His self-absorption extended beyond his immediate family. In the letters he wrote soon after sailing from New York, Barnum took uncharitable swipes at people he had met on his visit home who seemed to regard him with new respect:

I could hardly credit my senses, when I discovered so many wealthy men, who compose the codfish aristocracy of New York, extending their hands to me, and expressing their great delight at seeing me again, although before I left New York those same nabobs would have looked down on me with disdain if I had presumed to have spoken to them.[11]

He attributed this change in attitude not to his extensive self-promotion and name-dropping in the *Atlas* letters but to his having "accumulated a few more dirty dollars," something so many New Yorkers could have known only from the same Barnum letters. Still, he protested that "the very thought of money being the standard of merit makes me sick" to the point of wishing "I was not worth a shilling in the world!" And it was not just the rich at whom he now sneered. When he "met some good honest friends in humble circumstances, who almost appeared to approach me with awe — and then again I felt ashamed of human nature." His breast-beating continued with the declaration "I wish . . . all the world to know that my father was a *tailor,* that I am a *showman* by profession, and all the *gilding* shall make nothing else of me." To think that a shoemaker cannot be a gentleman, he continued, but that every rich person must be considered one — "Both notions are false and wrong, and never should be encouraged in a country such as ours." Which is a worthy enough sentiment, but it is hard to read the passage as anything but another way of exhibiting Barnum's recent rise in stature.

By far the ugliest aspect of his *Atlas* writings are his racist comments about a black man who watched Tom Thumb perform at the Egyptian Hall, having arrived with "a well dressed white woman on his arm" and himself "dressed off in great style, with gold chains, rings, pins, &c., (niggers always like jewels)." Barnum reported that he asked Tom Thumb to perform a racist song and dance numbers, and he seemed to take pleasure in the "discomfiture" they caused " 'de colored genman."

Toward the end of 1844, having arrived in Liverpool with his family and promptly ensconcing them at the Waterloo Hotel, he boarded the steamer *Princess Royal* to Glasgow to check in on the touring Tom Thumb. In another *Atlas* letter he wrote how, aboard the steamer, he entered into a debate about slavery with Scottish passengers who said that, but for the peculiar institution, "America would be the greatest, best, and justly the proudest nation in the universe." Barnum trundled out for the Scots the timeworn argument that it was in the interest of slave owners to treat their slaves well, "and that on the whole, they were much happier than the *starving workies* of this country." It is in this letter that he claimed not to be an "apologist for slavery" but added, "The rabid fanaticism of some abolitionists is more reprehensible than slavery itself."

Another piece appearing in the *Atlas* at about that time profiled Barnum as "Our Foreign Correspondent," using as its source "an intimate friend of Barnum's" — undoubtedly the foreign correspondent himself. In recounting the details of his life up until that point, the sketch reported that while Barnum was traveling with exhibitions through the South in the late 1830s he had in Vicksburg purchased a slave to serve as his valet and later received, in partial payment for a boat he had sold, "a negro woman and child." He sold all three people, according to the profile, after owning them for a short time, but not before he had administered fifty lashes to the valet for theft.[12]

His slaveholding, however temporary, is never mentioned in his autobiography, but he would later allude to it in a speech he gave while running for Congress in 1867, admitting he had not only "owned slaves" but "did more. I whipped my slaves." At this point, decades on in his life, he concluded, "I ought to have been whipped a thousand times for this myself." This shift does appear to be genuine. For all his casual racism and skepticism about abolitionism early in his life, Barnum, particularly as his interest in matters of temperance grew, would get to know several outspoken abolitionists and come to favor an end to slavery himself in the years before the Civil War.[13]

The dim view of humanity in general that Barnum expressed in many of the *Atlas* letters would evolve late in life into the more benign and bemused headshaking in his book *Funny Stories,* where everyone is fair game. Barnum was a man of his time, and his attitudes toward race, class, women, family, and status, many of them deplorable today, were often, but not always, also of his time. Still, living in a racist society does not ultimately excuse individual acts of racism. Living in an era of head-spinning fluidity of class status does not forgive hypocrisy and snobbery. Being the paterfamilias in a paternalistic culture does not make it understandable when a husband trivializes the emotions of his wife. Given Barnum's generosity of spirit in other contexts, his zest for living, and his facility for putting himself in the place of others, it is hard not to feel disappointed in him for being a worse man during these years than he would become.

By the spring of 1845, Tom Thumb had

traveled throughout England, Scotland, and Ireland, and Barnum and the Strattons — now equal partners in the business of exhibiting their boy — were ready to test his popularity on the other side of the channel. Barnum wrote in late spring to his *Atlas* readers, "The excitable Parisians talk of nothing but 'General Tom Pouce, les tres jollie charmant enfant!' " If Barnum's French was imperfect, the sentiment was clear. In Paris dozens of different lithographs and oil paintings of Tom had been created and widely displayed, confectioners made edible representations of him, and little statuettes of the general appeared in shop windows. Soon enough the general himself was appearing nightly at the Théâtre du Vaudeville in the Place de la Bourse in a play written expressly for him called *Le Petit Poucet.*

Tom had been exhibiting in the Salle Vivienne in the same neighborhood twice a day for only a month when a "grave personage, dressed in black, his hair powdered" and carrying a "splendid" cane, approached the general after a levee and presented him with a small silver snuffbox. According to the Paris correspondent for the *Illustrated London News,* Tom Thumb's delight at the gift soon vanished when he realized that the mysterious man had at the same time relieved him of the gold watch that the Queen Dowager Adelaide had presented him the previous year. The police were called, but the elegant thief was long gone.[14]

Barnum wrote that on the day he and his family arrived in Paris, March 18, he received an invitation to accompany Tom to the Tuileries Palace on the evening of the following Sunday — Easter Sunday — to meet the French king, Louis-Philippe, and the royal family. The king's daughter, Louise, the wife of King Leopold and thus queen of the Belgians, had seen the general at Buckingham Palace, and Tom's success with the British royal family was well known in France. This first Tuileries visit went much like the first appearance before Queen Victoria, with Tom now in court dress charming the king, queen, and assorted princes and princesses, dukes and duchesses in a grand reception hall. Barnum found the king easy to talk to, and Louis-Philippe regaled him with stories of his four-year exile in America, during which "he had roughed it generally and had even slept in Indian wigwams."[15]

After Tom performed, this time eliminating his impersonation of Napoleon, the king presented him with "a large emerald brooch set with diamonds," which he asked Barnum to pin on the general. Things were going so well that Barnum felt emboldened to ask the king to allow Tom's tiny carriage to appear in an upcoming parade on the Champs-Élysées of royal and diplomatic carriages headed to a celebration in the Bois de Boulogne. The king, perhaps not realizing that he was being drawn into a promotional scheme, agreed to make this possible. On the day of the parade, thousands of people lined the route, cheering for "Général Tom Pouce." Barnum concluded his tale of this event by modestly stating that "there never was such an advertisement," and where there had been excitement in London, there was now "furor" in Paris. Once again, Barnum's path to success passed through a royal household.[16]

Tom and Barnum visited the Tuileries three more times, twice to reprise his act for the king and his court and once, on October 6, to watch fireworks celebrating the king's birthday. They were also asked to visit the family at the Château de Saint-Cloud, the country palace west of Paris. There, Barnum wrote, the king requested that the general, for the first and only time in France, don his Napoleon costume and imitate the former emperor, something that had to be done "on the sly." The frisson of the inappropriate mirrored one of Tom's visits with Queen Victoria, when she asked him to pick a song to sing for her and he had chosen "Yankee Doodle," which he then incorporated into his act with up-to-the-minute new lyrics about the Buckingham Palace appearances themselves. At the end of the Saint-Cloud visit, the royal family "almost smothered" Tom with kisses, which seemingly every woman in every country he visited felt compelled to do. Tom, although still well short of puberty, enjoyed and eagerly encouraged these attentions, but perhaps his pleasure was less sensual and more pecuniary. Advertisements in the French papers of the time warned that in addition to the entry fee to one of Tom's levees, "those persons who wish to kiss him are to pay five sous more."[17]

In three months in Paris, during which, Barnum wrote, Tom was "as merry, happy, and successful as ever," Tom's father was able to save $500 per week from his share of the profits. As Barnum would write to a friend, "I suppose you will hear that General Tom Pouce hit them rather hard in Paris . . . [and] has not done hitting them yet, but we have all got as much money as we want and shall go home next summer." Barnum took Tom and what had now become a large retinue — twelve people, three vehicles, the tiny carriage and four ponies, and all of their luggage — through the French and Belgian countryside, with a quick visit to Spain to meet the Spanish Bourbon queen, Isabella II, in Pampeluna, as Pamplona was then known, where Barnum was her guest at a bullfight.[18]

Barnum began to act as an advance man for the troupe, traveling a week or more ahead of them to make arrangements and gather more material for his letters. In early August he wrote to Tom, "I am as usual tolerably sick, and intolerably homesick." Three weeks later he wrote to Kimball from Bordeaux, "This is a most charming country, & he who has not seen it has seen nothing." Later, during the grape harvest in the Médoc region northwest of the city of Bordeaux, Barnum accepted an offer to help stomp the grapes, jumping barefooted into a vat and dancing on them to a fiddler's polka tune. "Day after day," he reported to the *Atlas,* "have I reveled and run riot among thousands of acres of ripe luscious grapes."[19]

By the end of 1845, the troupe was back in London for a short run at the Egyptian

Hall, after which they turned to the English hinterlands for what was to have been a farewell tour. Charity and their daughters had returned home in June. Mrs. Barnum apparently never acquired her husband's enthusiasm for the French and their culture, which she found morally lax. She was pregnant with what would be their fourth daughter, and, as he had written in the summer, Barnum was ready to finish his European sojourn. But business remained so strong that he decided to stay in England with Tom for another year, a decision that undoubtedly contributed to a growing sense of unease between Barnum and Charity.

Tom Thumb would spend three years touring the British Isles, France, and Belgium and on the brief visit to Spain. In all, five million people had seen the general, Barnum estimated. The crowned heads of Europe had doted on him, and as Philip Hone, the former mayor of New York City, wrote in his famous and oft-quoted diary, Tom had "been kissed by a million pairs of the sweetest lips in Europe, from Queen Victoria down." Both Barnum and the Strattons had grown wealthy, one British newspaper reporting that the latter had made in the neighborhood of $350,000 — more than $10 million in today's dollars. Since the equal partnership lasted for only two of the three years abroad, Barnum made considerably more than that amount. He wrote only that "the General's father had acquired a handsome fortune," some of which Stratton gave immediately to his son and much of which he invested. The father would use $30,000 of the profits to buy land just outside Bridgeport and build a fine house on North Avenue, where he and his wife would live until his death on the last day of 1855. Cynthia would stay on there for another ten years or so before moving to West Haven to be with members of her family.[20]

Barnum's relationship with Tom's parents was often tense, an unsurprising situation given the amounts of money involved in their joint enterprise and the question of who ultimately controlled the source of that money, his parents or the man who had discovered and developed him. In letters home from abroad, including his letters published in the *Sun,* and later in both versions of his autobiography, Barnum spent a considerable amount of his time making tedious fun of the elder Strattons' penny-pinching and provincial ways. But he never wrote ill of Tom and often went out of his way to praise the boy's good nature, his talent, and his uncomplaining willingness to be almost always onstage. "The dear little General is cuter than ever," he wrote to Kimball in one of his last private letters from the European tour, "he is in fact a little brick and astonishes us all more and more everyday."[21]

EIGHT:
AT HOME

Barnum felt a lifelong tension between the comforts of domesticity and the excitement of the exotic, the satisfactions and responsibilities of family life and the challenges of business, and even the patriotic love of his homeland and the attraction of foreign lands and cultures. This tension was drawn tightest in his three heady but sometimes lonely years away and in the period immediately afterward. Barnum then spent his first half dozen years back in America struggling with the same predicament.

As early as August 1845, midway through the European interlude and feeling homesick, he had written to Charity in detail about buying land in Fairfield for a house he wanted to build. He urged her to get the project going if that was something she felt ready to do, only asking her to let him know the cost of any land she bought before finalizing the purchase. A native of Fairfield,

Charity apparently approved of settling there. Barnum's half brother, Philo, had recently been named deputy postmaster of bordering Bridgeport, and Charity and the children had also at times rusticated there while Barnum was in Europe. In April 1846, he returned for a visit to New York, where he met his new daughter, Pauline, who had been born on March 1. By then, Charity had scouted out the land for the house, and now he bought it, seventeen acres just yards from what was then the border between Fairfield and Bridgeport.[1]

While he was home on this visit, he expressed his weariness with some of the very things in Europe he had eagerly described in his *Atlas* letters. In late May, Walt Whitman, who had recently become the editor of the *Brooklyn Daily Eagle,* left his second-floor office overlooking the Fulton ferry and rode it across the East River to interview Barnum in Manhattan, where they talked about the showman's time in Europe and "his intercourse with the kings, queens and the big bugs," as Whitman put it.

We asked him if anything he saw there made him love Yankeedom less. His gray eyes flashed: "My God!" said he, "no! not a bit of it! Why, sir, you can't imagine the difference — There every thing is frozen — kings and *things* — formal, but absolutely *frozen:* here it is *life.* Here it is freedom and here are *men.*" A whole book might be written on that little speech of Barnum's.[2]

Barnum's enthusiasm for the land he had spent so much time away from suggests he was tiring of Old World pomp, however enamored of it he had been for a time. But even if the attraction of the far side of the Atlantic had grown weak and his appreciation for the vigorous ways of his native land strong, life at home on that short return trip had apparently become difficult, even rancorous enough to send him back to England earlier than he had planned.

Barnum wrote to Tom Thumb on May 14 that Charity was "in very bad health — she does not go out of the house except for a short ride in a carriage two or three times a week." Not only was she dealing with a newborn baby, having had to bury on her own her most recent child only two years before, but here was Barnum, bursting with success and self-regard, having spent most of the previous year squashing grapes, attending bullfights with a Spanish queen, and rhapsodizing about French landscapes in his *Atlas* letters. Charity had made it clear that even England was too risqué for her, so imagine her reaction when she read in one of his *Atlas* letters about the rapturous beauty of Spanish women, and then read his unpersuasive coda: "Suffice it to say this is a dangerous country to any except those who, like myself, have lived long enough to resist all temptations!" Does any wife, separated by an ocean from her husband, want to hear his loud protestations that he resists *all* temptation? To make matters worse, Barnum had continued to use Charity as an object of amusement in his letters, which, however forbearing she might have been, cannot have amused her.[3]

After his return to England in the summer, he wrote a letter to Kimball in Boston from Brighton on August 18, 1846, that is one of the most obliquely revealing letters of the many he wrote to his friend. In it, he apologizes for departing from the United States abruptly, apparently having left Kimball and others in the lurch in some financial way. He had intended to leave for England on July 16, he explained, but "in a fit of very desperation I resolved to leave the 25th June by G. Western." If he had waited for the later steamer, he would never have returned to England because he would have found himself in an "insane retreat." If that claim left any doubt, he added, "I never before experienced so much trouble, nay misery, in the same space of time as I was forced to endure during my stay in the States." Now that he was in England seeking some peace of mind, he was "hard at work and not very happy."[4]

Barnum never explicitly named the cause of all this misery, but if, as seems evident, the source was his relationship with Charity, this would explain his hesitation to say so to Kimball or anyone else. The purchase of the acreage in Fairfield and the idea of building a house there was well-timed as an attempt to mollify an irate Charity. But Barnum's determination to return to England for another year would have opened up another channel for her rightful disgruntlement. Although he protested to Kimball from England, "I have less troubles than when I was home," his continued unhappiness and his expressed determination to make things better next year, but not sooner, also suggest that his difficulties were domestic in nature. The final clue that Barnum was feeling the unremitting heat of Charity's indignation is that the letters to the *Atlas,* several of which had been written aboard the *Great Western* on his trip home to New York in April, now stopped and would not resume upon his return to England. His concession of ending the epistolary career that had given him so much satisfaction must have been penance for his long abandonment of his family and for his having enjoyed himself so much without them.[5]

Barnum might well have laid on the misery a little thick in the Kimball letter, given that its main purpose was to mollify its recipient, who was clearly miffed at him for something. Barnum referred to his early departure as "a shabby trick" and pled guilty to "selfishness, selfishness, selfishness." He also tossed Kimball a little pro forma flattery: "I hope you are succeeding in your stupenduous enterprise and that you will have a success exceeding your own most sanguine expectations, & I believe you will." After his repetition of the word *selfishness,* he signed off with the equivocal confession, "I plead guilty to this general crime & can only give as my poor excuse that it is a part of human nature."

The letter apparently did not succeed, for Barnum wrote Kimball again in October, alluding to his supposed friend's having written of "not wishing to continue friendship or advice where it is not wanted." But on January 4, 1847, Barnum wrote, "I am glad to see that you are willing to pull at your end of the yoke, and not let our correspondence flag," and he promised that when the steamer carrying him and Tom Thumb home to America stopped in Boston in late February, he would certainly see "my dear Moses" there in person.[6]

The plan had been to stay on in England well into the spring of 1847, but the wife of Fordyce Hitchcock, manager of the American Museum in Barnum's absence, died early in the year. The man's depression was so deep that Barnum feared he was "unable to manage business with his usual energy." So Barnum booked passage on the steamship *Cambria* out of Liverpool on February 4. The Strattons were ready to return home with him, and a parade with marching band accompanied Tom Thumb to the ship, where the crowd gave him three cheers and a hearty round of "For He's a Jolly Good Fellow." A rough crossing took them first to Halifax, Nova Scotia, then to Boston, where Barnum presumably had his promised meeting with Moses Kimball, and then on to New York, where Tom Thumb began to appear at the American Museum before unprecedented crowds.[7]

Soon after Tom's four-week run began at the American Museum on February 26, Philip Hone, who, like Tom, was the son of a carpenter, took his wife to see the general. In his diary entry for March 12, he wrote that the young general "performs four or five times each day to a thousand or twelve hundred persons; dances, sings, appears in a variety of characters with appropriate costumes, is cheerful, gay, and lively, and does not appear to be fatigued or displeased by his incessant labors."[8]

Admission to the American Museum was still only a quarter, but Barnum was now making more each day than he had formerly made in a week, since the building was "thronged at all hours, from early morning to closing time at night." Apparently he was able to reinvigorate Parson Hitchcock, who would not retire as manager of the museum for two more years.[9]

Once the triumphant run at the museum was up and the Strattons had returned to Bridgeport for a month of well-earned rest, Barnum induced the general to appear for two days in benefits for the Bridgeport Charitable Society, with which Charity was now associated. It was the first time the townspeople of Bridgeport were exposed to their most famous son since he had conquered Europe, when they could see that "a diffident, uncultivated little boy" had returned to them as "an educated, accomplished little man." In short, at least in Barnum's telling, he had in their eyes been "Barnumized."[10]

Barnum's own prosperity was such that the plans for his house had evolved into something more grand. He was now envisioning a stately pleasure-dome worthy of Kublai Khan, a fantasy of a mansion inspired by the minareted, multidomed Royal Pavilion of George IV at Brighton, which Barnum had visited and admired while in England. He had a London architect make preliminary studies inspired by John Nash's elaborate Oriental plan for the king's seaside palace. Back home, the Vienna-born architect Leopold Eidlitz designed Barnum's house, which would rest on a small rise in a treeless field overlooking Long Island Sound not quite a mile west of the heart of Bridgeport. The ferry to New York now took only three and a half hours, and two railroads met the ferry, so beyond his own ties to the area, and Charity's and Tom Thumb's, Fairfield was convenient to the American Museum, and the adjacent Bridgeport was, in Barnum's mind, a city "destined to become the first in the State in size and opulence."

Even as the "concurrence of my wife" about where to live had reassured him, the businessman in him could not help but weigh the possible financial advantages of settling in Fairfield.[11]

Although Barnum wrote that his sole concern was for the new house to be convenient and comfortable, unpersuasively suggesting, "I cared little for style, and my wife cared still less," he admitted that his "eye to business" did influence the dramatic design he picked. If the house was distinctive enough, he realized, it "might indirectly serve as an advertisement of my various enterprises." For the actual construction, Barnum employed what he called a "competent architect and builder" and bid him to spare "neither time nor expense" in completing the project. The builder, Thomas P. Dixon from down the coast in Stamford, must have been someone in whom Barnum initially had real confidence, since ground was broken even before Barnum returned from England, and then the showman went off touring with Tom Thumb for much of the time the house was rising.

The Tom Thumb tour began with a visit to the White House, where, on April 13, 1847, the general and the showman went to meet President James K. Polk, his family, and his cabinet, including future president James Buchanan. After that, they traveled for months throughout the United States and to Cuba. The little general appeared in Kimball's grand new Boston Museum on Tremont Row in June, where the take exceeded $6,000. Barnum made occasional trips home during this tour, but by May 1848 he agreed with the Strattons that his time traveling with them was now at an end. He pledged, not for the first time, to "henceforth spend my days in the bosom of my family."[12]

The exotic house on the edge of Bridgeport was completed in the late summer of 1848 and given the equally exotic name Iranistan, which Barnum translated as " 'Eastern Country Place,' or, more poetically, 'Oriental Villa.' " An advertising pamphlet produced in 1849 referred to the house as a combination of "the Byzantine, Moorish, and Turkish styles of architecture," and here and there Chinese elements were tossed into the mix. At the end of August a piece headlined "Iranistan" appeared in the *Brooklyn Daily Eagle* urging readers to hop on a ferry and go in person to Bridgeport to visit the mansion and its grounds, calling it "one of the most unique and magnificent structures in the country."[13]

Made of reddish sandstone, the villa measured 124 feet across, with a terraced, three-story central structure flanked by two-story wings, each of which featured a glassed, multisided conservatory. Deep loggias with Arabic arches and elaborate scroll-work fronted every floor, stretching the width of the house. Iranistan's most eye-catching aspect by far was its huge onion-shaped central dome, the top of which reached ninety feet above the ground, sur-rounded by four smaller domes and an end-less series of diminutive minarets. In front of the main house was a large fountain in the center of a circular driveway, and in back was a pond with swans and ducks. The whole acreage was landscaped into a park with hundreds of mature fruit trees and what Barnum called "forest" trees, which because of their size had been transplanted at great expense. Outbuildings, including glass greenhouses to shelter tropical fruits, an elaborate gardener's house, barns, sta-bles, pavilions, and so on, were also built in Oriental styles amid walks, statues, and formal flower gardens.

Inside, on the first floor, a frescoed draw-ing room stretched the entire depth of the house; also on that floor were a library with a Chinese theme, bedrooms, bathrooms with running hot water, parlors, and a baronial dining room with walls of oak painted with representations of Music, Poetry, and Painting. Objects in porcelain, a tea set in gold, and a silver service, all from Paris, were on display in the dining room, which could seat forty. The wide main hallway and grand walnut staircase were populated with marble statues, and on the second floor were more bedrooms and bathrooms and Barnum's princely study, dominated by a rosewood bookcase, its walls and ceiling lined with orange silk damask, and "window hangings, carpets, and everything else to match," as a visitor reported in the *Daily Eagle.* "Elegant and appropriate furniture was made expressly for every room in the house," Barnum wrote. The third floor featured a billiards room that could double as a ballroom, and above that, up a circular staircase, was the inside of the great dome, whose diamond-shaped windows, each a different color of stained glass, created a kaleidoscope effect for those sitting on a tow-stuffed circular seat that could accommodate forty-five posteriors.[14]

His interlocutor from the *Eagle* asked Barnum if he worried about burglars, given that the grounds were open to the public.

Barnum responded that they would have to get past several ferocious bulldogs before breaking in, and warned that, only a few nights before, the dogs had "attacked one of [my] ponies, tore him in pieces, and by morning had eaten him half up." Barnum, the master at attracting crowds through clever use of the press, here shows a facility for discouraging clientele of an unwanted sort, and one can hope that the half-eaten pony was only a useful fiction. But just in case the bloodthirsty bulldogs were not enough, Barnum had also installed a new-fangled alarm system.

The writer in the *Eagle,* who signed his report only with the letter *T,* concluded his visit to Iranistan by praising Barnum as "one of those off-hand, whole-souled, generous men who take your good will by storm. And his excellent lady, though more quiet in her manners, very soon makes you feel at your ease." As with anything published about Barnum, the suspicion always arises about whether he might have written the piece himself — was the *T* for "Taylor"? — or in some way dictated its contents. If he did not do so in this case, he at least displayed his ability to charm a visitor into writing an advantageous story.

Once everything "was finally completed to

my satisfaction" and the family was ensconced, Barnum undertook "the old-fashioned custom of 'house-warming.' " On November 14 a thousand guests, "including the poor and the rich," arrived to inspect Iranistan, to see what $150,000 (the equivalent of a mere six hundred thousand tickets to the American Museum) and the exertions of five hundred craftsmen, laborers, and nurserymen could produce. But the finished house was not just the work of many hands, from the architects who made the drawings to the men who shoveled out the pond. It was also a work of imagination, of aspiration and inspiration, the dream come true of a boy from a country village in Connecticut who as a man had seen and absorbed the most elegant trappings of imperial Europe and re-created them only a few miles from that modest place of his nativity. Surely the showman was warmed by the admiration of those who came from near and far, and also perhaps by their envy. As for the house itself, if a thousand close-packed bodies could not warm the autumn chill, then its proprietor could easily open the dampers and feel the hot air rising from his gas-fired furnace.

Now that Charity and their three daughters

occupied Iranistan, there began an extended period when Barnum tried to stay home but didn't always succeed. If it had not been obvious during her sojourn in Europe that Charity was no traveler, a less exotic trip she made with the family sealed her own intention to remain forever more a homebody. Some weeks before they moved into their new palace, Barnum had proposed a summer trip to Niagara Falls and Canada. They left on Barnum's thirty-eighth birthday, July 5, and began shadowing the tour of a certain famous miniature general. Within two days of their departure, they attended one of Tom Thumb's levees in Rochester, New York, and then joined him and his party crossing Lake Ontario to Kingston, at the mouth of the St. Lawrence River. Caroline, at fifteen the eldest Barnum child, kept a journal of their trip, focusing on the fun she often had along the way with Tom, with whom she had become friends in Europe. Together, for instance, they blew bubbles out a hotel window in Kingston, below which a raucous crowd of his admirers had gathered. The Barnums and Strattons traveled up the St. Lawrence to Montreal, and then on to Quebec City, taking in the sights between Tom's performances, before turning downriver and back to Kingston.[15]

Charity had become sick while in Quebec, but although she was now mostly recovered, she urged her husband not to start immediately back across the lake to Rochester. If she had a sense of foreboding, it was well founded, because after Barnum hustled them onboard anyway, the ship ran into a tremendous storm. Caroline, who would be a favorite of her father throughout his life and like him in her sense of humor, wrote in her diary that her mother became so frightened by the storm that "she forgot to be sick." The Barnums eventually reached dry land in Rochester and made their way to the American side of Niagara Falls. On August 3 they decided to cross by ferry to the Canadian side, but to do so required walking down 250 steps to get to the river, something Charity had to be encouraged to do. Halfway down, she grew dizzy and refused to go farther. Barnum and the girls, having grown resistant to her complaints, left her on her own. As Charity made her way alone back up the steps, she fainted, and some nearby men performed the gallant task of accompanying her back to her hotel. It is not hard to imagine the human torrent that Barnum, Caroline, and Helen received when they returned later in the day.

Even leaving aside this dramatic example of Barnum's inattention, Charity could hardly be blamed for any disenchantment with a family vacation that so closely resembled her unhappy experiences on tour with the Strattons in England and France. The exoticism of the new house in which her family now lived, with its evocations of Turkey, Persia, and China, could more than satisfy her underdeveloped interest in faraway lands. Her husband, having pledged himself to domesticity, would inhale it in a setting that reminded him each day of points on the globe where he had not yet been — the big world he was still culling for wonders to be displayed at his American Museum.

Whatever hard feelings the trip to Canada had produced or brought to a head in the marriage, the family seemed to be able to move beyond them and start to enjoy one another's company in the months that followed. On September 19, Barnum, Charity, and Caroline attended one of Tom's levees in Danbury, about thirty miles north of Bridgeport. It had begun at 10 a.m., and after it was over, the three accompanied Tom by carriage to the home of James White Nichols, a close friend of Philo Barnum's who also counted "Tale" as a friend. Nichols kept a diary for many years and in it described this day in some detail. Barnum carried Tom into Oak Cottage, as the Nichols house was called, where the little man expressed his eagerness for dinner and showed it by running about, eyeing the cheeses and peering into a pot where chickens were stewing. After the initial greetings, everyone went out into the yard, where Barnum passed the time by tossing into the air apples he found under a tree, warning Tom, "All that's *up* must come *down* / On the *head* or on the *ground*." Tom scurried around to avoid being brained, eventually hiding beneath Charity's apron. The meal was still being prepared, so Nichols led the party to the crest of a nearby hill, Barnum carrying Tom on his back. There they enjoyed the view until, "hearing a call for dinner from the house, we descended the hill, the little General being carried in Barnum's arms at a speed almost equal to a locomotive." Barnum tossed his small burden through a window of the house, and Tom was led right to the dining room, where he waited for the rest of the party. When they entered, he called out, "Come on, Barnum, I'm here." To which Barnum responded, "Ah, the general is something like *me,* he's not bashful." Over dinner Barnum reverted to his role as the straight man for his little companion, who "indulged in all manner of jokes and sarcasms on his friend and protector Mr. Barnum." Nichols found Barnum polished by his time in Europe, and the Barnum women amiable and diverting. After dinner, Tom, now ten years old, fished a cigar "almost as big as himself" out of Barnum's pocket and smoked it with "gusto" until he had to set off for Danbury for another performance.[16]

At Iranistan, Barnum took up the role of country squire with all the energy he expended on other parts of his life, soon buying a nearby parcel of a hundred acres of land suitable for gentleman farming. There he would keep milk cows and swine, plus an assortment of chickens, geese, swans, ducks, and pheasant. On the strength of this purchase, his neighbors elected him president of the local agricultural society, a job he held for the next six years. In his memoirs he poked fun at himself in this role, relating that, when he was asked to address the society in 1849, he realized that he knew next to nothing about farming, so instead "I gave them several specimens of mistakes which I had committed, and entreated them to profit by my errors." Besides giving speeches, Barnum's chief role as the society president was to oversee the annual agricultural fair. He could not help but bring his showman's flair to the job, deciding one year, when "a celebrated English pickpocket" was arrested at the fair, to put him on display the next day, after passing out handbills advertising this new attraction. Barnum modestly pointed out, "Our treasury was materially benefited by the operation." He would bolster his arcadian credibility when he bought several acres of land just to the west of his Iranistan property and fenced it, creating a deer park featuring Rocky Mountain elk, reindeer, and other species.[17]

Barnum wrote of this period of his life, "I am frequently in New-York, and occasionally in other great cities, yet I am never so happy as when I return to my 'homestead.'" Of course, like any other comparable period in his life, this one was also filled with dizzying activity. He went to New York each week to check up on the American Museum. And in 1849 he opened a museum in Philadelphia, at Seventh and Chestnut Streets, called P. T. Barnum's Museum of Living Wonders. He spent many weeks there around the opening, sometimes joined by Charity and Caroline. The new enterprise was briefly in direct competition with his former partners the Peales, and when their establishment went out of business he and Kimball together bought its collection at a "sheriff's sale, for five or six thousand dollars," and divided the exhibits between Kimball's in Boston and his own in New York.[18]

Still, while he remained engaged with his museums, Barnum implied that he was otherwise mostly at home. This stretch of time in the late 1840s was one of real contentment, of devotion and recommitment to family rather than to the intense striving that had come before it.

One source of his satisfaction was a dramatic change he made in his life upon returning from Europe, a change that led to better relations with Charity and to greater patience with domestic life in general, as well as a commitment to something bigger and more meaningful than growing rich and achieving fame. This shift was Barnum's pledge to give up alcohol and promote the cause of temperance. That he would take this new path at the highest point yet in his professional career, at a time when many people feel that success has confirmed their worth and redeemed their sins, makes it all the more striking.

In the autumn of 1847, during the months of touring with Tom Thumb after their return from Europe, Barnum dropped in at the New York State Fair, where Tom was holding levees in Saratoga Springs. "I saw so much intoxication," he wrote, "among men of wealth and intellect, filling the highest positions in society." He asked himself then and there if he too might be on the road to becoming a drunkard. Barnum had been around alcohol all his life, and both he and his father had sold it in quantity. But even when he had worked as a young man at a porterhouse in Manhattan, at a time in life when many people are most susceptible to the temptations of Bacchus, he claimed never to have drunk more than a pint of anything alcoholic. Even now, he told himself, he drank spirits only when he was with friends. But then, he admitted, he was with friends almost every day. He decided at the fair to give up "spirituous liquors as a beverage," by which he meant distilled liquors. At this point, he saw no harm in wine, which he had enjoyed immensely in Europe, where he "had been instructed . . . that this was one of the innocent and charming indispensables of life." In a retrospective interview in the New York *Sun* when he was seventy-three years old, Barnum was asked, "Did you drink much prior to 1847?"[19]

"Well, I wouldn't have allowed anybody to tell me so," he responded, "but when I look back over that time I know now that I did." He went on to say that, as proud as he was of Iranistan when it was built, he was "ten times prouder of my wine cellar than of anything else I had." Even after giving up spirits, he drank a bottle of champagne, wine, or beer each day at the midday dinner, resulting in "after-dinner feelings" and a reluctance to do any business in the afternoons. When his mother-in-law would accuse him of being "heady" at those meals, he would get offended and threaten "to go back to whisky" if she said it again, because "I really considered myself quite a temperance man."[20]

He was at least enough of a temperance man, never mind the wine and beer, that in 1851 he invited a friend, the Rev. E. H. Chapin, to travel from New York to Bridgeport to deliver at a local church a lecture on the perils of alcohol. As part of his talk, the reverend addressed the question of the "moderate drinker," which Barnum realized was a pretty fair description of himself, although Chapin didn't intend it that way, believing Barnum's invitation to speak meant that he was already a teetotaler. Instead the speech made Barnum realize "the bad example I was setting," and there followed a sleepless night at Iranistan.

"The next morning, I had my coachman knock the necks off all the champagne bottles I had in my cellar, some five or six dozen," Barnum said, and "pour their contents upon the ground." He gave away "the port and other medicinal wines" and sent the liquors back to the merchant. "I then called upon Mr. Chapin, asked him for the teetotal pledge, and signed it."

When he returned home and told Charity what he had done, he wrote, "I was surprised to see tears running down her cheeks." She "astonished" him by saying that she had cried on many nights, worrying that his "wine-bibbing was leading me to a drunkard's path." He continued, "I reproached her for not telling me her fears, but she replied that she knew I was self deluded, and that any such hint from her would have been received in anger." That he could reproach her and she could profess to be afraid of his reaction adds more paint strokes to the unflattering self-portrait of the husband Barnum had become in the months and years before taking the pledge. Still, making a resolution not to drink and then keeping it took both discipline and self-awareness and constituted another serious effort to turn his marriage and himself around. When he made the pledge, he remembered late in life, "that was the end of my drinking." And indeed, as best as can be known, he drank no more.[21]

The feeling of relief that came from forswearing alcohol gave his life a new sense of purpose. "I had been groping in darkness," he remembered, "was rescued, and I knew it was my duty to try and save others." On the very day he signed the pledge, he managed to gather more than twenty pledges from his neighbors. Like any evangelist, and true to his industrious nature, he was now full of the spirit and could not stop spreading it. First, he talked up temperance to everyone he saw in Fairfield and Bridgeport, then he went out to the nearby villages and towns, and then he spent the winter of 1851–52 traveling around the state of Connecticut, "at my own expense," seeking converts. He estimated that these early efforts turned hundreds if not thousands of people to the temperance creed. Soon he was lecturing in other states and in New York City and Philadelphia. His effectiveness as a temperance speaker, at a time when public lectures were a popular and respectable form of entertainment, now matched the literary abilities he had displayed in his letters from Europe to the *Atlas*. If his skill as a promoter had made him notorious and his newspaper letters had made him famous, then the lectures were a bid to be taken seriously.

While he was striving to redefine himself as a better man at home and a moral exemplar in public, he still had a bit of the old Barnum to get out of his system. In the late 1840s, then, he perpetrated one of his last famous humbugs. The summer after returning from Europe, while accompanying Tom Thumb to Cincinnati, Barnum saw a local exhibition of a small horse covered with a curly, wool-like coat but lacking a mane or any hair on its tail — "withal," as Barnum put it, "a very curious-looking animal." Of course he had to have the beast. But he wasn't sure, yet, what to do with it, so he kept it out of sight in a barn in Bridgeport. The following winter, he had an idea.[22]

John C. Frémont, the famous explorer known as The Pathfinder, was undertaking his penultimate great expedition in the West, attempting to find a route for the transcontinental railroad through the southern Rockies that would be passable even in winter. Frémont was a national hero who would soon run for president, so his expedition in southern Colorado was well covered in the press. In March 1849 Barnum managed to place a wholly fictitious news story claiming that a St. Louis merchant had received a letter from someone in Frémont's party reporting that they had captured, after a chase of three days, a "nondescript" animal looking somewhat like a horse but having the tail of an elephant and the speed of a deer. This would be Barnum's chance to make use of the animal fattening in his barn at home. What he did not know was that, within only a few more days, real reports would arrive in the East revealing that Frémont's expedition had met with disaster in December and January, while trying to push forward through unusually deep snow and extraordinary cold, sometimes as low as thirty degrees below zero. Ten members of his original party of thirty-two had died of exposure or hunger, and everyone had suffered greatly. Men had been forced to eat their mules, then the leather tack for the mules, and had even boiled ropes for sustenance. A rumor later surfaced that when the leader of one small relief detail separated from the main group had died, his companions had eaten his frozen flesh.[23]

The news of the expedition created, Barnum wrote, using an unfortunate metaphor, a "ravenous" appetite for "something tangible from Col. Frémont." Although Barnum's scheme had been hatched before the sobering facts arrived, he apparently gave no thought to canceling his humbug out of respect for what the expedition had gone through. The public was in such a frenzy that "they would have swallowed any thing, and like a good genius I threw them not a 'bone,' but a regular tit-bit, a bon-bon — and they swallowed it at a single gulp!" His punning is almost gleefully disrespectful, but in fairness to Barnum, he wrote these words many years later, and it should be noted that Frémont himself spent little time grieving for his men; he was soon off to California chasing the discovery of gold near a ranch he had recently bought in the Sierra foothills.

By the middle of April, Barnum had rented a hall at 290 Broadway to exhibit "Col. Frémont's Nondescript or Woolly Horse," which, the ads said, combined characteristics of an elephant, deer, horse, buffalo, camel, and sheep. Following his usual pattern, Barnum warned in advertisements that the animal would be on display for only a few days before being shipped off to the Royal Gardens in London. Then, conveniently, a new ad announced that the ship was not ready to sail, so the public would have three more days to see the "ana-gogetical" animal. (Where Barnum came up with this obscure bastardization of the word *anagogical,* which means "mystical" or "al-legorical," is anybody's guess.) Although the Woolly Horse never made it to London, it did tour some "provincial towns" and then went to Washington, where Barnum's agent was arrested at the urging of Frémont's father-in-law, Senator Thomas Hart Benton, for falsely charging a quarter to see the horse. The case was dismissed, however, which allowed Barnum to add to his receipts until he decided, out of deference to the powerful senator, to put the horse out to pasture. Thus, even in these transitional years for Barnum, when he began to yearn for a measure of respectability, he could not resist the allure of a headline-grabbing hum-bug.[24]

NINE:
THE VOICE

Barnum's most remarkable success as a showman began just as his relationship with drink was ending. The new venture would put to use all his skills and imagination as a promoter, and as fulfilling as the interlude at home had been, this undertaking would get him back on the road, giving him ample opportunity to moonlight as a temperance lecturer. It would also give him a chance to move beyond the days of Joice Heth, the Fejee Mermaid, the Woolly Horse, and even the most famous little man in the world, to establish himself as something more than a mere promoter: a serious purveyor of high-brow culture. It would also, conveniently, make him far, far richer than he had ever been.

Three months to the day after Barnum and the Strattons sailed home from Liverpool, a new sensation appeared in London, and a delirium outstripping the one associated with Tom Thumb seized the British public. The Swedish opera singer Jenny Lind, who was already acclaimed on the Continent, made her debut at Her Majesty's Theatre in the Haymarket on May 4, 1847, performing the role of Alice in Giacomo Meyerbeer's *Roberto il Diavolo*. Attempts to bring Lind to England had been protracted and very public, and even the *Encyclopaedia Britannica* declared years later that the ruckus created by the debut's elegantly attired ticket holders had "become historic." They began to gather outside the theater at 4:30 p.m., eventually blocking the street, and when the doors finally opened three hours later, the ensuing stampede left the evening coats and gowns of many ladies in disarray. Once calm was restored and the crowd seated, Queen Victoria and Prince Albert swept into the royal box along with the Queen Dowager Adelaide and other royal personages. Among those in the audience were Lind's close friend Felix Mendelssohn and the celebrated actress Fanny Kemble.

When Lind first appeared on stage, she received a standing ovation, and in the third act, as she sang the maiden's love song "When I Left Normandy," the audience applauded each verse and, at the end of the aria, interrupted the production for twenty minutes, "rapturously" calling for encores "with the most enthusiastic waving of hats and handkerchiefs," as *The Times* of London reported. At the first of Lind's three curtain calls following the performance, Queen Victoria herself tossed a huge bouquet at the singer's feet. In the next day's *Times*, the music critic wrote of Lind's voice, "The delicious quality of the organ — the rich, gushing tone was something entirely new and fresh. The auditors did not know what to make of it. . . . The sustained notes, swelling with full richness, and fading down to the softest piano, without losing one iota of their quality, being delicious when loud, delicious when whispered, dwelled in the public ear, and reposed in the public heart."[1]

Victoria would attend all fifteen subsequent operas in which Lind performed during that season in London, ending on August 21, and each engagement would feature the same crush of elegantly dressed fans and other royals, including the Duke of Wellington, who would call out a greeting from his box when she appeared on stage. People traveled from as far away as the Continent not only to hear Lind sing but also to watch her act, charmed by her naturalistic style. One special performance, for the Queen's birthday on June 15, added trumpets and the singing of the national anthem in Her Majesty's honor, once the nine carriages transporting her party had arrived. On July 22 Giuseppe Verdi himself conducted the premiere of his ambitious but not wholly successful opera *I Masnadieri,* commissioned for Her Majesty's Theatre and written in part with Lind in mind.

The Jenny Lind mania spread well beyond those who could afford to risk the integrity of fancy evening dress and spend the equivalent today of more than $500 for an orchestra seat. "The name of Jenny Lind became a household word among thousands and thousands who had never been to the opera in their lives," writes one of her biographers, Joan Bulman, "and had no prospect or intention of going." People stood outside the cottage in Old Brompton where she was living, hoping for a glimpse of her. Articles of clothing were now called Jenny Linds, as were certain cigars. "Her portrait appeared on chocolate boxes, matchboxes, pocket handkerchiefs," Bulman writes, "her name was given to horses and dogs and children's dolls, [and] a magnificent golden-yellow tulip was named after her."[2]

With his many friends and professional contacts in London, Barnum would have been well aware of Lind's conquest of queen and country. The American papers also covered it. On July 3 James Gordon Bennett himself wrote in a letter from London to his *New York Herald* audience about the rivalry between Lind and another opera singer performing in the city that summer, Julia Grisi: "I have heard both frequently, and they are both great artists." Lind, he continued, "is not beautiful, but extremely interesting. Her voice is wonderful in power, compass, skill." The rivalry had kept their respective opera houses brimming all season, "as full as they could be packed."[3]

In the later version of his autobiography, Barnum wrote that, although his American Museum and many of his promotions had been aimed at the masses, "I myself relished a higher grade of amusement, and I was a frequent attendant at the opera, first-class concerts, lectures, and the like." We know that even as a teenager living in New York he fancied himself in the know about the theater, and his time in Europe as a codfish aristocrat among the hereditary ones gave him more opportunity to develop and satisfy his inclinations toward sophistication. His exposure to both the highborn and the highbrow led to his wishing to construct a palace for himself bedecked with all the finest things the world could offer, and even more to reconstruct himself as someone sturdier than a promoter of humbugs, collector of curiosities, and manager of a dwarf. So it seems inevitable that Barnum would develop an interest in Jenny Lind, would seek to raise his own status by associating himself with a singer favored by the greatest composers in Europe. That she filled Her Majesty's Theatre throughout her first season in London — and continued to succeed admirably in subsequent seasons — would naturally only raise the stakes for an impresario such as himself.[4]

When Barnum finally met Lind in 1850, he admitted that he had never heard her sing. But a large part of what interested him went beyond her musical talent and reputation. These were the same qualities that had drawn so many people to her since she had begun to make a name for herself in Sweden in her middle teens: simplicity, modesty, piety, spirituality, and later, once she had the means, philanthropy. She had been born out of wedlock in 1820 in Stockholm to an ill-tempered mother who made it plain she did not want her and indeed sent her away to live with strangers more than once. By the time Jenny's innate musical talent was recognized at the age of nine, when she was enrolled with financial assistance in the Royal Opera School, her uncompromising Lutheranism was already unalterably established. In Sweden, as in the rest of Europe, the British Isles, and the United States, theatrical performers were morally suspect, and even the protection of the Royal Opera did not exempt Jenny from the possibility of censure. But as Bulman writes:

> Those who had feared for Jenny's moral development . . . could set their minds at rest. She detested immorality with a violent, instinctive repugnance. She was a natural Puritan; besides, art and religion were to her so intermingled, artistic gifts so clearly a gift from God, that the artist became almost by definition a sort of priest.[5]

Her reputation for purity became part of her public persona and was a large factor in why she was so widely loved. If in private she could be stubborn, blunt, and solitary and could at times act the part of the prima donna, there was nonetheless something authentic in her manner, and this authenticity came through on stage and off. She was

241

both otherworldly and self-contained. She cared nothing about fashion, always dressing simply, and seemed to be made uncomfortable by too much public adulation. She truly believed that her talent for singing and acting had been divinely ordered and not earned, and thus could be taken away on any given day. Her nerve often failed her when she made a debut in a new city or country, so uncertain was she that she could call forth her talent or translate it into a different context.

These attributes made a strong impression on Barnum. When in the autumn of 1849 he began to think about proposing an American tour to Lind, he was himself trying to become a better person, a good husband and father dedicated to the family hearth, and a more moderate drinker on the road to complete abstinence. As he gave several days of thought to whether he should attempt to engage Lind, his " 'cipherings' and calculations gave but one result — immense success." One of the calculations had to do with how much an association with "the greatest musical wonder in the world" would be worth to his own reputation. "Inasmuch as my name has long been associated with 'humbug,' and the American public suspect that my capacities do not extend beyond the power to exhibit a stuffed monkey-skin or a dead mermaid," he began in honest self-assessment, he felt that he could afford to lose $50,000 as long as he presented the "divine Jenny" in a way that lent "credit to the management." That is, whatever else came of the venture, the very hefty expenditure of fifty grand would be fair value for a boost in his public profile.[6]

The two years following her London debut were tumultuous ones for Lind. In the fall of 1847, her beloved friend Mendelssohn died, leaving her bereft for many months. A second season at Her Majesty's Theatre, in 1848, turned out to be even more triumphant than the 1847 season, and she gave the first of a series of benefit concerts for British hospitals that would raise tens of thousands of pounds. During this time she became engaged twice, first to a fellow Swedish singer with whom she had long been enamored, and then to a very young and very dull British army captain, who turned out to be a religious fanatic and a mama's boy. Her fiancé broke off the first engagement and she the second, after the officer and his mother teamed up on her to extract promises that she would not perform in the immoral theater again and that she would renounce everything she had done in her stage career to date. During this same period, she began to perform with a young German pianist, Otto Goldschmidt, who had studied with Chopin in Paris and also with Mendelssohn, about whom Jenny and he could share their fond memories. Goldschmidt eventually traveled with her in America and, in February 1852, having converted from Judaism to Christianity, he would become her husband.

Even before the hectoring by the British officer and his mother, Lind began to have concerns about continuing her career as an opera singer. Her own religious scruples about the morality of acting fed these doubts; added to them were her worries about the exhaustion produced by singing so many demanding roles and the toll this heavy schedule might take on her heavenly instrument. Mendelssohn, whom she had first met in Berlin in 1844, had encouraged her to sing, instead of operas, oratorios — unstaged but dramatic religious-themed choral works — and he also introduced her to his songs and those of Schubert and Schumann. He wrote a soprano part with her in mind for his own oratorio *Elijah.* But it took her months and even years to extricate herself from opera. After all, by the time she gave her last performance, she was the most famous and best-paid opera singer in the world, and many people, especially the manager of Her Majesty's Theatre, to whom she felt a loyal gratitude, were economically dependent on her. But her last performance in his house finally happened, on May 10, 1849, in the role she had first sung there, Alice in *Roberto il Diavolo.* After that night — her 678th performance in a dozen years in thirty different operas in five languages — she sang opera no more. "The applause which she received at the conclusion of the Opera was something remarkable," the *Times* critic wrote of her last performance, where Queen Victoria was as usual in attendance. "She was called three times, by an audience that occupied even the obscurest nooks of the edifice, and that universally rose when she appeared; and so continuous were the plaudits, that they blended with each other into one roll of heavy sound."[7]

She was set to marry the British officer six days after that farewell, but when he overplayed his hand, she put an end to the engagement and escaped to Paris in a state of near emotional collapse. Both the conclusion of her opera career and her broken relationships had taken place very much in public, and she felt humiliated by her role in the second aborted betrothal. But then "she was astonished and relieved to find that all England rejoiced that the marriage" to the prim officer — "who did nothing but read psalms and go to church," as Jenny wrote to a friend — "had come to nothing."[8]

One night in June she went for dinner to the Hôtel de Charost, the Paris house of the British ambassador, where she enjoyed meeting a famous Italian opera diva of an earlier era, Angelica Catalani. After dinner, the older singer asked Jenny to perform, saying she would like to hear her sing before she died. Jenny sang and a few days later learned that, sadly, Catalani had indeed died, the victim of a cholera epidemic that was growing in the city. Deeply rattled, Jenny and her party left the next day for Amiens, then Brussels, then Cologne and other places in Germany, ending up on doctor's orders not to sing for at least six months and to get rest at Bad Ems, an ancient Roman town that had become a world-famous spa. By the end of the year she was in the port of Lübeck, a jumping-off point for Sweden, marooned there when her female companion, Josephine Åhmansson, came down with the measles. From Lübeck she wrote a letter to an English friend, a baroness:

> My nerves are better, and I feel *much less* agitated and more quiet than before. I believe that my having left the stage may be the chief reason for this happy change; my whole nature and my way of feeling was always very opposite to that sort of being, who can bear the calumnies of a theatrical life.[9]

She thought of going to Russia to make money for her charitable causes, including music schools in Sweden and a foundation in Mendelssohn's honor in England. And she began to sing in public again, not opera but songs of the Romantics and Swedish folk songs, sometimes accompanied by Goldschmidt. Now that she was rested and feeling mentally strong, she was more determined than ever to take control of her own life, even turning down her beloved sovereign, King Oscar of Sweden and Norway, when he asked her to perform in operas celebrating the marriage of the crown prince.

At about this time she received a visit from an Englishman named John Hall Wilton, who had traveled to Lübeck all the way from New York with the hope of meeting her. Several letters from him had made little impression on her, but a musical contact had eventually made the connection. He was the representative of P. T. Barnum and was authorized to sign her to a contract for an American tour managed by the famous showman.[10]

Four other promoters had approached Lind with the idea of an American tour, among them a man named Henry Wikoff, who in 1840 had taken the Austrian ballerina Fanny Elssler to the United States for a successful two-year tour. According to Barnum, Wikoff — a man of dubious morals whose later friendship with Mary Todd Lincoln would damage her reputation as first lady — tried to undermine him when he heard from Lind that Barnum's agent had approached her. He warned her that, as Barnum put it, "I would not scruple to put her into a box and exhibit her through the country at twenty-five cents a head!" This alarmed Lind sufficiently to move her to write to a London banker who knew Barnum. In reply, the banker promised her "that she could place the fullest reliance upon my honor and integrity," Barnum claimed. Later she would tell Barnum that she had also been reassured by the stationery Wilton had used to write to her, which featured a large engraving of Iranistan. The magnificence of his house, Barnum would have us believe, had reinforced her confidence in his substance as a businessman.[11]

Once Lind realized that she should take Barnum seriously, she demonstrated that she was the showman's match as a negotiator. Barnum gave Wilton elaborate instructions about how to negotiate with her, including incentives that would reward the agent in inverse proportion to how much he spent to convince her to agree to the tour. Barnum made clear his willingness to pay every imaginable expense, which included footing the bill for an entourage to accompany her on tour, complete with a music director, a male singer, two servants, and a companion. Although he hoped that Wilton could engage her to share in the risk and profits, he authorized Wilton to, as a last resort, guarantee Lind $1,000 per performance for up to 150 "concerts or oratorios." Wilton's financial incentives notwithstanding, Lind quickly took him for everything, including a pledge that all the money Barnum would pay her — $187,500 — be deposited in a London bank before she set out. So much for her "fullest reliance" on the showman's integrity.[12]

Lind wrote to a German friend that she was very happy with the deal that would take her to America: "The offer from there was very brilliant and everything was arranged so nicely, that I would have been wrong in declining it. . . . I shall be able to gain there in the course of one or two years a very large fortune." She would use this money, she said, to create schools in Sweden, and thus saw it as "a gracious answer to my prayers to Heaven!"[13]

Barnum makes much of his trouble in coming up with so much money in advance, averring that Wall Street thought his scheme would bankrupt him, topping the story by saying that the last $5,000 he needed to reach his goal was loaned to him by a clergyman. If this were not proof of divine intervention in the matter of Lind's tour, it at the very least underscored the impeccable spiritual qualities of the performer herself.

Barnum exaggerated the problems he faced in introducing her to the American public. Given her subsequent fame, he later wrote, "it is difficult to realize that, at the time this engagement was made, she was comparatively unknown on this side the water." He underscored this point with an anecdote about a conversation he had on a train. On his way home from Philadelphia, where he was working when he heard from Wilton that the contract had been signed, Barnum chatted with the "gentlemanly conductor," whom he knew from his previous travels on that line. The deal with Lind had been announced in the papers that morning, so Barnum asked what he thought people would make of her tour. "Jenny Lind!" the conductor responded. "Is she a dancer?" Perhaps this trainman had been too much of a gentleman to take notice of the back columns of newspapers, but beginning as early as 1845, the American press had begun to follow Lind's successes in Europe, and her more recent triumphs in England had turned her into the sort of celebrity whose romantic attachments, real and imagined, regularly became tidbits for the news columns. In the advertising columns were notices of Jenny Lind blouses and other articles of Jenny Lind clothing. Even so, she had not yet become the cultural icon that Barnum would endeavor to make her.[14]

By the time Lind arrived in America in September, just over six months from the time Barnum learned she had been signed, his campaign to prepare the public for her had become something to behold. On February 20, 1850, the very day he quizzed the train conductor, he wrote a letter to the papers in New York, which would be picked up far and wide, describing Lind as "a lady whose vocal powers have never been approached by any other human being, and whose character is charity, simplicity, and goodness personified." In this first attempt at marketing her, Barnum reversed his usual strategy of emphasizing the great expense to which he had gone to procure an act. Although he did say he would pay her "enormous" sums, he emphasized that she had turned down better offers and that money was not "the greatest inducement that can be laid before her." He didn't explicitly say what greater inducements could be offered but implied that her eagerness to visit America (which she could have done anyway by accepting one of those better offers) and her freedom to give charity concerts (which she might well have negotiated with the others) made the difference. But the strongest implication was that the real inducement was working with Barnum himself. In this opening salvo, Barnum also began to use the tour to improve his own reputation, and indeed his letter to readers of the New York papers promised them that even his own motivation for bringing Lind to America was not primarily financial: "I assure you that if I knew I should not make a farthing profit, I would ratify the engagement." That was undoubtedly read with a disbelieving smile by many of those readers.[15]

Within just a few days, however, Barnum was up to his usual tricks. He leaked to the papers the figure of $300,000 as the amount he would pay her to tour, but within a couple of weeks he amended that to the real $1,000 per night payment. As part of his initial feeding of the press, he also released a letter from Lind thanking Barnum "for the anxiety you and your agent evince to render my intended tour replete with comfort." In the following weeks and months, he continued to release small items to the press, which were reprinted around the country, including his booking of Lind and her party at the luxurious new Irving House hotel in New York and later at the Revere House in Boston. He disseminated news that his huge payment in advance of Lind's tour had been shipped by steamer on May 1 to London for safekeeping at the Baring Brothers Bank there, as well as announcements of his intention to rebuild a hall on Broadway and to refurbish one in Philadelphia in anticipation of Lind's appearances.

He also released reports of her triumphs years earlier in Europe and her present activities there, along with a list of cities she would visit in America and the number of concerts planned for each. He spurred speculation about ticket prices and let it be known that he planned to auction off tickets for the most desirable seats.[16]

One of his largest promotions involved extracting a letter from Julius Benedict, a composer who would be Lind's music director on the tour, promising that he would write the music for a song, "Welcome to America," to be sung by Lind at her first concert in New York, "if I can obtain the poetry of one of your first rate literary men." The letter (likely composed by Barnum) promised that "Mlle. Lind is very anxious" to perform such a "national Song." Barnum added a letter of his own to Benedict's, offering $100 to anyone who would produce the words to such a ditty. The showman soon elicited another round of stories nationally by upping his payment to $200, and a third round by naming a committee composed of well-known journal editors and book publishers to judge the submissions, eventually totaling more than 750. Barnum later admitted that the entries, which came from around the country and

Canada, "were the merest doggerel trash, with perhaps a dozen exceptions."[17]

During the months when Barnum was preparing America for her tour, Lind sang in Hamburg with Robert and Clara Schumann and returned to Sweden for what was referred to scoffingly as "hymn singing" by a public that still saw her as an opera diva. She did sing (but not operatically) for the royal wedding there and for the Queen Dowager. When she left Sweden in late June for the last time before sailing to the United States, a large crowd gathered at the dock to send her off. She performed in benefits in Germany and then went to London, where she said goodbye to Queen Victoria. Before her party departed from Liverpool, she gave two more benefit concerts there with Julius Benedict and the baritone Giovanni Belletti, who would travel with her to America. Barnum hired a critic from London to cover the first concert and an agent to get the critic's glowing review in the *Liverpool Chronicle* for the next day and send copies by steamer to New York that very morning. When the papers arrived, Barnum wrote, they "had the desired effect." The *New York Herald* republished the review on its front page on the very day that Lind herself reached New York. The second

Liverpool concert was the more memorable, however. She sang for the first time what would become one of her standard oratorio works, Handel's *Messiah*. Even without Barnum's encouragement, the critics were impressed. "It was a leave-taking," the London *Times* wrote, "such as even Jenny Lind has rarely experienced."[18]

On the Sunday before her departure, Lind and her party went to have lunch with Capt. James West aboard the S.S. *Atlantic,* the two-masted paddlewheel steamer on which they would travel. She mentioned the ship in a letter she wrote to her parents the night before her departure:

Nothing grander of its kind, I should think, could be found in any country. The vessel is 300 feet by 80, and is decorated so magnificently that one can fancy oneself in a rich private house.

I look forward to the sea — the ocean![19]

As the *Atlantic* steamed nearer, Barnum's preparations became more frenzied. The Canal Street pier on the Hudson, where the ship would arrive, had been decorated with the flags of the United States, Sweden, and other nations and with evergreen and floral arches reading, "Welcome to Jenny Lind" and "Jenny Lind, Welcome to America." The crowd of tens of thousands who would show up to greet her was seeded with "a large number" of Barnum employees, elegantly dressed in black and bearing bouquets, and Barnum's private carriage, drawn by two handsome bay horses, would be parked at the foot of the gangplank. In his autobiography, he allowed himself a bit of false modesty about this elaborate scene, writing, "These decorations were probably not produced by magic, and I do not know that I can reasonably find fault with some persons who suspected I had a hand in their erection."[20]

Barnum himself would meet the steamer off Staten Island and accompany the singer as the ship passed through the harbor, into the Hudson, and up to the pier. Among Barnum's many friends was Dr. A. Sidney Doane, the health officer for the Port of New York, stationed at the Quarantine Ground on Staten Island, who agreed to let Barnum accompany him on the official quarantine inspection as the *Atlantic* idled in the bay. Because it was impossible to predict exactly when the ship would arrive, Barnum went to the Quarantine Ground the day before it was expected and spent the night with his doctor friend. The next morning, the first of September, was misty, and there was no sign of the ship. A reporter from the *Tribune* met them in the late morning, and then at about 1 p.m. two guns sounded from the southeast, the direction of Sandy Hook, the first bit of American soil the steamer would pass. "In a few minutes," the *Tribune* reporter wrote, "the Atlantic hove in sight, her giant bulk looming through the light mist which still lay on the outer bay." Dr. Doane had a German flag raised at the Quarantine since he didn't have a Swedish one, and another salute roared as the ship threaded its way through the Narrows, after which the coal-fired paddles of the ship were stopped and it floated slowly in on the tide.

Barnum had prepared for this auspicious first meeting with Jenny Lind. He wore a white vest under his suit and bore a large offering of red roses. Soon he and the reporter were accompanying Doane in the quarantine boat, "over the fresh, dancing swell, as fast as four pairs of strong arms could urge us." When their boat came alongside, the ship loomed over them "like a mountain," the reporter wrote, "and it was something of an undertaking to climb the rope hand-ladder to her deck." To do so, Barnum, still spry at age forty, tucked the bouquet into his vest, and then labored up the ladder and onto the deck. Captain West met him there and escorted him to the front of the vessel, where Lind and her companions Benedict and Belletti were seated, enjoying the welcome sight of land.

Looking "as fresh and rosy as if the sea had spared her its usual discomforts," Lind wore a black cashmere coat over a silvery silk dress, a light blue silk hat, and a black veil. A small Pekingese dog, also silky, lay at her feet — a present from her friend Queen Victoria. Barnum was a man who could be counted on to make the grand gesture, and when Captain West introduced him to Jenny he offered her his bouquet with a flourish. But for once he had been out-gestured. The owner of the steamship line, shipping magnate Edward Knight Collins, had boarded the *Atlantic* before him, off Sandy Hook, and had presented Lind with her first bunch of New World flowers. Collins's bouquet was not only first; it was three times bigger than Barnum's. But Lind didn't seem to notice, turning her round face up to the showman, all expectation at the success the two of them were about to share.[21]

Barnum wrote that he took her hand, and after a moment of pleasantries she asked him where he had seen her perform. When he said he had never done so, she responded, "How is it possible that you dared risk so much money on a person whom you never heard sing?"

"I risked it on your reputation," Barnum told her, explaining that he trusted that more than his own musical judgment.[22]

Also stopped at the Quarantine was a Swedish ship, the *Maria,* flying her nation's flag. Seeing her countrymen on the vessel, Lind grew emotional. She waved her handkerchief at the sailors, who would be in quarantine, Doane told her, for a total of thirty-five days.[23]

No such delay would detain the *Atlantic,* which soon got under way toward lower Manhattan. Lind told Barnum that the sight before her was the most magnificent she had ever seen, to which Barnum suggested, "Except the Bay of Naples." "Not excepting even that," she replied. As they approached the pier, thousands of people could be seen gathered on both sides of the river, people filling the wharves and piers, people leaning out of windows or standing on the rooftops of nearby buildings, and people on the decks of other docked vessels, some of whom had shimmied up their masts and were thick in their riggings. The bad weather early in Lind's voyage had slowed her ship's arrival by a day, and the size of the crowd had only swelled. It was a Sunday and people were off work, promenading on nearby Broadway and wearing their Sunday best. "Have you no poor people in your country?" the *Tribune* reporter heard Lind ask Barnum. "Every one here appears to be well dressed."

But not everyone was well behaved. As the ship went upriver past the pier and then floated slowly into its berth, the crowd pushed in, held back by a gate at the entrance to the pier. Once Lind disembarked down a carpeted gangplank, the pushing grew frenzied, the gate gave way, and dozens of people "lay crushed by the inexorable crowd, stretching out their hands and crying for help." The police were able to urge the crowd back and save those who were trampled. At least one man fell from a sloop into the river and had to be fished out.

Once Lind and her party made their way to his carriage, Barnum climbed up in front to sit beside the driver, knowing that he was now so familiar to the public that his presence there would tell those along the route, cheering from the sidewalks and windows, that this was the carriage carrying the Swedish Nightingale. The crowd was densely packed around the carriage, with people climbing up on the horses and on the top of the vehicle. Even when the coachman whipped the horses he could not induce them to pull. When he then began to whip members of the crowd to move them back, Lind stuck her head out the window and asked him to stop. "I will not allow you to strike the people," a *Herald* reporter heard her say; "they are all my friends, and have come to see me." In this fairy-tale-like telling, a cheer then went up and the sea of people parted. The carriage glided through the streets, Lind continually bowing to those she passed, as they "literally heap[ed] the carriage with flowers," managing to get more than two hundred bouquets into the compartment where she sat.

Once they arrived at the Irving House, at the corner of Broadway and Chambers, across from A. T. Stewart's latest emporium, the hotel staff quickly raised the Swedish flag in greeting and Lind went straight up to her rooms on the second floor to rest. Many of the more than five hundred guests in the hotel wanted a glimpse of her, as did the crowd of thousands that gathered on Broadway in front of her hotel, whose members spilled onto the corner of City Hall Park and climbed the walls of an addition that was being built for Stewart's.

Cheers rose regularly as women who might be the divine Jenny peered out the windows of her apartment, and at several points Lind herself stood at the window and repeatedly bowed to the assemblage.

At midnight a group of two hundred musicians, members of the New York Musical Fund Society, made their way up Broadway to Chambers Street accompanied by twenty companies of New York firemen — three hundred men in all, wearing red shirts and carrying torches. They had intended to lead a torch-lit procession from the pier to the hotel the night before, when the *Atlantic* had been expected, but now they cleared a space for the band in the still-crowded street. Barnum estimated the crowd was ten thousand strong; the papers went as high as thirty thousand. Hotel guests threw open their windows or gathered on their balconies for the concert. After Lind, her head and shoulders covered with a crimson shawl against the chill, received the sustained cheers of the crowd, "Hail Columbia" and "Yankee Doodle" rang through the night, and then the band played them again at Lind's request. They continued their serenade with several more songs and concluded with "God Save the Queen."

Lind must have been cross-eyed with

exhaustion at this point, but she endured a visit to her apartment by a committee of the music society, and naturally a long speech ensued. Lind, who had been studiously looking at her feet as the speech droned on, then offered a response, "her voice choked with emotion," and graciously thanked the visitors for their welcome. With that, the delegation mercifully withdrew, and "the Nightingale retired to her downy nest." For Barnum, the day could hardly have gone any better. He and Lind had each made an effort to put the other at ease, and both had succeeded. The reception to the New World that Barnum had gotten up for her seemed to have filled her with elation. She told Belletti before retiring that the day had "been like Liverpool" and danced him around the room. We cannot know what Barnum's last thoughts were as his head hit the pillow in his own nest that night, but it is safe to say that they were of the future, and that they induced a sound night's sleep.[24]

TEN:
TEMPLES OF ENTERTAINMENT

In the months when Barnum was preparing America for the arrival of Jenny Lind, he was anything but idle in other aspects of his business. He closed the American Museum in April 1850 for extensive renovations that would incorporate the Chemical Bank Building next door into "one grand structure, finished in the most tasty style, at a cost of Fifty Thousand Dollars!" The words are unmistakably Barnum's, taken from an advertisement in the *New York Herald* that ran to nearly two thousand words, appearing the day before the museum reopened to the public on June 17. The most prominent feature of his rebuilt "temple of moral entertainment" was its Lecture Room, which Barnum claimed could seat five thousand patrons. A reporter for the *Herald,* having attended the press opening the day before and spoken with the renovation architect, wrote in the same issue as Barnum's ad that the theater could seat only two thousand, but never mind. The reporter was otherwise impressed, writing that the renovations "succeeded beyond the most sanguine expectations." The Lecture Room was decorated in red velvet seats and wallpaper, columns and trellises and other trim of "dazzling" white and gold, and fifty feet up, above two tiers of box seats, was a broad dome. Patriotic images of all the presidents appeared beneath the dome, and the sixty-foot-wide stage featured a drop curtain painted with a scene of the U.S. Capitol and its grounds.[1]

Just as he was promoting the Swedish Nightingale for her moral virtue as much as for her singing ability, Barnum's pitch for the reopening of his museum and its impressive new theater centered on their suitability for the whole family. From his first days of owning the museum Barnum had believed it should be a place where families could comfortably go, and he would increasingly emphasize the wholesome nature of the enterprises with which he was involved. Given his commitment to the temperance cause, it is no surprise that his newspaper advertisements announced, "There is no bar, or intoxicating drinks, allowed on the premises," and in an illustrated guide to the museum he promised instead the availability of "refreshing and healthful drinks of the season." His patrons were not permitted to leave for a snort in a nearby saloon without paying the full price for readmittance, which, Barnum claimed, "reconciled them to the 'ice-water' which was always profuse and free on each floor of the Museum." He emphasized in his pamphlet how well lit and well ventilated his rooms were, including the Lecture Room, giving further assurance of their suitability for families.[2]

As for the exhibits throughout the museum and the entertainments offered within, he promised, "The most fastidious may take their families there, without the least apprehension of their being offended by word or deed." He was explicit about why he called his lavish new stage a Lecture Room rather than a theater: the "hundreds of persons who are prevented visiting theatres, on account of the vulgarisms and immorality which are sometimes permitted therein, may visit Mr. Barnum's establishment without fear of offence."[3]

Those hundreds of reluctant theatergoers were more like thousands and tens of thousands in Barnum's mind. His marketing strategy of appealing to members of the rising middle class, who had the means to buy tickets for the whole family, would come to fill his pockets. But Barnum kept his price at a quarter, half that for children, and admittance to the Lecture Room did not require an extra fee for ordinary seating. Like his friend Moses Kimball, Barnum was genuinely interested in the theater and determined to make a comfortable place not only for lectures but also for the performance of moral dramas, melodramas, and the occasional work of the Bard — although as Barnum later wrote in his defense against an accusation of pandering, "Even in Shakespeare's plays, I unflinchingly and invariably cut out vulgarity and profanity." This sort of statement and the distinctions he often made between the probity of his offerings and the moral laxity of the regular playhouses made more rarefied observers see him as a threat to the serious theater. However, A. H. Saxon, an expert on nineteenth-century American entertainment, credits Barnum, Kimball, and others like them with the growing respectability of American theatergoing in the second half of the century.[4]

The first play presented at the reopened American Museum was, appropriately enough, the temperance melodrama *The Drunkard; or, The Fallen Saved: A Moral*

Domestic Drama in Five Acts, which had first been adapted for the stage in 1844 by Kimball's Boston Museum stage manager, William H. Smith. Smith himself directed the play and acted the title role at Kimball's establishment, where it ran 140 times in its first season. Inspired by the growing temperance movement, the play became one of the movement's founding documents. In early 1848 Barnum had offered the play in his Philadelphia museum, where it was popular enough to be performed eighty times alongside a companion drama called *The Gambler,* which had also run at the Boston Museum. For the American Museum production of *The Drunkard,* certain Boston place-names were replaced with local references to Broadway, Trinity Church, Five Points, and even the American Museum itself. In its first four months in New York, the play was performed at Barnum's 150 times. Competing New York theaters that did not mind calling themselves theaters also offered productions of *The Drunkard* at the same time it was running at the American Museum.[5]

The Drunkard tells the story of a young man who lives happily with his comely wife and little daughter in a "pretty rural cottage" until a lecherous and unscrupulous lawyer, who has designs on the wife, tempts the husband into becoming a brandy-swilling lush. The young man turns into such a drunk that he abandons his family and heads to the barrooms of the Five Points. Eventually his now impoverished wife and daughter follow him to the city, hoping to reform him. Before that happens, when he is at his lowest point and his wife and daughter are near starvation, a Good Samaritan gets the husband to take the temperance pledge, cleans him up, and reunites him with his family. In the fifth act, they are back in the cottage, their finances restored, a Bible on the table, and the young man plays "Home, Sweet Home" on the flute as his daughter sings the first verse, eventually accompanied by her mother and, as the curtain descends, by other members of the cast. The fallen drunkard has been saved.

After the debut performance, the audience called out Barnum to speak, a possibility for which he had been prepared, since two days later the text of his remarks appeared on the front page of the *New-York Daily Tribune*. In it, he managed to say a number of things that, given his public reputation as a man who was not above a bit of exaggeration in service to making a buck, were humorously self-deprecating but at the same time self-promoting. He said, for example, that the expensive renovations to his museum were, "believe me, when I pledge my honor," not undertaken with any "thought of *gain.*" Heaven forfend! His only motive was to provide wholesome entertainment, so much so that "I pledge myself to withdraw into private life, if ever the moment arrives that the great mass of our citizens prefer immoral, and vicious, to moral and reformatory entertainments." His Lecture Hall audience and the readers of the *Tribune* were meant to believe that his remarks should not be taken "as reflecting in the slightest degree upon other places of public amusement" or as challenging the judgment of their managers, despite "their peculiar views." Finally, he invited his auditors to say whether "I fall short in my endeavor thus felicitously to combine innocence with pleasure, rational amusement with a proper sense of virtue and morality."[6]

Reading his words many decades later, and noting his glib overstatement ("During a somewhat eventful life, this is the proudest moment I have ever yet experienced"), his false modesty ("I was doing well enough pecuniarily"), his orotund phrasing ("vividly painting the positive and inevitable evil consequences of vice, in whatsoever form"), and his naked self-congratulation ("erecting and perfecting . . . the most beautiful, commodious, comfortable, and best-contrived Saloon in this country, and I verily believe in the world"), it is easy to imagine in every word of this well-tooled, tonally consistent speech its self-parodying wit. We can only imagine these lines delivered with a theatrical flair and a twinkle in the eye. At about this time, Barnum was described as a "handsome, medium-sized man . . . smooth shaven, with a wealth of curly black hair, and a smile all over his face." The hair would thin and the face would thicken, but for now he was in his prime, delivering his observations in his strong, well-enunciated tenor. How could he not have been flushed with the excitement of the moment, his whole being bursting with an understandable pride at his revamped museum, his elegant new hall, all renovated in a mere nine weeks? Barnum had been on stage often, going back to his traveling shows in the South and more recently for his appearances as straight man to Tom Thumb, and his growing success as a temperance lecturer attested to his ability to hold an audience. He was comfortable when he spoke this night, imbued with both a sense of purpose and a winking self-awareness.[7]

His audience would, as ever, be included in the humor. "There goes old Barnum again," they would be saying to themselves with an inward chuckle, while nonetheless admiring his actual accomplishments. The verbal pyrotechnics of this mostly self-educated man, the splendid setting that he owned outright, the famous temple in Connecticut where he lived, the promise of years of entertainment to come and the notoriety of the amusements he had already provided — all of these aspects of Barnum's success would be well-known to his mostly striving, middle-class audience, whose members were indeed looking for pastimes suitable for the whole family. And Old Barnum's confidence was so complete that he could mock himself even as he indulged in bold self-promotion. Is it any wonder that of all the attractions available in Barnum's newly commodious museum, few could rival its owner and impresario?

The frenzy that met Jenny Lind's arrival in New York only grew in the days before her first concert, on September 11, at Castle Garden, a covered theater that occupied what had been a circular fort built just off the Battery, accessible by a 200-foot wooden bridge. The army had used the fort from the time of its completion in 1811 until 1823, and then leased it to New York, after which the city opened the site in 1824 as a "place of resort." The next year, Castle Garden was the site of a 6,000-person reception for the Revolutionary War hero the Marquis de Lafayette, wrapping up a grand return tour to the United States.[8]

Barnum had paid $1,000 to have an awning built over the bridge to Castle Garden, which was brightly illuminated on the night of the concert, creating a "triumphal avenue" for the more than five thousand excited people who had already passed through an alley formed by sixty New York City policemen. Some two hundred boats bobbed outside the walls of the castle, bearing ruffians beating drums and raising a "hideous clamor of shouts and yells." At times they tried to force their way into the fort, but the police pushed them back. The theater, itself also brightly illuminated, was divided into four color-coded sections that helped people match their tickets to their seats. Facing the stage from above the balcony was a banner made of flowers with the words "Welcome, Sweet Warbler," and at the back of the stage, behind where the orchestra was seated, was a large wooden sounding board on which the flags of Sweden and the United States had been painted. The crowd was mostly male, which a reporter for the *Tribune* attributed to the $5 price for a ticket; the ladies, he wrote, "must stay at home, it seems, when the tickets are high, but the gentlemen go nevertheless."[9]

Lind's conductor, Julius Benedict, opened the show at 8 p.m. with his sixty-piece orchestra playing the overture from Weber's opera *Oberon,* followed by baritone Giovanni Belletti singing a tricky aria from Rossini's *Mahomet the Prophet.* After the applause for his performance stopped and the crowd grew silent, the Swedish Nightingale herself, dressed in white, passed through the orchestra to Benedict, who led her to the footlights. "The vast assembly rose as one man," the *Tribune* writer reported, "and for some minutes nothing could be seen but the waving of hands and handkerchiefs, nothing heard but a storm of tumultuous cheers." Bouquets piled up at her feet. Barnum claimed it was "by far" the most people she had ever stood before. When the audience calmed down, the violins and flute began the first strains of what was even then a bel canto warhorse, the "Casta diva" aria from Bellini's *Norma.* Although the critic for the *Herald* felt that nervousness caused Lind to falter at first, and that all in all her performance of the song "was not equal to her rehearsal," the *Tribune* writer was inspired to release a flood of adjectives. Her modesty, her sweetness, her power, and her birdlike trills were what most distinguished her in his mind.[10]

The highlights of the rest of her performance were a Rossini duet with Belletti from "Il Turco in Italia," an aria with two flutes from Meyerbeer's opera *A Camp in Silesia,* the Swedish "Herdsman's Song" and "The Echo Song," and, as a finale, the song that won Barnum's contest, "Greeting to America." Benedict had hurriedly matched the poem to music "in the style of the Marsellaise," as the *Herald* critic described it, almost getting the spelling right. The *Tribune* writer noted that the cheers at the end of her concert were somewhat "less vehement" than those at the beginning, but perhaps this could be attributed to voices in the audience gone hoarse with overuse. The applause was sufficient, however, to draw Lind out for a final bow, after which people in the crowd began to call for Barnum. Naturally he had a speech prepared for just such an eventuality.

Among the calls was one, "Where is Barnum?," that had lately become a question people applied to any new curiosity, suggesting that he must be behind it in some way. Like so many things that were said about Barnum, this phrase seems to have originated with the showman himself. In any case, when he took the stage at Castle Garden, Barnum seemed to acknowledge his authorship by saying, "If there has ever been a moment when I aspired to have the question generally asked, 'Where Is Barnum?' that time has passed by forever." Why? He pointed in the direction Lind had gone upon leaving the stage and asked the audience if, "in the presence of that angel I may be allowed to sink where I really belong — into utter insignificance." Thus the answer to the question, he said, had become "Barnum is nowhere!" Jenny Lind's superiority to himself, he said, was proven not only by the talent she had just put on display but more significantly by her decision to donate $10,000 from her share of the proceeds to charities in the city. Barnum then read the names of the dozen lucky organizations, after which three cheers were raised. Calls for Lind to return to the stage went unanswered, as she had already departed the theater.

The second beneficiary on the list Barnum read was the Musical Fund Society, which had played for her on the night of her arrival. When word of her gift reached them, off they went with a band to the New York Hotel, where Lind had moved to be less conspicuously located. Another crowd of thousands gathered and persuaded her to greet them from her balcony. As it happened, Barnum would write, her share of the receipts from that night did not reach $10,000, but the next concert, two nights later, easily made up the difference. Barnum professed to have worried that he might have overdone the publicity for Lind, that the hype could have led to disappointment and a reaction against the singer. But the first concert had allayed those fears. "The Rubicon," he writes, "was passed."[11]

Lind gave five more concerts at Castle Garden, the last coming on September 24. When the crowds grew to as many as eight thousand, Barnum's first-night competence at seating five thousand customers in an orderly way was overwhelmed; at the next-to-last concert, some fifteen hundred standing-room-only ticketholders first blocked the gate to those with seats and then, when they were admitted, "acted more like rowdies than gentlemen . . . actually trampling over ranks of persons already seated."

The next stop on her tour was Boston, for which Lind and Barnum departed on the afternoon of the 25th on the steamer *Empire State,* leaving from a pier near the Battery and sailing past Castle Garden on an overnight trip via Newport and Fall River, where they boarded a special train in the morning. Barnum's agent for the Jenny Lind tour, Le Grand Smith, had gone ahead to make the arrangements. Among the things Smith arranged were enthusiastic crowds to greet the steamer at Fall River and the train when it arrived in Boston. Soon after her carriage reached the Revere House, where she was staying, another crowd materialized in spite of a persistent rain. The mayor turned up, and in the course of his tedious prepared greeting, her patience with the overnight boat ride, the nearly impassable crowds, and the bloviating politician addressing her came to an end. She interrupted his encomium about her character with the icy query, "What do *you* know of my private character? . . . Sir, I am no better than other people; no better." Her tone alone made her point and finally earned her some rest.[12]

Things had generally gone so well in New York that the Boston preparations followed the same plan. One of Barnum's most successful publicity gambits had been to auction off the first ticket to the first Castle Garden performance. Ticket auctions were not his invention, but his goal was less the dollar amount he could squeeze out of that sale and more the publicity it could inspire. He persuaded his next-door neighbor on Broadway, a hatter name John Genin, to go all out at the auction so that he too could soak up some of the publicity it generated. The scheme worked out at least as well for hat sales as it did for ticket sales. Genin won the auction, which took place before an audience at Castle Garden, with a bid of $225, after another friend of Barnum's, who had gotten the same encouragement to participate, lost his nerve. Genin received national attention for his winning bid, and owning a Genin hat became a sign of sophistication, making him as rich as he was well known. Le Grand Smith arranged a similar auction for the day before Lind's Boston arrival, and a local singer named Ossian F. Dodge bid up to $625. When Lind got word of this, according to her attorney, her reaction was "What a fool!" But afterward attendance at his own recitals more than compensated Dodge for his investment. Ten days later, in Providence, Rhode Island, a

Col. William Ross paid the largest amount of anyone on Lind's tour, $650, but, contenting himself with the publicity, didn't bother to attend the event for which he held the most expensive ticket.[13]

The first Boston concert took place on September 27 at the Tremont Temple, which had been built as a theater but was now owned by the Baptists. Presumably Moses Kimball had no hard feelings about the choice of venue, since the Tremont seated twice as many people as his theater in the Boston Museum. The program repeated the selections from the opening night in New York, and the reception by the again largely male audience was considered enthusiastic by the more reserved standards of Boston. One departure was that Barnum, when called to the stage after the performance, had very little to say. He did, however, speak at the Tremont two nights later, delivering a temperance lecture to another full house, and was so well received that he was asked to deliver another talk on the following Sunday.[14]

Lind gave a second concert at the Tremont and, after a day trip to perform in Providence, devoted an evening's performance to charity. Perhaps because it was the least well attended of the three so far in

Boston, Barnum decided to change the venue for the last two Boston concerts. He chose the upstairs hall of the Fitchburg Railway Depot, which had a much larger capacity than the Tremont but only two narrow entrances and, up a long flight of stairs, a square, low-ceilinged room with bad acoustics. The first concert went off without a hitch, the crowd being much smaller even than those at the Tremont, but Barnum's advertising and aggressive ticket sales in outlying towns pulled in a huge crowd for the last Boston performance, on Saturday, October 12. According to one report, the six thousand people who turned up made it the largest crowd ever for a Boston event, and since the hall was meant to accommodate only half that number, chaos resulted.[15]

Ninety minutes before the concert began, so many standing-room customers had arrived that those with seats could not enter. At 7:30, when the promenade or standing-room customers were admitted, the crowd surged into the building and a scene ensued like that of Lind's first London concert. Doors were smashed, clothes were torn, women fainted, and once people reached the upstairs lobby they pushed into the hall and took seats that were not theirs. Even after the orchestra began to play, the pandemonium still unfolding in the hall made it impossible to hear. What *could* be heard was the sound of glass shattering, as the atmosphere in the room became suffocating and the many windows, which could not be opened, were broken in a matter of minutes. First a representative of Lind and then, to hisses, Barnum himself came onto the stage and told the audience that they could have their money back, and word spread to the many people who were still outside waiting to be admitted. Some people then left and the concert went on. But after angry customers surrounded Barnum, shaking fists in his face, he retreated to the Revere House, returning later to make sure Lind could leave the hall safely.

Charles Rosenberg, who attended the concert while following Lind's tour for a book he would write, put much of the blame for the mess on the Boston police, whose officers stood idly by when they might have brought order outside the hall. But the Boston newspapers were unanimous in condemning Barnum for selling far too many tickets in advance and then selling discounted tickets before the concert began. Barnum did stay in Boston long enough to deliver another temperance speech, in

Roxbury on Sunday night, and to write a long defense of his actions for the Boston papers, but he let others who worked for him handle the unpleasant task of repaying the still-angry customers demanding refunds. Rosenberg writes that Lind "bore the annoyance with tolerable energy . . . but she was undoubtedly much terrified." The next day, her fears were replaced by anger toward "those who had made the arrangements for the concert." But her anger must not have lasted long, for only three days later she was strolling the grounds of Iranistan, arm in arm with its squire.[16]

P. T. Barnum in London in 1844, when he was touring with Tom Thumb and writing for the *New York Atlas*. Portrait by Charles Baugniet.

Charity Hallett Barnum in an 1847 oil portrait by Frederick R. Spencer. "Without Charity, I am nothing," Barnum would quip, but his wife often stayed at home during Barnum's many travels.

3

This advertisement for an exhibition of Joice Heth in December 1835 claimed she was 161 years old and the former nursemaid of George Washington. The outrageous nature of this humbug would permanently damage Barnum's reputation.

Moses Kimball, a museum owner in Boston and Barnum's frequent collaborator, brought a "mermaid" to Barnum.

4

5

What Kimball offered Barnum looked like the upper torso of a monkey joined to a fish. It became another early humbug, which Barnum dubbed the "Fejee Mermaid." People flocked to see the dried-up specimen when Barnum exhibited it in 1842.

6

A primary reason for the crowds was Barnum's vigorous advertising, depicting not the Fejee Mermaid itself but idealized images of the mythical creatures.

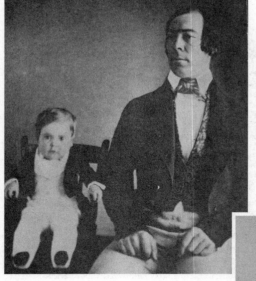

Charles Stratton in the early 1840s, at about the time Barnum discovered and transformed him into General Tom Thumb. The man with Charles is his father, Sherwood Stratton.

8

This carte de visite from the early 1860s shows Tom Thumb dressed for his most famous impersonation, that of Napoleon Bonaparte. He delighted Queen Victoria in this role, but only performed it for Louis-Philippe, the king of France, when explicitly asked.

9

A publicity photo probably taken in about 1850 of Barnum and Tom Thumb in one of the many outfits in which he performed while touring in the United States, England, and much of the rest of Europe.

10

Soon after Barnum acquired the American Museum on lower Broadway in 1842, he not only made it his own, but turned it into the premier tourist attraction in New York City.

11

This 1855 lithograph, titled "Sleighing in New York," celebrates the exuberance of life on lower Broadway in those times, with Barnum's museum very much in the mix.

Three Barnum daughters, Caroline, Pauline, and Helen, painted by Frederick R. Spencer in 1847. Another daughter, Frances, had died three years earlier.

Iranistan, the "Oriental villa" Barnum built for his family in Fairfield, Connecticut, was completed in 1848. Modeled on the Royal Pavilion in Brighton, England, it showed off the wealth he had attained while touring overseas.

The singer Jenny Lind, "the Swedish Nightingale," was already a sensation in Europe and Britain when Barnum signed her at great expense for an American tour. Barnum promoted Lind not only for her remarkable voice and stage presence, but also for her modesty and morality, traits not always evident in performers of the day.

Barnum and his new find, dubbed Commodore Nutt. The two men visited Abraham Lincoln and his cabinet in the White House in October 1862.

The 1863 "fairy wedding" of Tom Thumb and Lavinia Warren distracted the nation from the bloody battles of the Civil War. The two are flanked here by Commodore Nutt and Lavinia's sister Minnie.

Several of Barnum's properties went up in flames during his long career. An 1865 fire that destroyed the American Museum is depicted here in a painting by Christopher Pearse Cranch.

After the fire of 1865 Horace Greeley, editor of the *New-York Tribune*, told Barnum that he should "quit, and go a-fishing." But Barnum would soon open a new museum farther up Broadway.

Near the end of the Civil War, Barnum ran for the Connecticut legislature as a candidate from Fairfield so that he could vote for the constitutional amendment to abolish slavery. In all, he served four terms in the legislature and one as mayor of Bridgeport.

In the years after the war, the Barnums bought a town house on Fifth Avenue, where Charity oversaw the arrangements for their many guests and where they enjoyed Central Park and other amenities of city life.

But Charity's health declined over a number of years, and in 1873 she died while Barnum was in England. Within a matter of weeks, Barnum secretly married Nancy Fish, the daughter of an English friend.

Barnum with Nancy and his children and grandchildren on his sixty-fifth birthday, in 1875. His youngest daughter, Pauline, third from right, would die in April 1877.

In 1880, Barnum joined forces with James Bailey and others. Eventually the two men realized that they complemented each other perfectly, and the Barnum & Bailey Circus was born.

Barnum had for years wished to display a favorite of British schoolchildren, Jumbo the elephant. In 1882, despite protests from Queen Victoria and many of her subjects, Barnum acquired the great beast and shipped him to America.

Jumbo was Barnum's last big national sensation on the order of Tom Thumb and Jenny Lind. But in 1885 Jumbo was struck and killed by a freight train, and was mourned around the world.

Undaunted, Barnum put both the stuffed hide of Jumbo and his skeleton on display, the latter depicted here in a poster for his first Greatest Show on Earth.

The picture of prosperous old age, taken in the late 1870s, at a time when Barnum had begun to give away parts of his vast wealth.

A postcard of Barnum & Bailey's Winter Quarters in Bridgeport. The showman's fifth and final devastating fire occurred here in November 1887.

Barnum built Marina (right), the last of his four mansions in Connecticut, just a few feet from his previous home, Waldemere, which was torn down when the new house was completed in 1888. Barnum gave Nancy the deed to Marina.

This poster for his final hurrah in London at the vast hall called Olympia shows both Barnum and his partner Bailey, but mentions Bailey only in small type.

The cover of a pamphlet about the spectacle created by Imre Kiralfy called "Nero, or the Destruction of Rome," which featured 1,200 players and was the grand finale of the Olympia show.

Barnum and his beloved great-grandson, Henry Rennell, who was born in 1884. As Barnum got older, he styled himself "The Children's Friend."

Eleven:
Before the Fall

Soon after she reached Boston, Jenny Lind wrote to her former guardian in Sweden, "Mr. Barnum has shown, and is still showing himself, extremely generous, and reasonable; and seems to have made it his first object to see me satisfied." The statement to the press that Barnum released nearly two weeks later, the day after the Fitchburg Depot fiasco, was in part intended to dispute rumors of a falling out between "the great Northern Light" and "the small Drummond light," as a writer in the *Herald* characterized the singer and her promoter. "In no instance," Barnum wrote, "and at no time whatever, has the slightest difference taken place between the lady and myself. Invariably I have been treated by her with the greatest kindness, and the most perfect confidence in my exertions of her behalf." For some, the fact of Barnum's denial proved the accuracy of the rumor.[1]

On Monday morning, October 14, 1850, Barnum took an early train from Boston to New Haven and then home to prepare for the arrival later that day of Lind's party, which included Benedict and Belletti. The group spent the night at Iranistan, and the next morning Lind asked Barnum to walk her around the grounds. As she took in its gardens and fanciful outbuildings, she said, "I am astonished that you should have left such a beautiful place for the sake of travelling through the country with me." That day, he remembered, she was in a "playful mood." Perhaps as her way of assuring him that the rumors of their disagreements had not come from her, she told Barnum she had heard a quite contrary report: "that you and I are about to be married." When she asked him how such an absurd rumor could have gotten started, he claimed to have responded, "Probably from the fact that we are 'engaged,'" at which she "laughed heartily." If Charity shared in the laughter, Barnum didn't say so. But it is unlikely she was present: in her biography of Lind, Gladys Denny Schultz writes that Charity was "shy and retiring" around the singer and allowed her daughter Caroline to step forward as hostess during the visit. But Charity nonetheless secured an unwitting revenge for Lind's intimate stroll in the gardens with her husband: a day or two later in Philadelphia, Lind developed a debilitating headache blamed on a reaction to Iranistan's flowers.[2]

Both Lind and Barnum found themselves under pressure in these first weeks of the tour. Barnum wrote that during the whole of their travels, "I did not know a waking moment that was entirely free from anxiety." Not only was he dealing with unmanageably large crowds of people, but he was also exerting energetic and sometimes incautious efforts at generating those crowds. He was constantly feeding the newspapers new tidbits about Lind's acts of generosity and at the same time often being lambasted in those same papers when things went wrong, and even when they went too right, meaning that Barnum was raking in profits. Lind herself had the stress of being constantly in the limelight, on stage and off, her every movement detailed and critiqued in the press. Her fans would repeatedly gather even on the supposition that she would be at a particular place at a particular time. Her generosity created an onslaught of crazily determined would-be recipients of her charity, and Barnum was criticized for pocketing his share of the profits while she gave hers away. She was also of course at the beginning of a long interlude in a strange land, mostly at the mercy of a man she hardly knew at all, one whose past could give her pause. Still, even three months into the tour, Lind wrote to a German friend, "Mr. Barnum behaves extremely well towards me: and I could not wish for anything better."[3]

However cordial their personal relationship remained, trouble was beginning to develop elsewhere. When Lind arrived in New York, she had, on the advice of Baring Brothers Bank in London, which held Barnum's large deposit for her tour, retained attorneys in New York to represent her interests in the United States. One of the attorneys, Maunsell B. Field, had worked with her in her first days in America, as her contract was altered and altered again to give her a larger share of the profits from the tour and to give her the right to cancel it after either the sixtieth concert or the hundredth, if she no longer wished to work with Barnum. On his side, Barnum was able to retrieve the money he had deposited at Baring Brothers and gained the right to represent her outside the United States if she agreed.

Relations between Barnum and Field were

apparently amicable, and it initially seemed that these contractual rearrangements would generate little friction. In his memoirs, Field was highly complimentary about the showman and his behavior toward Lind. The three of them worked cordially on the first changes in her contract, Field wrote. He also reported admiringly that when the receipts for the first concert came up short, Barnum made up the difference from his own pocket. And then he added:

Again and again Miss LIND desired changes made in the contract to her own advantage, and every time Mr. BARNUM yielded. Whatever his motive, he was most obliging and complaisant, and although I have never since met him, I have always esteemed him for the good-nature and liberality which he exhibited at this time in his business relations with Miss LIND. I believe that she received every farthing that belonged to her, and that he treated her with the most scrupulous honor.[4]

Field represented Lind for the first month that she was in America, and then his cousin and partner John Jay, who had been off in Europe, returned and took over her representation. Jay was the grandson and namesake of the Founding Father and Supreme Court justice, and was himself an active abolitionist who would go on to help found the Republican Party. Soon after Jay took control, things went bad, presumably because Jay felt that even the revised contract was too favorable to Barnum. Midway through Lind's tour, then, its future began to look doubtful.

On October 23, when Barnum and Lind were back in New York after concerts in Philadelphia, Barnum wrote to Joshua Bates, a friend of his at Baring Brothers, which, having recommended Jay's firm, presumably had some influence with him. His letter emphasized the warm relationship he had with Lind, but warned that their friendship was being traduced by people "moving in the first classes of society," specifically by Jay, who "has been so blind to her interests as to aid in poisoning her mind against me by pouring into her ears the most silly twaddle." Barnum attributed the ill will of Jay and unspecified others to envy, "and envy soon augments to malice."[5]

Barnum's reference to "the first classes of society" hints that his enmity toward Jay was exacerbated by his sensitivity to questions of class as refined by his experiences in London, since Jay was the scion of one of

New York's most prominent families. Jay's "silly twaddle" also seems to have itself been based on class. In Barnum's letter to Joshua Bates, he wrote that Jay's argument against him had much to do with his "regret that I was a 'showman,' exhibitor of Tom Thumb, etc., etc." In any case, Barnum warned Bates in his letter that "continual backbitings" could harm a successful business relationship he had worked hard to achieve, and he added ominously, "I cannot allow ignorance or envy to rob me of the fruits of my enterprise." Barnum asked Bates to advise Jay to back off, but the eventual dissolution of Barnum's partnership with Lind gives evidence that the main effect of Barnum's letter was to allow the showman to blow off steam.

The more Barnum promoted Lind for her generosity, the more he was criticized for maximizing his own profits. In truth, he often picked up the expenses for Lind's benefit concerts and gave her all the credit for donating the proceeds. After all, the notion of Lind the angel was a central theme of his marketing strategy, so Barnum not only did not mind being her foil, but he actively encouraged the false impression of his role. A close friend and advisor in St. Louis, Sol Smith, an impresario, a lawyer, and, improbably, a comedian, dedicated a volume of his memoirs to Barnum, writing, "The following conundrum went the rounds of the American newspapers: 'Why is it that *Jenny Lind* and *Barnum* will never fall out? Answer: — because *he* is always for-*getting* and *she* is always for-*giving.*'" Smith had long suspected that his dedicatee had himself come up with the joke, and Barnum, who quoted the full dedication in his 1869 autobiography, did not deny it. Barnum added that when he showed Lind a newspaper quoting the conundrum, she replied, "O! Mr. Barnum, this is not fair; you know that you really give more than I do from the proceeds of every one of these charity concerts." Her private appreciation of his generosity apparently offset whatever she might have been demanding through Jay. During the tour, Barnum held his tongue and took his lumps from the press.[6]

The *New York Herald,* with whom Barnum always had a strained relationship, covered Lind's every concert and movement assiduously but did not hesitate to call Barnum "the veriest charlatan that ever exhibited his sleight of hand before the stupid gaze of the multitude" and to observe that, given "the antagonistic qualities of the two distinguished individuals," the wonder was "that

Barnum and Lind did not fly off from each other by the natural laws of repulsion." Her own generosity expressed itself in more ways than in her charitable gifts. After Barnum was criticized in all four cities where Lind had appeared so far for the price of tickets, she pushed Barnum when they returned from Philadelphia to Tripler Hall in New York to lower prices and not sell tickets to speculators. The *Herald,* having lobbied for lower prices itself, saw fit to run a letter from Lind to Barnum and his letter in reply, in which she expressed these wishes and he agreed to accommodate them, pledging that, given the size of the hall, the cheapest tickets could go at $3. "This," the *Herald* added complacently, "is as it should be." Barnum undoubtedly wrote both letters.[7]

Lind performed fifteen times at Tripler Hall — ten concerts and five oratorios — including an unfortunate performance of the *Messiah* marred by amateurish local singers and a poorly tuned organ. But she admired the acoustics in the hall and filled it every night she performed. On November 26 the troupe, including sixteen of the sixty musicians who had been accompanying her so far, departed with Barnum and his daughter Caroline on a twelve-thousand-mile southern tour, first returning to Philadelphia for four concerts, followed by four in Baltimore and then two in Washington.

Because Washington had no theater large enough to accommodate a Jenny Lind concert, and because efforts to engage the House of Representatives chamber of the Capitol were undermined by pesky congressional rules, Barnum engaged an unfinished theater called the National Hall, which could seat three thousand people. Despite efforts to complete the building in time for the first concert on December 16, on opening night it still lacked ornamentation, smelled of fresh plaster, and required temporary seating, including armchairs for dignitaries and hard benches for everyone else. President Millard Fillmore and his wife attended, but his reception upon entering the hall was less robust than those that others received. When the Mexican war hero Gen. Winfield Scott made his way to the front, he got three cheers from the audience, and Kentucky's senator Henry Clay, standing humbly at the back waiting for the prelude to end, also got rousing cheers when the crowd detected him. When the president arrived, the applause had been perfunctory, and to make matters worse, the seats reserved beside him in the front row for his cabinet and their wives remained empty through the first half of the concert, a bibulous reception at the Russian ambassador's house being the bigger draw.

Lind and her party had a full schedule the next day, receiving visits at Willard's Hotel from the president, Secretary of State Daniel Webster — an admirer who had already seen Lind in Boston and New York — Clay, and other dignitaries. In the afternoon she rode on a steamer with Barnum, Caroline, and others in her party, accompanied by Col. John A. Washington to visit his home, formerly that of the first president, down the Potomac at Mount Vernon. There they stopped at George and Martha Washington's graves, toured the mansion, and were served a "sumptuous and splendid collation." Lind was deeply moved to be given two books from the president's library, both containing his handwriting. That night her entourage was received at the White House.[8]

The cast of Washington dignitaries, including the president, attended both of her concerts there, and the newspapers were largely laudatory. But one thing that happened mars the visit from today's perspective. Rumors spread in the city that Lind had given $1,000 to an abolitionist group in the North, which at the time would have dimmed considerably her prospects and Barnum's for her concerts in Richmond, Charleston, New Orleans, and elsewhere as her tour swung to the south and eventually up the Mississippi. The Washington *Daily Union* published a letter from its editor to Barnum inquiring about the truth of the rumor and also published his response, in which he hastily denied it, emphasizing that *"there is not the slightest foundation for such a statement."* One of the *Daily Union* reporters asked Lind herself about the rumor, and she too denied it. Lind had indeed given smaller amounts of money to "colored" old folks and orphans groups, but in the weeks after the passage of the Compromise of 1850, including the controversial Fugitive Slave Act, her public support for abolition could have seemed like meddling in the nation's politics. In response, Barnum practically tripped over himself rushing to deny the rumors of her abolitionism.[9]

From Washington, the tour went to Richmond for one concert, followed by a train ride to Wilmington, North Carolina. The party then boarded a steamship for Charleston and suffered a frightening, storm-tossed passage that took nearly twenty hours longer than expected, so long that a report was telegraphed north that the ship had been lost. During the ten days they spent in Charleston waiting for a scheduled steamer to Havana, Lind gave two concerts and hosted parties for her retinue on both Christmas and New Year's Eve. She had been planning the Christmas party for some time, having written home to her former guardian for traditional Swedish presents so that she could put on a Swedish Christmas. Barnum wrote that among the presents attached to the decorated tree, which included both serious and joke gifts for each person, was a small statue of Bacchus for him, to tweak him about his teetotaling. On New Year's Eve she asked Barnum to join her in a dance, and when he said that he had never danced before, her response was "I am sure you can do it." He good-naturedly gave it a try, and even more good-naturedly reported in his autobiography, "I never saw her laugh more heartily than she did at my awkwardness. She said she would give me the credit of being the poorest dancer she ever saw!"[10]

The Havana newspapers had campaigned against the high cost of tickets for Lind's concerts there, and on opening night the audience hissed her when she took the stage, something she had never experienced before. When she reached the footlights and saw the reaction of the crowd, according to a *Tribune* reporter who was present, "her countenance changed in an instant to a haughty self-possession, her eye flashed defiance, and, becoming immovable as a statue, she stood there, perfectly calm and beautiful." There followed a performance that triumphantly won her doubters over, after which Barnum "could not restrain the tears of joy that rolled down [his] cheeks." When he greeted her offstage, she draped herself around his neck: "She, too, was crying with joy, and never before did she look so beautiful in my eyes as on that evening." Even though Lind was called back for five encores, the papers did not let up in their criticism of Barnum, and her next two concerts in Havana were the worst attended of the entire tour. Barnum had announced a dozen concerts in the city, but after Lind gave a fourth performance as a benefit, he canceled the final eight, unwilling to accede to the call for lower prices.[11]

The entourage would spend much of January 1851 in Cuba, where Barnum, Caroline, and others joined Lind in staying at a villa she had rented on the outskirts of the capital. There, Barnum recalled, she would "romp and run, sing and laugh, like a young schoolgirl." During this period she was "merry as a cricket," Barnum wrote, often asking him to play catch with her in the courtyard behind the house, stopping only when Barnum was tired out. "Then her rich, musical laugh would be heard ringing through the house, as she exclaimed, 'You are too fat and too lazy; you cannot stand it to play ball with me.'" By this time, Lind was thirty years old, Barnum a decade older, and in a daguerreotype from later that year he still looks fit, vigorous, and brimming with self-confidence, his dark curly hair perhaps beginning to recede, his neck only hinting at the jowliness to come. She was teasing him, and he was enjoying the attention. Many men — including Belletti, who was helplessly in love with her — fell for Lind right and left, and at the least Barnum appreciated her charm. Lind herself had shown a tendency to be attracted to men who were safe — older, younger, established friends, as well as that one religious fanatic. But while both their accounts grew warmer in Cuba, it seems doubtful that there was anything more than friendship between Barnum and Lind, especially given the presence of his daughter Caroline at the villa.[12]

Despite whatever glow this Havana respite cast upon Barnum's mood, which was ever bright and cheerful, it did not prevent him from writing a truly unpleasant letter to the owners of the New York *Sun* about their rival and Barnum's nemesis, James Gordon Bennett, and his wife. The couple happened to be in Havana at the same time, and even happened to take the same boat from Cuba to New Orleans as the Lind tour continued. Barnum's letter, marked "Confidential," accused Bennett of having been bought off with bottles of "champaigne" by a local aristocrat so that the *Herald* would provide favorable coverage of the Cuban government. It also reported Mrs. Bennett's "strange antics in Havana," namely hanging out regularly at a bar with "a gang of rollicking men gathered around her," even though her husband had scolded her for frequenting the place. More cruelly, perhaps, he accused the Bennetts of unpopularity, reporting that she had had to cancel a ball in Havana because too few people would come and that on the steamer to New Orleans they had been snubbed by the ship's other passengers, including Lind and Barnum himself. In a signed postscript to the letter, sent from New Orleans on February 10, 1851, Barnum revealed one of his ways of dealing with the press, writing to the *Sun*'s owners, the Beach brothers, "Please make what use you can of these facts & keep my name <u>secret</u>, though I hold myself responsible for all that I write."[13]

Lind gave a dozen concerts in New Orleans, then the party headed up the Mississippi on a steamboat that Barnum chartered to Natchez, Memphis, and on to St. Louis, where she gave five concerts before they went back down the river and then overland to Nashville and north to Louisville. From there they followed the Ohio upriver to Cincinnati for five more performances and finally to Pittsburgh, where the unruly nature of the crowd on the first night persuaded Lind to leave town early the next morning, forcing Barnum to cancel a second planned concert. Barnum followed Lind by steamer, stage, and rail to Baltimore, where Charity met him and Caroline. Because of exhaustion, Lind had to delay an announced benefit concert in Baltimore for two days, until May 1, raising $3,700 for the needy. She gave another benefit concert in Philadelphia on May 3, netting $5,000 there, and then everyone returned, with relief, to New York.

Since arriving in the United States, Lind had given seventy-eight concerts for profit, forty-eight of them on the tour just ended, and another dozen for charity. Barnum too was weary after the long tour, and once

Lind was back under the influence of her advisors in New York, and again hearing reasons to be discontented with his management, he recalled, "I . . . cared little what course they advised her to pursue." Starting on May 7 at Castle Garden, she gave fourteen more concerts there or at Tripler Hall, and following one more performance in Philadelphia, her ninety-fifth in conjunction with Barnum, he offered her the opportunity to buy her way out of a commitment to seven more, and she agreed. She also had to pay him a flat fee of $25,000 for another fifty concerts projected in the original agreement. But by Barnum's estimation — and he kept careful track of every penny — Lind netted $177,000 even after paying Barnum for her escape, while he grossed, after paying up her share, $536,000. Inflation makes an 1850 dollar worth about thirty times that today, so Lind's nine months of work earned her roughly $5.3 million in today's dollars. Barnum is less forthcoming about his other expenses in putting on the ninety-five concerts, but it seems safe to say that he made two or three times more than she did.[14]

The outward cordiality of the business breakup suggests that both of them were ready to move on. He wrote, "After so many months of anxiety, labor and excitement, in the Jenny Lind enterprise, it will readily be believed that I desired tranquility." After a half year away from Charity and his children, he seemed relieved at the prospect of renewed domesticity. The family spent a week at Cape May, New Jersey, and then returned home to Iranistan for the summer. The fortune he had acquired through the Jenny Lind tour would make any number of new ventures possible, but would also make him a target, as Lind was, for scores of people who wanted a piece of that fortune.[15]

TWELVE:
PUTTING OUT FIRES

Even before he went out on the road with Jenny Lind, and while he was dedicating himself to family life, Barnum had been working at a dizzying number of ventures, some of which had now come to pass. When those projects relied on his instincts and experience as a showman, they tended to be successful. But when he was tempted by schemes in areas where he was less familiar, the results were uneven. Eventually, as his attention turned in so many directions and he bankrolled so many initiatives, his long run of good luck, stretching back to his purchase of his museum a decade earlier, would come to an end. But for several years he was able to overcome small setbacks, to sample his opportunities, and to learn from his mistakes. A series of ventures in the early 1850s reveals the breadth of Barnum's interests and the range of risk he was comfortable with — as well as how capable he was at adapting once he'd pushed too far, eventually turning failure into future success.

As Barnum had been renovating and expanding the American Museum in 1850, he was also working on a plan he had hatched the previous year to start a new circulating show, "a great travelling museum and menagerie." His partners included Tom Thumb's father, Sherwood Stratton, and a circus man named Seth B. Howes, whom Barnum put in complete charge of the new venture, not having "time nor inclination to manage such a concern" himself. Barnum could hardly have chosen a better man for the job than Howes, who is sometimes called the father of the American circus. He was born five years after Barnum on a farm less than fifteen miles from Bethel, in Brewster, New York. His much older brother Nathan had started a small traveling circus when Seth was eleven, and Seth performed in it on horseback and helped with the management. He would be connected with one circus after another for most of the next quarter century, up until his association with Barnum. In 1848 he and his brothers started the Great United States Circus, considered then to be the biggest of its kind ever assembled in this country. After Howes worked with Barnum, he would import a hippodrome from Paris and establish it on Broadway, and then he managed a circus in England for seven years, returning home to help start what would be called the Great European Circus. Like Barnum, he also managed individual performers, working with Tom Thumb and also with Eng and Chang, the Siamese Twins, whom he took on a year-long tour in 1853. After he left circus life, Howes made a princely fortune in real estate in Chicago, at one point owning the land that is now Hyde Park, and retired to Brewster, where he built on his family's property a lavish, turreted, stone castle of a house that he called Morningthorpe.[1]

What would be called P. T. Barnum's Great Asiatic Caravan, Museum and Menagerie was still being put together when in 1850 the three partners sent a ship to Ceylon with the goal of capturing or buying a "herd" of a dozen elephants and "such other wild animals as they could secure." The *Regatta* sailed out through the Narrows in May, carrying five hundred tons of hay to be stored on St. Helena, halfway between New York and Ceylon, to be used as feed on the journey home. After a year, the *Regatta* returned to New York with ten of the thirteen elephants it had set off with from Ceylon. One of the elephants was captured with a calf, which with its dam survived the passage to America, where it became the steed of Tom Thumb in the caravan. Barnum's agents had also acquired a huge Burmese bull in Ceylon, and brought back a native elephant handler, now transformed as a promotional matter into the chief of a "wild and wandering tribe" from the island. Six lions would also be on parade in the traveling show, along with other beasts "selected at immense cost," and a cortege of 110 horses and ninety riders. A large selection of curiosities from the American Museum would accompany this menagerie from town to town, and a tented pavilion large enough to accommodate fifteen thousand people would be erected at the end point of the procession, which would pass through the streets accompanied by a brass band and a military band. Admission to the exhibition would be Barnum's usual charge of twenty-five cents.[2]

Barnum did not seem to regret the death of the three elephants in shipment from Ceylon, perhaps because so many others had perished during their procurement. "Large numbers" had been killed, Barnum reported, dwelling not on the loss of life but on the "most exciting adventures" and "numerous encounters of the most terrific description" that proved necessary in the capture of those thirteen. It seems that his agents had not been able to buy elephants, so they had hired dozens and dozens of local people to help them drive the animals into places where they could be captured. To capture as many as he requested, however, required being willing to kill or maim many more.

This is one of those places in Barnum's story where a modern sensibility must struggle to understand him. Our own sense of moral responsibility toward elephants and other large mammals led directly to the closure of the circus that bore Barnum's name for 125 years after his death. For most of those years most people did not see the harm in parading elephants and other wild animals and doing what was necessary to train them to be performers. In his day, procuring wild beasts and shipping them long distances involved harsh realities that Barnum accepted without apparent regret, and keeping them alive after they came under his care was also a challenge. The financial incentive existed to make the whole process of exhibiting wild beasts more humane and efficient, and Barnum would hire people with the expertise to make this happen. But he also resigned himself to the frequent deaths of the beasts in his care, more readily than we would expect today. Still, while he never hesitated to mention the expense and trouble this aspect of his business created, he was circumspect about sharing with his audience how many elephants were killed in the process of capturing his troupe. His early advertising for the Asiatic Caravan said only that the elephants captured in the Ceylon jungle had been subdued and made no mention of those killed in the process.

Once the Great Asiatic Caravan, Museum and Menagerie was out on the road in the spring of 1851, Barnum was willing to use his wealth for ventures beyond showmanship, trying his hand as an investor. By summer's end, he had a visitor in Bridgeport representing a new British invention called a fire annihilator, which would put out fires without using water, by suffocating them with steam and chemical vapors. The overstatement in its name should have been a warning to Barnum, the master of overstatement, but its British and American pedigrees soon persuaded him to invest. After visiting Washington, where he met with former congressman Elisha Whittlesey, who had become the first comptroller of the U.S. Treasury and was angling to hold the American patent for the Phillips Fire Annihilator, Barnum agreed not only to invest but to become an officer in the company that was set up to sell it to Americans. He also became its "general agent," meaning he was involved in sales but also in creating franchises across the country and in opening a New York office for the business. According to Barnum, he collected only a small percentage of the $180,000 that was soon pledged to the enterprise but personally guaranteed that amount and urged investors to hold the bulk of their money until a grand demonstration of the annihilator should take place.[3]

W. H. Phillips, the British inventor of the contraption, would be present with Barnum for the public display of its annihilating powers. After a successful demonstration before about thirty people on December 17, 1851, on Hamilton Square, in the remote precincts of Manhattan at Sixty-Ninth Street and Third Avenue, the big trial was set for the same place on the following day. Barnum's advertisements and fliers brought a crowd of some three thousand spectators on a bitterly cold afternoon to watch as fires were set to the shell of a house constructed for the demonstration and then to marvel as the annihilators did their work. Phillips's plan, as he would write to the papers the next day, had been to start two separate fires, one small and one large. But after a fairly unimpressive first fire was quickly snuffed out by four annihilators, rowdies in the crowd swarmed into the house, tossed a number of pre-positioned annihilators out the windows (seriously injuring one small boy), and then themselves set the house ablaze. Phillips, who was knocked down twice trying to get the intruders out of the house, refused to intervene as it now burned down. Members of the crowd called out the familiar refrain "Where's Barnum?" as a chorus of "Humbug" also rose above the ashes. A small group carried one of the annihilators to a nearby pub, where they chalked the name *Barnum* on it and hung it above the door to much laughter. A piece in the *Tribune* the next day was headlined, with a jaunty disregard for spelling, "Annihilition of the Fire Annihilator." Despite Phillips's call for another demonstration, Barnum returned the money he had already collected and eventually sold his share in the company. Although Phillips would succeed in getting an American patent for the machine, on October 31, 1852, the factory in Battersea where the Fire Annihilator Company built and stored its product itself caught fire, and neither the annihilators nor an old-fashioned bucket brigade could save the building. Passengers of steamboats passing by on the Thames were reported to have been "greatly inconvenienced" by the showers of steam the burning annihilators emitted. The factory fire would be the fire annihilator's fatal blow.[4]

The number of business schemes presented to him during this period, Barnum wrote, had "neither limit nor end," and most were "as wild and unfeasible as a railroad to the moon." Many of these speculators assumed that Barnum's greed was bottomless and that he would have no compunction about lending his name to any sort of swindle. But he often responded to these proposals, he wrote, by saying that what he wished for, far more than money, was tranquility. Still, he was amused by the variety and persistence of the offers that came his way. In his 1869 autobiography he described a few of them, sharing his own witty responses. The last came from a fellow who wanted to use camels to carry people overland to California: "I told him that I thought asses were better than camels, but I should not be one of them."[5]

Among the projects Barnum did take on at about this time was one that reached back to his roots in the newspaper business. He and the brothers Alfred and Henry Beach, who had given up joint editorship of the *Sun,* each invested $20,000 to found a weekly illustrated newspaper, modeled on the *Illustrated London News.* Barnum was a worthy third to these two members of a newspaper family, having established the *Herald of Freedom* two decades before and in his career since having been intimately involved with the newspapers of his and other cities, as advertiser, writer, source, and friend or enemy of prominent editors. The first issue of the *Illustrated News* appeared on the first day of 1853, and although the circulation grew to exceed 150,000 (and by Barnum's estimation its number of readers reached half a million), it closed after forty-eight issues. The paper ambitiously aspired to cover "Intelligence, Literature, Art, and Society." Its chief engraver was Frank Leslie, whose own subsequent illustrated weekly paper would become an American mainstay and an important chronicler of the Civil War. The first editor of the *Illustrated News* was an excitable literary man named Dr. Rufus Griswold, and his assistant was Charles

Godfrey Leland, a young journalist who later became a prominent folklorist. It was generally believed by "the entire American press" that Barnum's interest in the paper was to create a frictionless vehicle for promoting his own interests, and Leland himself claimed in his memoirs to have been sufficiently concerned about it to explain to the showman that "this would ere long utterly ruin the publication." Leland credited Barnum for avoiding that path, so much so "that in his own paper he was conspicuous by his absence." Barnum assisted his editors by soliciting articles from the likes of William Makepeace Thackeray, who was in America at the time, and his old friend Edward Everett, who as U.S. minister to Great Britain had set up the first meeting between Tom Thumb and Queen Victoria and was, at the time Barnum wrote to him, U.S. secretary of state.[6]

According to Leland, Barnum also liked to stop by the office to share his latest joke or puzzle and to help him fill a regular humor column. "There was a great deal of 'boy' still left in Barnum," Leland recalled, adding that Barnum would delight in sitting down to hear the best bits from the next column. Leland was unstinting in his admiration for Barnum, even though his tenure as editor of the *Illustrated News* (where he soon replaced Griswold) was brief and in his memoirs he emphasized how hard he was worked and how little he was paid. When he once complained to Barnum about his salary, Barnum doubled it, which still left Leland lagging behind what others in the newspaper business were being paid. But given that Barnum had put out the *Herald of Freedom* by himself, and given the older man's general indefatigableness, Barnum was probably not the person to feel great sympathy for how hard Leland was working.[7]

The *Illustrated News* ran its last issue on November 26, 1853, and Barnum had again lost money. But he soon allowed himself to be drawn into another investment in Manhattan, one that at least depended in part on his skills as a showman. The famous Crystal Palace exhibition in London's Hyde Park in 1851 had inspired a group of New York businessmen to erect their own Crystal Palace in what was then called Reservoir Square and is now Bryant Park, located behind the main New York Public Library at Fifth Avenue and Forty-Second Street. Barnum wrote that he was approached by the initial group of investors but declined to participate, because he thought it was too soon for New York to try to emulate the successful world's fair in London. Besides, he thought the site, "four miles distant from the City Hall, was enough of itself to kill the enterprise," being too far from the population center of the city. But the investors were undeterred by Barnum's doubts and went ahead without him. The American Crystal Palace had a footprint following the Greek-cross plan of a central square with four equal wings, topped by a dome a hundred feet in diameter, the whole built of iron and glass, with enough wood to make it as flammable as the British original would turn out to be. The exhibition opened on July 14, 1853, with President Franklin Pierce as the featured speaker, but by the following winter the novelty had worn off sufficiently for its owners to approach Barnum again in the belief that he and his old friend John Genin, the now quite-rich hatter, could revive it. Barnum again "utterly declined," but in almost no time he somehow found himself the president of the enterprise and a big investor in it. He immediately planned a "re-inauguration" ceremony, a Fourth of July celebration, and other Barnumesque events. But after three months of his focused attention, he realized that the enterprise was doomed, so he resigned.[8]

He made at least one cursory attempt to fob the structure off on his friend Moses Kimball, proposing that the building be disassembled and rebuilt on the Boston Common, but he was honest enough to begin his letter floating this scheme with the admission "I was an ass for having anything to do with the Crystal Palace." Still, he went on to make a spirited defense of the idea, even asserting, "New Yorkers who now think the palace *too far off* to visit would positively go to Boston to see it." Kimball declined his friend's offer.

Barnum was nowhere specific about how much money he invested in the enterprise. But when he mentioned to Kimball a new project he had begun immediately after resigning his presidency, he added, "I *hope* [it] will make up my losses by Crystal Palace." After a series of questionable ventures, he turned to one that put his best qualities forward. It would rely on his instincts as a showman, his impressive verbal skills, and his dedication to hard work.[9]

For this new endeavor, he anchored himself at home, spending what was left of the summer and much of the fall in the elegant second-floor study he had built for himself at Iranistan. Over the next four months, he would write his autobiography. Given its length, its coherence, its wit, its polish, and its depth of self-reflection, his speed in writing the four-hundred-page book is remarkable. *The Life of P. T. Barnum, Written by Himself,* was published in a first edition of fifty thousand copies in mid-December 1854, only a few weeks after its completion. Considering Barnum's latter-day reputation, it's worth noting that the book is not dramatically more, or less, mendacious than the usual autobiography by a famous person, and rivals Rousseau's *Confessions* in its eagerness to reveal his own foibles, misdeeds, and missteps.[10]

Yet it is not as though when Barnum sat down at his desk, cocooned in the orange silk damask that covered the walls and ceiling of his study, he was starting from scratch as a novice writer. He had been inventing his persona ever since he had gone to work in his father's store, and he had polished and polished again his anecdotes about himself in his years as a public speaker and a person in whom the press and the public took an eager interest. He had his hundred letters to the *New York Atlas* from 1844 to 1846 to draw on for his time in England and Europe; he had journals he had kept in the 1830s that formed the basis of his mock autobiography of Barnaby Diddledum, which had also been published in the *Atlas*, in 1841; and he had his daughter Caroline's journals from trips she had made with him in 1848 and 1850–51. He wrote Kimball as he was getting started, "Pray tell me if the story of the old sailor getting [the Fejee Mermaid] in China was really true, and also give me all the particulars of its origins that you can." In the same letter he asked Kimball if he had a copy of a pamphlet Barnum had written about mermaids. He wrote such letters to other friends to help him jog his memory or recover things he had already written about himself or his undertakings, since he had always been a writer of real productivity, dashing off advertisements, articles, squibs, pamphlets, letters, and on and on. Nothing he wrote ever feels labored: his prose seems to flow easily from the same stream that made him such a good talker. Even the many letters in which he apologizes for the haste with which they were composed exude his high spirits and unwillingness to do things perfunctorily, although the haste sometimes means things tumble out in a stream of consciousness.[11]

As he was writing his book, Barnum was also busily preparing for its reception. In

October 1854 he announced to newspaper and journal editors hither and yon that "fifty-seven publishers have applied for the chance of publishing" the book and also sent out two letters to journalists claiming that "Boston, New York, and Philadelphia publishers are all after the book in a swarm." In the first letter, he undercuts the claim about the fifty-seven publishers by adding, "Such is the *fact* — and if it wasn't, why still it ain't a bad announcement." He makes his appeal to publishers in the second letter "as a whilom brother of the Order Editorial." The jaunty tone of both announcements makes clear that he knew his news would find friendly editors eager to publicize it, especially when he leaked parts of the book to them. Only four days after the second letter, he purchased a notice in New York newspapers, addressed "To Publishers," asserting "Circumstances having occurred by which the publication of my 'Autobiography' is again thrown open to the trade" and encouraging publishers to submit bids for the almost-finished book. Appended to the notice was the book's preface, consisting of seven short paragraphs, in which he offered his subsequently well-known self-analysis: "On the whole my life has been a merry one. I have looked chiefly on the bright side of things." He promised that the book would not cover up his humbugs and admitted that some people might find his "confessions . . . injudicious," a selling point if ever there was one and an observation that presaged the book's strongest condemnations.[12]

Barnum's efforts to publicize the eager competition among publishers to acquire his book came after he had already written to a friend in late August that his publisher would be the firm of Julius Starr Redfield. He never said whether there had been a subsequent falling out with Julius Redfield — a fellow Universalist who attended the same New York City church as Barnum — or whether the idea of a competition was only a ruse to get publicity. But his notices about the competition were reprinted widely, along with the preface, and certainly added to the general interest in what Barnum would produce. The *Sun* reported that twenty-one bids from publishers came in response to his invitation, and the highest bidder was Julius Redfield! Reporting also had it that Barnum would receive $.56 for each $1.25 copy of the book that was sold, but in fact he signed a contract with Redfield calling for him to get 30 percent, or $.375 per copy. This is the precise deal that

Barnum had described in another letter to a friend nearly two months earlier.[13]

By the middle of March, three months after Redfield unleashed it on the world, *The Life of P. T. Barnum* had received more than a thousand positive reviews in the United States alone (many seeming so due to selective quotation), and not a few negative ones, and within a year it had sold an astounding 160,000 copies, for which Barnum's share would have been $60,000. It was published at the same time in England, where pirated editions soon appeared, and was also translated into French, German, Swedish, and Dutch.[14]

A piece in the *New-York Times* acknowledged the divide in critical opinion, calling *The Life* "a very amusing book, which every one will read, half the world will abuse, and nobody can help laughing at and with." Underlining this divide in its own pages, the *Times* published a second review asserting that the book established Barnum as a shameless liar, unaware of his own faults, and concluding that it "will be very widely read and will do infinite mischief." The *Herald* managed only two snide paragraphs and change for Barnum's book, suggesting, "It would be hard to find a more disgusting mess of trash, and the book seems to have been published to show to what vile uses printers' ink may be put." Overstatement went in both directions, one review calling Barnum's life "the most readable work ever published." Barnum himself favored a review in the *Springfield Republican* of Massachusetts, which suggested that a reader should go beneath the book's humorous surface to find a "lesson that mere humbugs and deceptions generally fail" to turn a profit and that the showman's intention was always to employ humbuggery only to publicize his "real and substantial exhibitions, such as his Museum, Tom Thumb in England, and Jenny Lind."[15]

Only two of the negative reviews seem to have gotten under Barnum's skin. The principal one appeared in the *Trumpet and Universalist Magazine* in March 1855. Its reviewer was indignant that Barnum could associate himself with the Universalist faith and with some well-known Universalist preachers. The other was a devastatingly negative review in *Blackwood's Edinburgh Magazine,* which published both a British and an American edition. It concluded that Barnum "has left nothing for his worst enemy to do; for he has fairly gibbeted himself." *Blackwood's* and other British publications took delight in attributing what they saw as Barnum's worst characteristics to his being an American. "Mr. Phineas Taylor Barnum is, we are thankful to say," the magazine chortled, "not a native of this country." *Punch* declared him to be the "type and symbol of the glorious Republic" and saw fit, as the title for its review had it, to propose "Barnum for President," an idea more absurd in 1855 than it seems today. Barnum undoubtedly encouraged such disparagements by dedicating the book to "The Universal Yankee Nation, of Which I Am Proud to Be One." The section of the autobiography where he tells how he sold Tom Thumb to the British by setting himself up as a gentleman, renting a fine house and a liveried servant, could not have helped, nor could the sting of his overwhelming acceptance by the British aristocracy and the British people.[16]

Many of the negative reviews on both sides of the Atlantic were concerned, both overtly and by implication, with the coarsening of public life that Barnum's book represented. His plain speech, his delight in practical jokes and silly anecdotes, his willingness to admit and forgive himself his faults — all of this punctured the gentlemanly façade of the literary establishment, even as his approach was playing into prejudices in intellectual circles, on both sides of the Atlantic, against Americans who rose in class status through mere commerce. The publication of an autobiography necessarily invites criticism not only of the book but also of the life it portrays, and although Barnum admitted, "There are some things in my Autobiography which may honestly be objected to," he added plaintively, "I only ask the acknowledgment that there are some *good* streaks in me and in my book, for I do not admire the doctrine of total depravity."[17]

The decision to tell his life's story at the age of forty-four, just past what would turn out to be his life's halfway mark, might seem brash in retrospect, but his father had died before turning fifty and life expectancy in general did not promise Barnum the decades that, as it turned out, remained to him. Besides, he had a story to tell and had every right to believe that he could tell it well. Some critics who despised the book saw it as just another of his humbugs — an attempt to fool the public into believing that he really could mean both to confess his sins and absolve himself of them — but clearly the autobiography was not intended as humbug. And if he really thought there was more profit in serious enterprises than in humbuggery, then its financial success proved his point. It has been estimated that his autobiography has sold more than a million copies down through the years, and it did well enough in the decade after its publication to encourage him to greatly expand it fifteen years later.

Barnum had been eager to enhance his public reputation as a serious person since before he began to pursue Jenny Lind. His emphasis on moral drama in his Lecture Room, the family-friendly educational aspects of the American Museum, and his energetic lecturing on temperance all show that he was sincerely putting shameless humbuggery behind him and turning to more substantial and respectable pursuits. His autobiography was meant to emphasize this change in him, admitting (if a little too robustly) his sins and touting his virtues. But the negative aspects of its reception were unexpected. That his efforts at transformation could be so easily ignored and adamantly rejected in so many quarters stung and even staggered him. It must have been especially hurtful to be treated so harshly in Britain, where he had first been accepted by many people at the top of society — a continuing source of pride. Barnum would indeed recommit himself to

become a more serious and more worthwhile person in the years after *The Life of
P. T. Barnum* appeared. And although he
never admitted it, the dismissive things said
about his book and about himself must have
motivated this change to come as much as
the difficulties that still lay ahead.

THIRTEEN:
A RUINED MAN

After the Jenny Lind tour ended, Barnum briefly but seriously considered moving the family to Philadelphia, where he owned a museum and a country house, but between them Charity and Caroline persuaded him to stay in Fairfield. With that, he redoubled his commitment to his adopted hometown, involving himself in an ambitious real-estate development project in adjacent Bridgeport that would draw more on his energy and his wealth than his wisdom.

Across the Pequonnock River from Bridgeport lay what Barnum called a "beautiful plateau" and what an early travel writer named Timothy Dwight IV called a "cheerful and elegant piece of ground," the "surrounding country . . . gay and brilliant, perhaps without a parallel." At the time the travel piece was written, about 1815, Bridgeport consisted of a hundred houses situated on both sides of the Pequonnock, near its mouth. The bridge connecting them gave the village its name. The eastern portion of the community did not develop over time as the western portion had, something Barnum blamed on "want of means of access" to the beautiful plateau. He decided to solve the problem directly, and with a prominent attorney in the town, William H. Noble, set about creating on this fine piece of land the new city of East Bridgeport. Noble had inherited a fifty-acre homestead on the eastern bank of the river, half of which Barnum bought for $20,000 on the last day of October 1851. Together the two men quietly purchased another 174 acres of adjacent land, and then set about, in conjunction with the city of Bridgeport, building a series of new bridges across the river. Barnum and Noble quickly laid out a grid of tree-lined streets on their property and marked off lots for residences and businesses. At the heart of the new city would be a six- to eight-acre grove of trees preserved as Washington Park. (To this day, Barnum Avenue and Noble Avenue cross at the northwest corner of the park.) Soon they began selling the lots at cost, keeping every other one for themselves, expecting to make their money when the value of the lots increased. If that were not enough, they also lent the new landowners the money to buy the land and build on it, allowing them to draw down their debts in irregular payments as small as $5.[1]

This remarkable deal had a few stipulations: the property must be developed within a year, the style of the houses and buildings had to meet with their approval and be situated back from the street, and the lots must be surrounded by fences and kept tidy. Barnum did not say where the ideas behind these restrictions came from, but the general principles by which they developed their new city anticipated by half a century those of the Garden City movement in England and the City Beautiful movement in the United States. The principles also resemble the ideals of the New Urbanism movement that began in the United States in the 1980s.

With head-spinning rapidity, the first factory in the new city rose, and by New Year's Day 1852, a group of young coach makers had leased it and moved in. Other businesses and residents followed quickly, and after just thirty months there were "dwellings, stores, factories, etc., which have cost an aggregate of nearly one million dollars." By the middle of 1853, the new city also boasted its own hotel, church, schoolhouse, and sawmill, and the lots themselves had increased in value tenfold, meaning the value of the land that Barnum and Noble still held had increased by at least this much. Barnum wrote with some satisfaction that he had made a handsome offer to buy out Noble and that his partner had turned him down.

At this point in his autobiography, Barnum unfurled for the first time one of his most memorable phrases, describing what would be a guiding philosophy for his investments in and around Bridgeport: "profitable philanthropy." He would build bridges to the new city, pay for the laying out of streets, the planting of trees, and the preservation of land for a park, and even lend money at a favorable rate to those who wished to contribute to the overall beauty and desirability of the place. But he would do it in a way that enhanced his own investment. He would undertake good deeds that would benefit himself as well as others. The idea of improving the city and richly sharing in the financial advantages of those improvements would guide his relationship to the two Bridgeports for the rest of his days. In the end, the ledger would be very much in favor of the Bridgeports.[2]

This "pet scheme" of developing East

Bridgeport soon became an obsession of Barnum's. He had "East Bridgeport on the brain," and thus was perhaps too open to new proposals to see the city grow and prosper. Having made so much money from his museum, Tom Thumb, and Jenny Lind, he became increasingly eager to leverage that wealth in new speculations, but he became increasingly careless about how he did so. Once involved, he was lax about keeping tabs on his investments. In addition to his East Bridgeport development, he held properties in Bridgeport and elsewhere in Connecticut, farther off in Manhattan and Brooklyn, and even farther afield. One of his cousins, a scoundrel who had followed the Lind tour scalping tickets, was by this time operating out of Cleveland, where he forged Barnum's name on notes amounting to $40,000, which he then blew on gambling and female companionship. He later claimed in court that Barnum had known about and not objected to the forgeries, which led to years of legal troubles for the showman.

One of Barnum's other projects was to move a small clock-making business in which he owned stock from the nearby town of Litchfield to an "immense" building in East Bridgeport, from which, he believed, would eventually emerge more than five thousand clocks a month. He estimated that it would bring six hundred new residents to the city. The Litchfield clockmaker merged with another small clockmaker that had already moved to the city, the merger was incorporated as the Terry and Barnum Manufacturing Company, and in 1852 they built a factory for this business. As successful as this venture was as an example of the sort of development Barnum wished to see in East Bridgeport, it led directly to a much bigger outlay and greater risk for Barnum.

Just a few years later, he would write, a visitor named Chauncey Jerome called at Iranistan. He was an inventor and the president of the Jerome Clock Company, a large and well-known clockmaker in New Haven, which employed in good times as many as a thousand people. Jerome had paid for an impressive new church in New Haven and had recently been elected mayor of that city. The company would relocate to East Bridgeport, Jerome said, if Barnum would help his business secure a substantial loan. In the autobiography, Barnum went on at length about the due diligence he did to be sure Jerome's company was solid. But in the end it was not solid. Barnum never addressed what would seem to be the best reason for him to have been skeptical of the deal: that a newly elected official would willingly initiate a plan to move a thousand workers out of his city. Jerome himself had a different story to tell: that he never called at Iranistan to begin with; that his company, which had by then been run by his son and other investors, had been in good financial shape until it got involved with the Terry and Barnum Company; and that Barnum and Terry's manufacturing company was itself in debt. If Jerome's account were the true one, it seems that Barnum could have just as easily blamed his coming financial troubles on Terry as on Jerome, but he did not.[3]

In any case, Barnum made the decision to involve himself with the Jerome Clock Company, offering to endorse up to $110,000 in notes to help it through a lean time. At this point, Barnum seems to have relied too heavily on his bookkeeper son-in-law, David W. Thompson, husband of Caroline, who oversaw for the busy Barnum all of the East Bridgeport businesses. Barnum began to endorse notes for the Jerome Company willy-nilly, wittingly or unwittingly putting his name on nearly half a million dollars in notes. These notes were used to prop up the Jerome Company, until it went bankrupt in early 1856, paying its debts at only twelve to fifteen cents on the dollar. "To cap the climax," Barnum wrote, the company "never removed to East Bridgeport at all."

When the Jerome Company went bankrupt, all but a few of the many balls Barnum had been juggling came thudding to earth at once, "and then," he admitted, "I failed!" His financial situation was so complicated that he was forced to file for bankruptcy. In his later autobiography, he made his bankruptcy out to be a complete shock. In that book, from the distance of years, he was able to blithely write that his agent brought him "the refreshing intelligence that I was a ruined man!"[4]

However, as early as the previous summer, Barnum had begun to make moves to protect parts of his fortune, proving that he knew his financial footing was growing increasingly risky. First he sold for a dollar his long-term lease on the first of the two buildings now housing the American Museum to his chief assistant, John Greenwood Jr., who the next day sold it to Charity Barnum for the same amount, thus protecting that asset. At about the same time, he sold the contents of the museum to Greenwood and Henry D. Butler, another associate, for twice what he had spent to create the collection — but he held their notes for "nearly the entire amount." Greenwood and Butler then rented the museum building from Charity for $19,000 a year above the annual lease amount, which would provide the Barnums with steady income no matter what happened next.[5]

In a letter he wrote in early February, Barnum began, "The clock folks have *wound me up*. Never mind. My wife owns the Museum lease, which will give her an annual income for the next 23 years that will support us." He also moved other properties in Bridgeport into Charity's name. In the two weeks after he declared bankruptcy, he had mortgaged Iranistan several times for a total of $102,000, an amount more than three times its assessed value. He then used this money to pay his Bridgeport debts to bankers and shopkeepers and made good to local banks some $40,000 in notes they held for the Jerome Company.[6]

Within days, courts in Connecticut had appointed assignees to handle his assets there, including his East Bridgeport holdings and Iranistan itself, from which the Barnums moved immediately. On February 14 the *New York Post* reported, "Iranistan is untenanted, all of the furniture having been removed to this city and sold." The

Barnums now lived "in a very frugal manner" in a furnished rental house on West Eighth Street, near Sixth Avenue, many blocks north of the museum that was no longer, at least legally if not in any other way, his. To punctuate their change in circumstances, Barnum wrote that his new landlady and her family were boarding with his family, which was sadly reminiscent of a time in the city when the Barnums had taken in boarders out of immediate financial necessity; he added that he was "once more nearly at the bottom of the ladder."[7]

Neither Charity nor her husband could be anything but depressed by this situation, and by April they had moved again, this time on the "orders" of Charity's doctor, to "a secluded spot on Long Island where the sea wind lends its healthful influence." Charity was evidently having a hard time adjusting to the loss of their elegant home and servants, and Barnum was himself affected. He wrote that even his "own constitution . . . through the excitements of the last few months, has most seriously failed." He was, understandably if uncharacteristically, "in the depths."[8]

But even now he could not keep his hands off his business. In early February he wrote to a friend in hopes that the friend's dental assistant, who was Turkish, could help the museum's nominal proprietor Greenwood acquire "two beautiful Circassian slaves." The Circassians inhabited a region that touched on the eastern shore of the Black Sea, and the women were famous for their beauty and much desired by sultans as concubines. Barnum reported that he had already written to the U.S. consul in Constantinople, but he was hoping to gain further Turkish assistance for Greenwood. "For my own part," he wrote disingenuously, "I have renounced business & care forever." He and his family would stay on Long Island for four months, living on the seaside farm in Westhampton of a man who had often sent shells and other curiosities to the American Museum. One day Barnum and the farmer were out walking on the beach when they came upon some men and a twelve-foot black whale, dead but still "hard and fresh." Barnum immediately counted out a few dollars to the men who had found it, and shipped it to the museum, "where it was exhibited in a huge refrigerator for a few days." People swarmed to see it, as Barnum knew they would, and Greenwood and Butler sent him a portion of the receipts, enough to pay the boarding bill for his family for their whole stay in Westhampton. The farmer could not believe Barnum's luck, especially since it was the first black whale he had ever seen washed up on that shore. "I wonder if that ain't 'providential,' " the farmer remarked, with a laugh that "resounded, echoed, and re-echoed through the whole neighborhood."[9]

Barnum's financial misfortune inspired the glee of those who had long despised what he stood for, as well as those who no longer felt the economic need to pretend to be his friend; he included a number of newspaper editors in the latter category. But it also became a morality tale of a man brought down by his vanity, of one who had often played fast with others now being the victim of such "cuteness." Even before his bankruptcy became official, Ralph Waldo Emerson, in a letter to his wife, pointed out "that P. T. Barnum has assigned his property, — which is what old people called — the gods visible again." By "old people" he meant the ancients and their belief that the gods would step forward to administer justice where it was deserved. James Gordon Bennett and other newspapermen saw Barnum's downfall as the final chapter of his autobiography: "The author of that book glorifying himself as a millionaire . . . is completely crushed out. . . . It is a case eminently adapted to 'point a moral or adorn a tale.' " As for the Richmond *Daily Dispatch,* always eager to see any situation through a regionalist lens, it blamed Barnum's troubles on his Yankee sharpness and delighted that a different Yankee sharper, the Connecticut clockmaker Jerome, had "stopped the clock of Barnum, and prevented it from ever *ticking* again." The paper predicted, prematurely, that Barnum's "sayings and doings will no longer be chronicled by the New York press," and scolded that when his bankruptcy was "added, by way of appendix to his autobiography, [it] will prove an antidote to the bane of that shameless production."[10]

But, as Barnum related, a strong gale of support arose from "hosts of hitherto unknown friends" who were eager to offer him "something more than sympathy." Many people proposed to lend or give him money to get back on his feet or to organize public benefits "by the score, the returns of which would have made me quite independent." A letter signed by more than a thousand New Yorkers, among them Cornelius Vanderbilt, journalists, businessmen, hoteliers, the Delmonico's restaurant family, and at least one prominent general, appeared in New York papers in early June, expressing support and proposing benefits on his behalf — and drawing the predictable scorn of the *Herald.* Theater owners such as Laura Keene and William Niblo offered the proceeds of an evening's performance. In Bridgeport a large meeting of citizens, called by the mayor to express their collective sympathy and support, featured addresses by prominent citizens, resolutions, and the reading of a letter from Barnum, an event such as he himself might have organized. (Aware that people could see his own hand behind this gathering, Barnum felt the need to assert in his letter, "I knew nothing of this movement until your letter informed me of it.") In the days after the meeting, a group of his neighbors across the city line in Bridgeport offered him a loan of $50,000.[11]

With some exceptions, Barnum declined these many outpourings of financial support, publicly stating, "While favored with health, I feel competent to earn an honest livelihood for myself and family." His unwillingness to accept help had several sources. He was, and had every right to be, proud of the things he had accomplished largely on his own, and that pride and the self-confidence that went with it were not likely to evaporate even in this moment of distress. Because he was still besieged by creditors both honest and conniving, and was and would continue to spend many hours defending himself in court, any gifts or loans publicly known might soon be attached in legal proceedings. But, finally, he could fall back on the truth expressed by one of his favorite witticisms, drawn from the King James Version of First Corinthians: "Without Charity, I am nothing." Because enough of his wealth had been put in Charity's name, safe from legal challenges, he could afford to take the time he needed to wade through the mess he had created — or as he constantly emphasized, the mess created by the deception of others.[12]

Perhaps the most welcome and the most heartfelt of all the offers Barnum received in his first months of bankruptcy came from Tom Thumb, now all of eighteen years old. Filled with the usual dreadful puns about his size, Tom's letter acknowledged the many people who had offered Barnum help and asked to be remembered as someone who belonged to "that mighty crowd." Although he was in Philadelphia at the start of a western tour, he pledged himself "ready to go on to New-York, bag and baggage, and remain at Mrs. Barnum's service as long as I, in my *small* way, can be useful." He mentioned that he had pulled in two thousand customers at a single performance that very day and volunteered to help Barnum "attract all New-York." Whether or not the letter was intended for publication, it feels, for all its sincerity, like a performance, and Barnum soon saw it published in the *Tribune.* The showman declined even this offer from his friend, but soon enough he and the little general would be collaborating again, although far from Philadelphia or New York.[13]

Taken together, the reactions to Barnum's autobiography and bankruptcy provided an unusual, and unusually intense, public evaluation of a person still in his forties who was not a presidential candidate, a general, or an explorer. Barnum had become so familiar a public figure that by this time in his life his name was often used in the newspapers, and presumably in private conversation, as shorthand for a number of qualities: energetic promotion or self-promotion, interest in the odd or the exotic, business acumen and the ability to beat out competition, and, finally and foremost, the vast realm of humbug. In the United States, the British Isles, and Europe, Barnum embodied an identifiable American type — the go-getter — and was also one of the most renowned examples of the growing fluidity in social class that was a central factor of life on both sides of the Atlantic throughout the nineteenth century.

Barnum's financial success was one thing, but his acceptance by the British upper class in the 1840s and by such prominent Americans as Commodore Vanderbilt and Horace Greeley in the 1850s suggested that a person could move not only from rags to riches but even from obscurity to respectability. This proposition was what made him such a controversial figure, someone whom Bennett and many other editors could routinely denounce to an audience eager to see Barnum put in his place, a man whom Emerson and members of the intelligentsia in the United States and Britain could find both sneer-worthy and also alarming. That the middle classes responded so readily to what Barnum offered — to his hoaxes and publicity stunts but also to the way he challenged them to see with their own eyes and rely on their own judgment — was partly what defenders of tradition, the perquisites of class, the intellectual elite, and culture itself, as they saw it, were railing against when they attacked Barnum. Yes, his smugness was irritating, but it was his role as a leader of the mob assaulting the citadels of culture — for example, by undermining serious theater with his moralistic melodramas — that made him a palpable threat.

Even those who sneered, however, could get Barnum's place with the average American just about right. John Delaware Lewis, the British son of a Russian merchant whose sneering came by way of Eton and Cambridge, made a jaunt to the United States and brought back sketches collected in 1851 as *Across the Atlantic.* "By 'going-a-head' to an extent hitherto unprecedented in his trade — devoid of any absurd delicacy as to the means by which the ends are to be accomplished," Lewis observed, Barnum "has endeared himself to the middle and lower ranks of his countrymen, and seems to stand forth proud and preeminent as their model of a speculator and a man." Lewis might not have fully approved, but he recognized Barnum's preeminence. The perennial popularity of the American Museum, the robust sales of the autobiography, the widespread appeal of his nostrums for success in business, and the eagerness of newspapers across the land to print any snatch of news or gossip about him all proved that, for all his faults, "Old Barnum" was, in our striving, democratic country, the object more often of respectful affection than of scorn.[14]

By early December 1856, weary of the financial shell game and legal wrangling that took up so much of his time, and longing for his old life as a showman, Barnum set sail for Liverpool, where nearly thirteen years earlier he had landed with Tom Thumb to begin their successful campaign to win over the British public. The little general himself would soon join him again, but for the moment, Barnum accompanied "an exceedingly talented *trio,* Mr. & Mrs. Howard & their little daughter, Cordelia, an exquisite actress of eight years." The Howards were known for playing in the musical version of *Uncle Tom's Cabin,* and little Cordelia broke hearts as the soulful Little Eva. Once he reached Liverpool, Barnum went back to the Royal Waterloo Hotel, where he was now friendly with the staff, marveling over how little they and the hotel had changed over the years, and ordered again the meal he had first had there, "fried soles and shrimp sauce."[15]

As was the case on that first trip to England, he came without bookings but soon approached theater managers with the pitch that, given his dire financial straits, "I should never have crossed the Atlantic with an attraction which I did not *know* possessed every element of immense success." Soon both the Howards and Tom Thumb were "making much money" for Barnum in London and other English cities, and as a result, "my health & spirits are much better than I would like to have many suppose." Charity was also feeling stronger, and by late spring she and two of their daughters, Helen and Pauline, joined him in London. Meanwhile he was dining often with old friends like Thackeray, Albert Smith, Julius Benedict and Giovanni Belletti, and various theater managers and journalists. Otto Goldschmidt visited him with an offer of help from Jenny Lind and encouraged him to move to Dresden, where he and Jenny lived and where he said that Barnum could live frugally.[16]

But the financial picture was brightening, and after the Howards returned to America, Barnum and Tom Thumb went to Germany, via Paris and Strasbourg. The general appeared at various spas in Germany, including Baden-Baden — "a delightful little town, cleaner and neater than any city I had ever visited." The high-rolling clientele, who visited these spa towns as much for their gambling establishments as for taking the waters, supported large admissions charges for Tom's exhibitions. These performances soon became "the most profitable that had ever been given," permitting Barnum to send thousands of dollars back home to help clear his debts and buy back some of his former holdings. The two men went on to Holland, where Barnum was once again hugely impressed by the local neatness and cleanliness, in which the country was "evidently not next to, but far ahead of godliness." But the frugality of the Dutch made it harder to fill seats for Tom's performances, so he and the general spent most of their time sightseeing before returning to England.[17]

In early summer, almost before his family had had time to settle in with him in a London suburb, he was off again by steamship from Liverpool to New York. When he walked along the familiar blocks of Broadway he had the opposite experience of the one he had had when he first returned from London, when people who had formerly turned away from him cozied up because of his newfound wealth: "I saw old and prosperous friends coming, but before I came anywhere near them, if they espied me they would dodge into a store, or cross the street . . . or they would become very much interested in something that was going on."

He calls these people his "butterfly friends" and professes to have been delighted for "the opportunity to learn this sad but most needful lesson." He stayed in America long enough to be rejoined by his wife and daughters for the marriage of his second daughter, Helen, in Bridgeport on October 7.[18]

After the wedding, having been advised that his staying around might make it easier for his agents to settle his remaining debts, he returned to New York. His financial outlook was now such that he took up lodging in the luxurious confines of the Astor House. One thing that had not been settled was Iranistan, which had not been lived in since the Barnums had decamped two years before. His Bridgeport assignee had not been overly eager to sell the place, perhaps sympathetic to Barnum's wish to reclaim it if his finances improved enough to allow him to do so. But the attorney did hire workmen to keep the house in sufficiently good shape to sell if necessary. Barnum wrote that these carpenters and painters had been warned not to smoke in the house but had developed the habit of eating lunch in the large dome room and then smoking a pipe afterward, which Barnum suspected led to an errant ash.

For on December 18 his half brother Philo telegrammed Barnum in New York with jarring news: Iranistan had caught fire the night before and was now ashes. "My beautiful Iranistan was gone!" Barnum wrote. During his financial troubles he had failed to make all the payments on his insurance policies for the house, and those he held were valued at only $28,000. Eventually the grounds and outbuildings were sold for $50,000, and both of those sums went into retiring his debt, but it was a marked loss for Barnum. The sewing-machine inventor Elias Howe Jr. bought the grounds in the summer of 1859, intending to build his own impressive house there, but somehow he never did. For his part, Barnum had a narrow, mile-long, artificial lake in East Bridgeport dredged out in the fall of 1859, with the idea of rebuilding Iranistan there, but nothing came of that plan either.[19]

Barnum soon returned to England, leaving Charity and their youngest daughter, Pauline, living in Fairfield with Caroline and her husband, David. The showman joined Tom Thumb again to tour Scotland and Wales, once more taking in good profits. But after some months he realized that the general could generate plenty of cash without his personal oversight.

Hearing the "old clocks" ticking in his ear, Barnum now reinvented himself again, as a public lecturer. He took the advice of American friends in London to get up a talk called "The Art of Money-Getting." The basis for the talk would be a list of ten rules for business success that Barnum had created in 1852 for a prolific Philadelphia author named Edwin T. Freedley, who published the list in his 1853 book, *A Practical Treatise on Business,* which also included a chapter by Horace Greeley titled "The True Man of Business." Freedley told his readers that he delayed the book for three weeks while waiting for Barnum's response, referring to the showman as "the ablest tactician, and one of the most successful business men of the age." Barnum had published a slimmed-down version of the list in *The Life of P. T. Barnum* in 1855, and now he would greatly fatten it up with examples, anecdotes, funny stories, and a great dose of common sense masquerading as wisdom.[20]

Or perhaps it *was* wisdom. Commonsensical advice included the following: pick a business you are suited for; work hard and persevere; hire good people; and don't count on others to do your job for you. Advice that came out of his own experience included "let your pledged word ever be sacred"; "be not too visionary"; "engage in one kind of business only"; "advertise"; and "live considerably within your income." His wisdom, hard won, also included "Prosperity is a more severe ordeal than adversity, especially sudden prosperity."[21]

Barnum seems to have spent a good deal of time preparing the lecture, joking to his friends that, given the clock catastrophe and his own bankruptcy, he should call the talk "The Art of Money-Losing." But they spurred him on by reminding him that he could not have lost money without first having made it and that the public was well aware (thanks to Barnum himself) of how much wealth he had accumulated from the Jenny Lind tour and other ventures.

He gave his lecture for the first time on December 29, 1858, at St. James's Hall in Piccadilly, a concert venue decorated in Moorish style that had opened earlier in the year with a choral performance led by his old friend Julius Benedict. Seated on the narrow, light-green horsehair benches in the hall were the Americans who had encouraged him, plus "all my theatrical and literary friends" and critics from the press.[22]

The next day's *Times* gave his lecture high marks, pointing out that there was no odor of the charlatan about Barnum, but that he came across as a "thoroughly respectable man of business." The paper's critic praised his "fund of dry humor that convulses everybody with laughter, while he himself remains perfectly serious." The text of the speech appears in the 1869 autobiography, refined and expanded after much use over the ensuing decade. It does not contain many opportunities for convulsive laughter, so Barnum must have ad-libbed freely, his deadpan delivery magnifying the humor. The critic made a point of praising his "sonorous" voice, which is of particular note because there has long existed the myth that his voice was squeaky.[23]

The *Times* was not alone in its high opinion of his performance. Barnum exulted, "My own lavish advertisements were as nothing to the notoriety which the London newspapers voluntarily and editorially gave to my new enterprise." Here Barnum did not exaggerate. The victory must have been especially sweet since he had learned years before that the London papers could not be bought off with advertising money, unlike many of their American counterparts of the time. Barnum concluded, "The city thus prepared the provinces to give me a cordial reception."[24]

He would deliver the speech nearly a hundred times in the first five months of 1859, both in the provinces and in the city of London. Advertised as the "Science of Money-Making," not the art, and promising "an original definition of HUMBUG," the presentation would also include "pictorial illustrations." Having managed to procure from his friend Moses Kimball that desiccated thing the Fejee Mermaid, he exhibited it on his tour through the countryside. He seemed especially pleased with his performances in Oxford and Cambridge, where he had years before received the usual rough treatment from the undergraduates and was prepared to receive it again, "fully resolved to put up with whatever offered." When a Cambridge student interrupted his lecture on February 21 by calling out a question about Joice Heth, Barnum pushed back by saying he would gladly give the student "all the information I possess concerning your deceased relative." The quip feels ugly today, but Barnum believed it made the students less eager to tangle with him. A local newspaper had a different impression, calling the students "very disorderly" and subjecting Barnum to "many interruptions and shouts of derision." The newspaperman dismissed Barnum's talk as "nothing but a string of anecdotes" about how he had humbugged the public, and his wounding conclusion was that "Barnum appears to be a vain, elderly man, on the best possible terms with himself."[25]

At Oxford on February 25, Barnum announced at the outset, "You have paid me liberally for the single hour of my time which is at your service," and pointed out that they could spend that time listening to him or indulging in their own tomfoolery. When the audience tested this proposition by energetically singing "Yankee Doodle," Barnum took a seat on the stage and contentedly waited them out. Several more such interruptions happened, but he kept both his good humor and an eye on his watch. When the hour was up, he stopped abruptly and the audience swelled forward, congratulating him on "a jolly good time." Ticket sales for that single hour in Oxford amounted to £169, or about $850 in 1859 dollars.[26]

Barnum returned home in early June on the steamship *Africa* to be with Charity, whose health was failing. As he wrote to Moses Kimball, "My poor Charity continues very ill." She and their unmarried daughter were now either boarding with Caroline and her husband or living cheaply in a small rented house. In his note to Kimball he added about his own health, "I am not quite well as the *clock wheels* are running in my head yet & make me dizzy sometimes." He had left behind in England an eight-page pamphlet of his speech, selling for two shillings. If the advertising for the text was not quite as energetic as that for his public deliveries of it, still it kept his name before the British public. Although the provincial halls had not always been full and, especially in the smaller towns, the reception had not always been as enthusiastic as in London, all in all, his lecture tour was the "source of very considerable emolument to me."[27]

He spent the rest of 1859 actively overcoming that clock-wheel dizziness, focused on the American Museum from behind the scenes, booking acts, finding new dramas and new exotic objects. In the fall he went into business with the singers Henri and Susanna Drayton to offer opera bouffe or parlor opera to New York and other cities, which the couple undertook with an ambitious series of appearances. Before 1860 had progressed very far, Barnum could write to a friend that the American Museum was bringing him $90,000 a year, although he told a much different story to those still making claims, legitimate and not, on his Jerome Clock paper. But even the *Herald* admitted in late 1859 that Barnum had in effect pulled himself out of debt and vowed to sin no more in a financial way. Combining the income from his various ventures, selling lots in East Bridgeport and other property, adding in Charity's own income, and relying on her frugality if not always his own, he had over a period of five years paid off the bulk of what he owed and was now ready to tell the world, "Richard's himself again."[28]

Although advertisements in the New York papers had continued to tout "Barnum's American Museum" throughout the years when Greenwood and Butler were nominally its proprietors and Barnum simply its agent, he was now ready to regain his status as the legal owner, showing everyone that he was in every way again in charge. He bought back the rights to the museum's contents on March 17, 1860, and then took official possession of the museum a week later. That night, before he closed the building for a week of refurbishment, he spoke from the museum's stage to a sympathetic full house, giving his side of the story of his financial recovery; offering thanks to those who had helped him through, starting with

Charity and ending with John Greenwood (to whom "I owe much of my present position of self-congratulation"), who would stay on as his second in command at the museum; and pledging to rededicate himself to the museum "as a popular place of family resort." Barnum wrote, "This off-hand speech was received with almost tumultuous applause," but whatever the decibel level of its reception, the speech was clearly anything but off-hand and soon was being peddled as a pamphlet titled "Barnum on His Feet Again."[29]

In a notice headed, with the standard editorial indifference to spelling, "Barnum's Last Pronunciamiento," the *Herald* was eager to poke fun, calling the speech a "refreshing piece of blarney" and referring to the showman as "Chevalier Barnum," accusing him of "giving a great many words and very few facts, and meaning nothing in particular." Comparing his career with that of William Niblo, the *Herald* suggested, "Something is wanting in the furniture of the Chevalier's mental household": namely, common sense. Barnum and Niblo were both "naturally clever men," Bennett's paper conceded, but Niblo kept to the show business he knew, while Barnum was "overrating his own powers" and involving himself in businesses he should have left alone. Niblo, it concluded, was now retiring as a millionaire, "while Barnum goes to work again a poor man, looking for another Joice Heth."[30]

Leaving aside the now long-standing animus Bennett had exhibited toward Barnum, the paper can be forgiven for its skepticism about the sincerity of a speech that even Barnum saw as filled with self-congratulation. Given that the American Museum had continued to buy almost daily ads in the newspaper that Bennett owned, his enthusiasm for taking Barnum on was in admirable contrast to the prevailing journalistic ethics of the day.

One sign that Barnum was back on his feet was his breaking ground on a new house that would be next door to one he had constructed for his daughter Caroline after her 1852 marriage. He and Charity had been without a permanent place to live since leaving Iranistan, and now his wife's health "was much impaired, and she especially needed a fixed residence which she could call 'home.' " The site was about six hundred yards northwest of where Iranistan had been, also in the town of Fairfield. With the help of Caroline and his old friend the poet Bayard Taylor, he would name the Italianate-style house Lindencroft, not in honor of Jenny Lind but because a grove of linden trees adorned the grounds. "All that taste and money could do," Barnum declared, "was fairly lavished on Lindencroft." Saxon writes that the house was a hundred feet deep. Although substantial, it was not nearly as imposing from the front as Iranistan. Like the earlier house, the new one featured a large fountain out front, but otherwise "no attempt at ostentation" was made, Barnum said, hardly needing to add that Iranistan had been all ostentation. Lindencroft was not meant to be a symbol of his success or a calling card for his business, but was built purely for "convenience and comfort." Charity, who had become an accomplished gardener, filled the grounds with "rare and beautiful flowers" to go with its walks, arbors, lawns, gardens, trees, and shrubs. For both of them, the house was "a labor of love," and Barnum hoped to live out his days there.[31]

Barnum had undoubtedly been deeply rattled by his financial comeuppance, but when his natural disposition to look on "the bright side of things" began to pull him out of the doldrums, Charity did not escape them as easily as he did, and continued to feel downcast. He also had to contend with the unhappiness of his children, who "had been brought up in luxury; accustomed to call on servants to attend to every want." Even if he was back on his feet, his family's circumstances remained for a time diminished from what they had been at their height. It is not hard to imagine that one reason he had returned to England to tour with Tom Thumb was to escape their misery. Once he started to make money again, his life soon enough became all fried soles and shrimp sauce in the best hotels. Still, he had made a conscientious effort to pay off his debts, and he had publicly vowed to continue improving himself.

In his letter to his Connecticut neighbors soon after his bankruptcy and in his speech at the museum four years later, Barnum claimed to have learned that "there are, in this world, some things vastly better than the Almighty Dollar!" But in the same speech he acknowledged that "business activity is a necessity of my nature" and emphasized that, on the cusp of fifty years of age, he had no desire to retire. His natural inclination for business would never leave him, and given his genius for it, he would continue to accumulate dollars, almighty or not. But his faith led him to believe that his troubles had been God's way of teaching him to be a better person, and in the three decades left to him, he managed, in this regard, to do what he saw as God's will. The charitable way in which his true friends had treated him, offering him loans and often buying up his debt and allowing him to discharge it at less than its face value, had also made an impression on him. His quip about his being nothing without Charity seems to have been a lesson he now took to heart. He would become more generous in his dealings with others, and as his wealth accumulated again, he would give more and more of it away, not only in "profitable philanthropy" but in the sort that has no strings attached beyond proving to himself that he was not nothing.

FOURTEEN:
THE WAR AND A WEDDING

Even as Barnum was putting the pieces of his life back together, events in the nation were leading toward the great cataclysm of the Civil War. The month before Barnum reclaimed his museum, Abraham Lincoln had given his Cooper Union speech in New York, which led to his nomination for president in May and his victory in November. With the election, the fragile bonds between slave and free states began to break. Barnum was a Lincoln man and a passionate defender of the Union, although many of his neighbors in Connecticut and his customers in New York City were not. He did what he could for the Union cause, while getting back to his museum and returning to some of his usual humbuggery. He would also, during one of the bloodiest and most dispiriting periods of the war for the North, manage to create a welcome distraction for a weary Union, a celebrity wedding that was part enchantment, part absurdity, and all showmanship.

On March 27, 1860, an ad half a column deep appeared on the front page of the *New-York Tribune,* headed "BARNUM'S AMERICAN MUSEUM," followed by his name as "Sole proprietor and Manager," with John Greenwood described as assistant manager. Announcing the museum's grand reopening, the ad used the word *new* some ten times, liberally augmented with *now* and *renovated:* "COMPLETELY RENOVATED AND REARRANGED, so as to meet, in all particulars, the views of the most exactingly critical." The stage and Lecture Room were refurbished, the gaslights replaced throughout, the resident acting company shot through with new performers. On the day of the reopening, two different dramas and one farce played. Fireworks began at sundown. Among the familiar exhibits like the Happy Family that he had acquired years earlier in the English countryside (new family members replaced the old ones as they died off) were a grizzly bear named Samson, a sea lion, and a "learned seal."[1]

In the year following the publication of Charles Darwin's *On the Origin of Species* in 1859, thrusting evolution into the spotlight and contradicting the biblical story of humankind's creation, Barnum had a new act that showed up in this ad — one of the most objectionable humbugs of his later years. "WHAT IS IT! WHAT IS IT WHAT IS IT!" the advertisement cried out, and what it just might be, the ad claimed, was "the long-looked-for connecting link between man and monkey." The exhibit featured an eighteen-year-old, mildly mentally challenged, and microcephalic black man named William Henry Johnson, who stood only four feet tall and weighed only fifty pounds. Barnum dressed him in a furry ape costume and fitted him with a long pole, supposedly an aid in the transition from walking on four legs to two. The showman had Johnson's head shaved — the ape suit went neck high — and taught him to smile foolishly and speak, when he spoke at all, in screams or gibberish. A white lecturer presented him to the museum visitors, telling stories about his capture in Africa and the attempts that had been made to civilize him. Huge numbers of people paid their quarter in order to enlarge their scientific knowledge or reinforce their preconceptions about race, or both. Even as sophisticated an observer as the New York lawyer and diarist George Templeton Strong went to the 1860 exhibit two days in a row soon after it opened, calling Johnson "clearly an idiotic negro dwarf," but also "fearfully simian . . . a great fact for Darwin."[2]

But, interestingly, as the white man talked, Johnson would subtly undermine him to the audience, with, as the *New York Clipper* put it, "many sly manoeuvers that lets in the light on the humbug terribly." When he was first exhibited in February, a number of New York newspapers swallowed the story hook, line, and sinker, but soon they, like the *Clipper,* began to express their serious doubts. This followed the pattern that Barnum had eventually settled on in presenting a new "scientific" discovery: offer it as true, adding, as Barnum did in a pamphlet for the exhibit, that its authenticity had been confirmed by "some of the most scientific men we have"; encourage doubts to be raised; and then invite his paying customers to make up their own minds. In the ad, Barnum slightly distanced himself by describing the possibility that this was the missing link as something "pronounced by so many people" — not necessarily including himself. He had long before explained to Moses Kimball that the point of this sort of exhibit was not to say one way or another if the actor is "human or animal": "We leave that all to the sagacious public to decide." That is what made it a humbug, by Barnum's definition, and not an outright fraud.[3]

Barnum's involvement with missing-link exhibits preceded Darwin's book, stretching back to about 1845, when he showed an orangutan at the American Museum and described it as a "link between man and brute." Then, in 1846 in London, he tried to fob off a misshapen American actor as a "wild man." A longish advertisement in the *Times* of London asked, "Is it an animal? Is it human? Is it an extraordinary freak of nature? Or is it the long sought for link between man and the Ourang-Outang?" The ad explained that the exhibit's "What Is It?" moniker applied "because this is the universal exclamation of all who have seen it." But there was not much time for exclamation because, within half an hour of the exhibit's opening at the Egyptian Hall, a visitor recognized the actor and exposed the fraud. Barnum had been wary of this, writing to Kimball only the week before, "I half fear that it will not only be exposed, but that *I* shall be *found out* in the matter. However, I go it, live or die."[4]

William Henry Johnson's act was a final attempt at Barnum's earlier ploy, and one that would succeed over a long period of time. In the more than six decades of Johnson's career, which would last until his death in 1926, he would be viewed, according to one estimate, by a hundred million people. For many years after Barnum's own death, Johnson was a prime exhibit for the Barnum & Bailey and Ringling Brothers shows and became one of the most famous circus characters of his day. Barnum apparently treated him well, sharing in the profits and even buying Johnson a house in Bridgeport, and there was real affection between the two men as their relationship continued well into Barnum's own circus days in the 1880s.[5]

Nothing can or should mitigate the overtly racist nature of the "What Is It?" presentation and reception. In Barnum's mind, if not in ours, this exhibit must have been different from that of Joice Heth, if only because the element of doubt was the very point of the exhibition, making it not the outright hoax that Heth's act was. Barnum was never ashamed of exhibiting Johnson as he came to be of exhibiting Heth, and there was not the public outcry that there had been about Heth.

Among those who would see Johnson in his first year at the American Museum was the Prince of Wales, Albert Edward, who was making a four-month tour of Canada and the United States, every moment of which was followed by the press. At the age of three, the prince had met Barnum and Tom Thumb at Buckingham Palace, and now he was nearly nineteen. On the third day of his October 1860 visit to New York, he and his royal entourage stopped at Barnum's. The proprietor himself was off in Connecticut, so Greenwood, who was British by birth and nervous as a cat to receive the prince, showed him around. He hustled Albert Edward up to the second floor, where the first exhibit he saw was "What Is It?" "His Royal Highness manifested much curiosity" in it, the *Tribune* reported, and asked Johnson's "keeper" to give his "regular account of the animal." Then they went on to see the vast array of other displays, Greenwood leading with backward steps.[6]

As always, Barnum described the royal visit colorfully, if second-handedly:

The tall giant woman made her best bow; the fat boy waddled out and kissed his hand; the "negro turning white" showed his ivory and his spots; the dwarfs kicked up their heels, and like the clown in the ring cried "Here we are again!"; the living skeleton stalked out . . . ; the Albino family went through their performances; the "What is it?" grinned.[7]

At the end of a fairly brisk visit, which the *New-York Times* reporter said "seemed to afford him a great deal of amusement," the prince turned to Greenwood and said, "I suppose I have seen all the curiosities; but where is Mr. Barnum?" Barnum's own interpretation of this moment is that the prince, when hearing that Barnum was not in the museum, was actually saying, "We have missed the most interesting feature of the establishment."[8]

Having himself missed this signature moment at his museum, Barnum hustled up to Boston, which was the last stop for the royal visitors before returning home. Albert Edward received him there at the Revere House, and when the showman reminded the prince of his visit to Buckingham Palace with Tom Thumb, the moment elicited a royal smile. Barnum tells a good story about being whisked through the streets surrounding the Revere House, crowded with royal watchers, because he had been mistaken for the presidential candidate Stephen A. Douglas. When Douglas later campaigned in Bridgeport, a friend asked Barnum if he had ever seen the senator. Yes, Barnum's story goes, "I said: 'He is a red-nosed, blear-eyed, dumpy, swaggering chap, looking like a regular bar-room loafer.' " To which his delighted friend responded that that morning's paper had said that Douglas was "the very image, in personal appearance, of P. T. Barnum."[9]

When Lincoln was in New York for his Cooper Union speech, he had stayed at the Astor House, just across the street from Barnum's American Museum, but he did not visit. Perhaps the widely publicized "What Is It?" exhibit was enough to keep the would-be president away. Even so, Lincoln would be linked to Barnum's "What Is It?" during the presidential campaign, in the form of a Currier & Ives cartoon called "An Heir to the Throne or The Next Republican Candidate," showing the diminutive Johnson with his pole standing between a disheveled Greeley and Lincoln holding his trademark split rail. In his speech balloon, Greeley introduces Johnson as "this illustrious individual in whom you will find combined all the graces and virtues of Black Republicanism" and proposes him as the next Republican presidential candidate after Lincoln. And in his speech balloon, Lincoln refers to Johnson as "this intellectual and noble creature" proving "to the world the superiority of the Colored over the Anglo Saxon race" and calls him "a worthy successor to carry out the policy which I shall inaugurate." At least in this instance, however, it can be said that race-baiting in a presidential election campaign did not work as planned.[10]

A year later, Lincoln was back in New York as president-elect, on his way from Springfield to Washington to be inaugurated. This time he stayed at the Astor House with his family, and Barnum pushed through the crowds in the hotel late on the beautiful mild afternoon of February 19 to invite them to visit the museum the next morning. The president-elect replied that "he would certainly attend" at some point the next day. To which, the *Herald* reports, as always adding a bit of brassiness to the showman's tone, Barnum responded, "Don't forget. You're 'Honest Old Abe'; I shall rely upon you, and I'll advertise you." Barnum was as good as his word, rushing the ad into the papers, but perhaps because of Barnum's attempt to use him as a marketing tool, or more likely because he was pretty seriously in demand, Lincoln himself did not go to the museum, but Mrs. Lincoln and their children did visit.[11]

Barnum's own views on politics and slavery had evolved over the years, even if his eagerness to make money off the "What Is It?" exhibit never changed. "I began my political life as a Democrat," he wrote in his 1869 autobiography, and he claimed in an 1865 speech to have voted for every Democratic presidential candidate from Jackson to Pierce. But "Bloody Kansas" in 1854 "shook my faith in my party," and by 1860, with secession and war looming, he had become a Republican, joining the antislavery party that had emerged in opposition to the Kansas-Nebraska Act. He was publicly pro-Lincoln, and when a local group of Wide Awakes, the movement of young Republicans in support of Lincoln, announced a plan to direct one of their torchlit marches from the center of Bridgeport to Lindencroft, Barnum bought enough candles to light up every window in the house, demonstrating his support with "a flood of light," while his Democratic neighbors showed their opposition by keeping their houses dark.[12]

After the First Battle of Bull Run in July 1861, northerners who sympathized with Secession began to hold "peace" rallies. At these events, a white flag would often be flown above the Stars and Stripes. Barnum's region of Connecticut was especially active in this way, and so he decided to accompany about twenty like-minded friends to attend one of the meetings happening ten miles north of Bridgeport, in Stepney, "and hear for ourselves whether the addresses were disloyal or not." As they were leaving Bridgeport, they came upon two omnibuses carrying about twenty-five three-month militia volunteers who had just been mustered out and returned from the war. They and a number of other Bridgeporters were also headed to Stepney in a skeptical frame of mind. Barnum's crew beat the slower omnibuses to the "very large gathering" and were present when, as the preacher was delivering his benediction, the omnibuses appeared over a hill, filled with the soldiers hollering pro-Union cheers and displaying Union banners.

In a later account written by William A. Croffut, who had been at Bull Run as a correspondent for the *Tribune,* and a local divinity student and future journalist named John Moses Morris, the soldiers went straight to the flagpole where the peace flag, white with a black eagle and the word PEACE, had just been raised, as well as "an ancient Jackson war-flag." As a soldier shimmied up the hickory pole and tore down the offending flags, the rally's speakers fled the stage in a panic — "Bull Run on a small scale" — and hid in a nearby cornfield. The soldiers then raised Old Glory and carried Barnum on their shoulders to the stage, where he delivered "a speech full of patriotism, spiced with the humor of the occasion." The loyalists in the crowd passed pro-Union resolutions and sang "The Star-Spangled Banner." Among others who spoke was another member of the Bridgeport contingent, Elias Howe Jr., the sewing-machine magnate. Some of those at the peace rally had somewhat betrayed the cause of peace by drawing weapons, but the soldiers managed to disarm a few of them, though not before at least one pistol was fired. In his speech, Howe, who despite his great wealth would soon serve as a private in the war, told the crowd, "If they fire a gun, boys, burn the whole town, and I'll pay for it!"

Before that was necessary, the Bridgeporters decamped, with what was left of the white peace flag dragging in the mud behind one of the omnibuses. But the soldiers remained in a riotous mood, and when they returned to Bridgeport and a crowd of several thousand people had appeared in the streets by evening, they sacked the offices of the *Bridgeport Farmer,* a Democratic, pro-secession newspaper. Barnum had wired several New York papers about the events of the day, ending his first dispatch by saying that the soldiers had been talked out of attacking the *Farmer* office, but a short time later, at 8:30 p.m., he sent a second telegram saying that the newspaper "ha[d] just been gutted. . . . The windows were smashed, the type all thrown into the streets, and the presses destroyed." He wrote in his autobiography, "I did not approve of this summary suppression of the paper, and offered the proprietors a handsome subscription to assist in enabling them to renew the publication." One of the editors escaped over rooftops during the riot, fleeing to Canada and eventually ending up in Augusta, Georgia. The other did restart the *Farmer.*[13]

Less than a week later, after the arrest of one of the principal peace-meeting activists on orders of Secretary of State William H. Seward, Barnum wrote to President Lincoln from Lindencroft, reporting that the arrest had "rendered Secessionists *so scarce,* I cannot find one for exhibition in my museum" and praising the effectiveness of the administration's *"strong arm."*[14]

As early as 1855, Barnum had written to the militant abolitionist Unitarian preacher Thomas Wentworth Higginson, telling him that Charity "attends the Unitarian church, but her hatred of slavery is so strong that they are *too tame* for her." His own views on slavery had been affected by his travels in the South, where he had "grown to abhor the curse from witnessing its fruits." His letter to Higginson continued, "I have spent months on the cotton plantations of Mississippi, where I have seen more than one 'Legree.' " It is more likely that his experience of cotton plantations anywhere could be measured in hours or days rather than in months, and this letter was not the time to confess his own brief ownership of slaves and the beating of one of them. But it seems clear that his opinion had evolved since 1845, when he told the group of Scots on a steamboat to Glasgow that the views of some abolitionists were more reprehensible than the institution itself. He also told Higginson in his 1855 letter, "I am quite your disciple as to woman's rights," and asked if Higginson could put him in touch with the suffragist Lucy Stone, whom he would like to invite to Bridgeport, having listened to her speak on the topic in New York and been "enchained to the seat" during her lecture.[15]

Friends he had made in the temperance movement influenced this general liberalizing of Barnum's views. Several of these friends were preachers who were also deeply involved in abolition, women's suffrage, and other causes. Barnum himself remained a fervent member of the Universalist Church and increasingly acted on his religious principles. And his own financial humbling had also made him more cognizant of the hardships others faced, and more sympathetic to them.

As the existence of the peace-movement Democrats in Connecticut implies, the North was anything but united in the cause of Union, let alone abolition and rights for women. Barnum's ardent antisecessionism and disdain for Copperheads, as the peace Democrats came to be known, undoubtedly cost him business. But throughout the war the museum supported the Union, offering a series of patriotic, war-themed dramas beginning with one called *Anderson,* which dealt with Maj. Robert Anderson's failed attempt to hold on to Fort Sumter. Barnum also filled the museum with artifacts from the war, created wax figures of Union generals who were in the news, and even commissioned an automaton of a young Union soldier on crutches. A living twelve-year-old Union drummer boy who had been injured at Fredericksburg drummed at the museum, and the glamorous northern spy Pauline Cushman spoke there as well.[16]

So closely was Barnum associated with the federal side of the war that after the Draft Riots in New York in 1863, soldiers sometimes volunteered to guard Linden-croft, which was rumored to be in danger of being torched by southern sympathizers. The soldiers even gave him flares that he could shoot up in the event of an attack, warning those at the Bridgeport arsenal to come to his rescue. Barnum explained that he did not have to use them until much later, when a burglar alarm went off in the house one night and he sent up flare after flare, so that "the whole place was as light as day." Half-dressed but fully armed neighbors streamed into his yard to offer assistance, and Barnum claimed that in the light of the flares they could see two burglars making their escape. An engraving that portrays this scene appeared in his 1869 autobiography.[17]

Barnum's enthusiasm for show business never faltered, even as the war progressed. In the spring of 1861, at about the same time Fort Sumter was under siege, he learned of a little person from New Hampshire whom he wanted to exhibit, repeating the routine he'd developed with Charley Stratton. After months of negotiations with the boy's father, a prospering farmer in Manchester, Barnum signed a five-year contract to exhibit the boy, named George Washington Morrison Nutt, for a modest amount. Barnum immediately christened him Commodore Nutt and floated the fiction that he was still trying to sign him up, prompting other promoters to make handsome competing offers. In advertisements meant to look like a press account, Barnum chronicled the offers of these competitors and released a letter of his own directing his agent to acquire Commodore Nutt, offering his father up to $30,000 for a three-year contract, plus all expenses. Other newspapers picked up this account verbatim, and soon Barnum's new exhibit was going by the name the "$30,000 Nutt."[18]

Nutt, who was nearly fourteen years old, was, at twenty-nine inches, four inches taller than Tom Thumb had been when Barnum first met him, but over his years of success Tom had eventually grown taller and considerably more rotund. Nutt was what Barnum called "almost a *fac-simile* of General Tom Thumb as he looked half-a-dozen years before." So much so that many people suspected Barnum of simply renaming Tom in order to create a new sensation. Eventually Barnum would allay most of these suspicions by bringing the two little men together on stage, but in the meantime he gave the Commodore the Tom Thumb treatment, creating costumes for him and constructing a carriage driven by Nutt's brother and attended by a footman, both in livery, and pulled by two Shetland ponies. But this time Barnum was inspired by his new star's surname to have the cab of the coach built in the shape of an English walnut, which would open on hinges, exposing the young Nutt within.

After Barnum signed Tom Thumb for a month of appearances with Nutt, beginning on August 11, 1862, the crowds came as usual, but Barnum asserted that many people still believed Nutt to be the real Tom Thumb and the real Charley Stratton to be a fake — "no more like the General than he was like the man in the moon." Barnum found amusement in such people who "deceive themselves by being too incredulous." A month after their joint appearance at the American Museum ended, Barnum accompanied both men to Washington as part of what was billed as "Barnum's Museum, Circus, and Mammoth Amphitheatre," which also featured the established museum exhibits of an Albino family from Madagascar and twelve performing grizzly bears under the direction of Grizzly Adams, as well as equestrian performances. In the newspaper ads, Nutt got billing above Tom Thumb, even though, as Margaret Leech dryly notes in her famous book about the wartime capital, *Reveille in Washington,* "Tom Thumb was the most admired general in town."[19]

On the Sunday afternoon of October 19, the *Evening Star* reported, Barnum lectured on temperance for an hour on the grounds of the Capitol to "a large audience," urging "total abstinence upon his hearers in a most convincing style." Two days later, he and the Commodore called at the White House at the invitation of President Lincoln. When they arrived, they learned that the president was in a cabinet meeting but had asked to be interrupted when Barnum and Nutt showed up. The president "received us cordially, and introduced us to the members of the cabinet." After a bit of joshing with secretaries Salmon P. Chase and Edwin Stanton, Nutt was addressed by the president himself, who bent over to tell the little commodore that if he ever engaged the enemy with his fleet and was in danger of being captured, "I advise you to wade ashore." In a display of Thumbian wit, Nutt gave Lincoln's long legs the once over and said, "I guess, Mr. President, you could do that better than I could."[20]

Barnum remarked that this meeting took place during "dark days of the rebellion," and indeed they were. The sad slaughter of Antietam had happened only a month before, and Lincoln had visited his worrisomely confident but cautious commander, Gen. George McClellan, near the bloodied battle town of Sharpsburg earlier in October. While Barnum was in Washington, his former neighbor Mathew Brady was displaying images in his New York studio that his men had taken at Antietam, giving the public its first photographic view of the wages of war. Although it had not been much of a victory, Antietam was victory enough for Lincoln to have announced without seeming desperate his intention to sign an Emancipation Proclamation at the beginning of the new year.[21]

Still, with all his burdens, Lincoln always seemed ready to be amused, as were the members of his cabinet on this October day, and indeed in wartime Washington the public could find distraction in many more entertainments besides Barnum's traveling show.

The war news only got worse for Lincoln and the Union as the autumn wore on. The president fired General McClellan in early November for his unwillingness to press the advantage over Robert E. Lee after Antietam, and in December the new commander of the Army of the Potomac, Maj. Gen. Ambrose Burnside, oversaw the "butchery" of his Union troops at the disastrous first battle of Fredericksburg. He would be relieved of his command at the end of January 1863.

In the meantime, Barnum was making moves that would result in one of the great distractions of the war years, which the *New-York Observer* would call, tongue in cheek, "the event of the century, if not unparalleled in history."

Barnum learned in the fall of 1862 of a perfectly proportioned and charming female little person, and he hurried to engage her. Her name was Mercy Lavinia Warren Bump, and she was twenty years old, thirty-two inches tall, well educated, and plumply attractive enough that Barnum dubbed her the "Queen of Beauty." She had worked briefly as a schoolteacher in her hometown, but a cousin had lured her to perform as a singer and dancer, appearing alongside a giant on a riverboat plying the Mississippi and Ohio Rivers. Barnum put out the usual stories of her reluctance to be signed, even for a handsome sum, and of his full use of his persuasive powers in sealing a deal with her parents, themselves fourth cousins from a well-regarded family in Middleborough, Massachusetts.

In his autobiography, Barnum wrote that once he had her under contract he kept her out of sight at the house of one of his daughters in New York, while he had a "splendid wardrobe" made for her, including "scores of the richest dresses" and "costly jewels." Then he arranged for her introduction to the New York press at appearances at the St. Nicholas Hotel in late December, where she drew raves for her beauty and composure. By early January she was appearing at the museum, and "from the day of her début she was an extraordinary success." In an advertisement on January 13, Barnum claimed that a hundred thousand people had been to see her in her first week on display, during which she had worn a different new dress each day.[22]

Tom Thumb had given an interview to the *Bridgeport Standard* in October 1862, expressing his hope "one of these days to get married," and at the age of twenty-five and as a man of real means, he was a suitable match for Lavinia. Barnum devoted many pages of his 1869 autobiography to the courtship that came to pass between Tom, who supposedly fell in love with the Queen of Beauty at first sight, and Lavinia, who supposedly had no interest in marriage and therefore had to be won over by the persistent general. The implication in this long telling was that the wooing was stately and dignified, although largely consisting, in Barnum's description, of Tom's showing off his wealth to her. But on January 13 those same newspaper ads announced the impending wedding. Barnum claimed that the wooing happened while Lavinia was appearing at the museum, where Tom first met her, after which he went straight to Barnum's office and declared, "I believe she was created on purpose to be my wife!" But Barnum mistakenly recorded that her levees at the museum had begun in the autumn; instead they had begun on January 5. He likely got this wrong on purpose to make the courtship seem longer than it was, because if it was as short as seems evident — possibly less than two weeks — it would tend to support the suspicion that Barnum had arranged the marriage, a suspicion he raised and denied in the autobiography. His protracted tale of the courtship was also meant to absolve him of these charges and prove that the marriage was a love match. In the end, the marriage would prove to be sturdier and happier than many, even if Barnum had indeed been rushing it along.[23]

The great event was set for February 10, after which, Barnum claimed in his ads, Lavinia would retire to the country house of her wealthy new husband, so if the public wanted to see her at all, they had better do it quickly. Barnum recalled, "Lavinia's levees at the Museum were crowded to suffocation, and her photographic pictures were in great demand." Sales of cartes-de-visite images of the Queen of Beauty amounted to $300 a day, and Barnum was taking in more than ten times that much each day at the ticket office. To further promote the "fairy wedding," as Barnum began to call it, he displayed Lavinia's wedding dress in a store window on Fifth Avenue, and he had photographs made by Mathew Brady of the bride and groom in their wedding outfits. Bishop Horatio Potter of the Episcopal Diocese of New York first agreed to officiate, and named Trinity Church across from Barnum's museum as the venue, but the rector of that church said no, and at the last minute the bishop himself announced that "too much publicity [had been] given to the affair," and backed out. So the setting was changed to the Gothic, James Renwick–designed Grace Church up Broadway across from Brady's new studio, and Tom Thumb's own minister, Rev. Junius Willey from Bridgeport, did the honors.[24]

On the spring-like day of the great event, carriages began to arrive at the church at 11 a.m., having passed through streets crowded with onlookers and closed to other traffic between Ninth and Twelfth Streets on Broadway, which was lined on both sides with policemen. As the organ pumped out the overtures to *William Tell* and *Oberon,* the *Tannhäuser* grand march, and more, into the church filed governors and congressmen and the wives of John Jacob Astor III, William Henry Vanderbilt, and the warring newspapermen Bennett and Greeley. Perhaps the most surprising guest in the glittering crowd was, among a number of generals in attendance, Burnside, who had only days before been cashiered by President Lincoln. "The gallant soldier looked well and hearty," the front-page story in the *New-York Times* reported the next day, "and received the evident regard of the audience with ease and dignity." One wonders what his reception might have been had he not foolishly sacrificed the lives of thousands of Union soldiers at Fredericksburg only two months earlier.

But this was a day of celebration, and at last Barnum could be seen making his way up the center aisle to a seat at the front of the church, along with the families of the betrothed, soon followed by Commodore Nutt and Minnie Warren, who was Lavinia's sister and also a dwarf, and then the "Loving Lilliputians," as the *Times* labeled them. As the bride and groom passed by, the *Times* unkindly reported, "A sense of the ludicrous seemed to hit many a bump of fun and [an] irrepressible and unpleasantly audible giggle ran through the church." But once the service began, the crowded church pews and the ceremony proceeded with appropriate dignity. For once, Tom Thumb did not play an audience for laughs but said his vows clearly and reverently. After Lavinia spoke her own vows with her usual composure, and the Rev. Thomas House Taylor, rector of Grace Church, dispensed the benediction, "the General honestly kissed his wife," the *Times* wrote. That *honestly* was perhaps a reference to the "many millions" of kisses he had sold over the years.

Down the aisle the two strode to the sounds of Mendelssohn's Wedding March, and out again into the "breath-expurgating, crinoline-crushing, bunion-pinching mass of conglomerated humanity," held back by a double row of policeman bordering a tapestry that had been laid down the steps of the church and out to the waiting carriage. More policemen helped the nuptial vessel move out of the clamorous crowd surrounding the church and down Broadway. Hundreds of people ran after the carriage, and the sidewalks and overlooking windows were crowded for the whole ten blocks until the party reached the site of the reception, the elegant Metropolitan Hotel at the corner of Broadway and Prince Street, beside Niblo's Garden.

Although Barnum had paid for the wedding, he had somehow resisted selling tickets to the church service itself, even though as much as $60 had been offered for a pew seat. The same could not be said of the reception, where tickets were priced at $75, and even so, Barnum said, several thousand people paid up and twice as many who wanted to buy tickets were turned away. On arriving at the hotel, the newlyweds went up to their room, where Lavinia changed from her wedding gown to an ornate taffeta reception dress, both of which Barnum had paid for. When the happy couple returned to the reception, they were hoisted onto a grand piano, where they could greet the members of the throng and be seen by them. Soon Nutt and Minnie were lifted alongside, and the four were as much on display as the many wedding gifts in one of the hotel parlors, some of which, including jewelry and silver, were locked in glass cases to protect them from sticky fingers.

A wedding cake weighing eighty pounds, atop which stood a sugary Egyptian temple, had been confected for the reception, and more than two thousand guests went home with a small box containing a piece of it. After two hours the newlyweds retired to their room and the guests dispersed. Later that evening the New-York Excelsior Band appeared outside the hotel, where some five hundred spectators soon joined them. After their serenade, Tom appeared on the balcony of his room to give a gracious little speech of thanks to the band and to everyone who had celebrated with him and his bride that day.

In the first few days after the wedding, they would visit Baltimore, Washington, and

Philadelphia. While in Washington, they were invited to a reception in their honor in the East Room of the White House, where President and Mrs. Lincoln hosted members of the cabinet, generals, senators, "and many other gentlemen of distinction," along with their families. When the president offered his congratulations to the pair, who had donned again the clothes in which they had been married, he took Lavinia's hand "as though it were a robin's egg, and he were afraid of breaking it." So remembered the journalist Grace Greenwood, who was present at the event. The president kidded Tom Thumb that he himself was now in the little general's shade, since Tom "was now the great center of attraction." When the president asked how he, "as a military man," would be conducting the war, Tom responded, "My opinion is that my friend Barnum would settle the whole affair in a month."[25]

A. H. Saxon suggests that "the wedding was," for the showman, "too great a coup to let the public ever forget it." Barnum had a pamphlet prepared that described the whole affair in detail, not omitting many of the newspaper accounts, and distributed it and highly profitable souvenir photographs wherever the four members of the bridal party appeared, which in the next decade was almost everywhere in the United States, England, and Europe and on a three-year world tour that included India, Asia, Australia, and the Middle East. Until 1867 Barnum would continue to be the primary sponsor of the Tom Thumb wedding tour, but then Tom started his own company and, now only a shareholder, Barnum saw his profits shrink considerably. Barnum knew that Tom didn't need him anymore, since he had his own very competent manager, and later Barnum would write to Tom and Lavinia to thank them for "friendship and fidelity to me," admitting, "You could easily have thrown the old man overboard long ago."[26]

FIFTEEN: FIRE!

After Lincoln's reelection on November 8, 1864, as Gen. William Tecumseh Sherman's incendiary march through Georgia to the sea was under way, the Confederate government in Richmond, working with operatives in Canada, hatched a plot to send dozens of agents into New York to set the city ablaze in retribution. Richmond had appropriated $20,000 to support this quixotic effort. The hope was that the many Copperheads in the city (where the vote had gone two to one against Lincoln) would rise up from the ashes in general rebellion and unite New York with the Confederate cause.

The agents, who were equipped with black leather valises containing turpentine and bottles of phosphorus, checked into at least thirteen of the city's most prominent hotels with the intention of dousing their rooms in the turpentine and uncorking the combustible phosphorus. They also set fires, or tried to, on docks along the Hudson, and in lumberyards and other places of business, including Niblo's Garden, the Winter Garden, and Barnum's American Museum. The fires, set on November 24 and 25, mostly failed to catch, and those that did caused only minor damage rather than the general conflagration the Rebels hoped for. The fire at Barnum's was started at 9 p.m. on November 25 on the main building's fifth floor, while a performance was under way in the Lecture Hall below. The flames were soon put out, but not before a cry of "Fire!" led to the chaotic emptying of the theater, with some people sliding down iron pillars supporting the balconies. Thanks to the quick and calm response of museum employees, however, no injuries and only a few torn dresses resulted. Barnum's response was to create and display a wax figure of the captured Rebel arsonist Robert Cobb Kennedy, who would be executed the following spring for his role in the citywide attack.[1]

The fire, the panic, and the calm response of Barnum's staff presaged a much more catastrophic event at the museum eight months later, and Barnum's eagerness to put the museum's waxworks in action again might have been a contributing factor. The spring of 1865 was among the most momentous seasons in the history of the nation, with General Lee's surrender at Appomattox Court House on April 9, the assassination of President Lincoln on April 14, and the capture of Jefferson Davis, president of the Confederacy, in Georgia on May 10. Northern newspapers and many cartoons reported falsely that Davis had been caught wearing his wife's petticoats. Barnum capitalized on the patriotic zeal of the press by creating a wax figure he called "The Belle of Richmond," depicting Davis in a bonnet and a plaid dress. Barnum was soon running newspaper advertisements announcing that "JEFF. DAVIS IN PETTICOATS" was at the museum. But the Belle's run would not be a long one. Less than two months later, soon after noon on July 13, fire broke out somewhere in the bowels of the museum, and within half an hour "forked tongues of flames were darting through every window, wreathing the painted medallions outside with chaplets of fire, and sweeping away at a single touch the veracious canvas representations of the whales, giantesses and alligators within."[2]

As Barnum's employees tried to save some of the museum's purported million objects, and as visitors made off with them as keepsakes, a large crowd gathered on Broadway and the other streets around the museum, so densely packed that when the first of what would be thirty fire companies arrived at the scene, it caused "some severe accidents." The police tried to push the crowd back, but when one of the steam-powered fire engines let off a blast that sounded like an elephant's trumpet, panic flared among those still thronging the streets and people were trampled. Despite the chaos, nobody was killed.

The dusty museum itself, so crowded with objects, was a vast tinderbox, and soon the flames were leaping high into the sky. Every person inside escaped, some by making heroic leaps onto balconies and from there to the ground; one facetious report suggested that the giantess Anna Swan had to be hoisted down from a third-story window that was enlarged on the spot to get her through. The trained seal named Ned made its way out of the museum and through the crowd before it was safely captured. One bear supposedly climbed down a ladder to the ground, and some of Barnum's rare birds were set free to fly away. But most of the animals in the large menagerie were not saved. Two recently arrived whales from Labrador, which were being exhibited on the second floor in a tank twenty-five feet in diameter, were sacrificed when firemen broke the tank's glass walls so that the tons of Croton Reservoir water within might douse the fire below. The crowd outside could hear the pitiable sounds the whales made as they burned to death; monkeys, tigers, alligators, a kangaroo, and numberless other exotic animals perished in their cages, and some of the huge snakes that escaped their glass box were said to be seen slithering down stairways before they died.

Newspapers reported that the crowds in the streets were more amused than horrified by the whole scene, eager to get free glimpses of Barnum's albinos and other human curiosities as they escaped through the crowd. Spectators hollered out what passed for witticisms about the many animals, as well as objects of real value, that were being lost in front of them. Before the smoke and fire grew too dangerous, some objects were tossed from the windows to the streets below. Although most of Barnum's many wax figures simply melted into fuel for the fire, the figure of Jefferson Davis did sail out a window, its petticoats exposed to the crowd, where it (or perhaps just its head, as one report had it), was hanged from a lamppost on Fulton Street, beside St. Paul's Church. The crowd made merry reference to a line in the famous Union marching song "John Brown's Body," which spoke of hanging "Jeff Davis from a sour apple tree."

Soon the roof collapsed, and the inside of the building was likened to the crater of an active volcano. Then, according to a report the next day in the *New-York Times:*

> At 1:30 came a crash resounding like the explosion of a powder magazine. The whole wall on the Ann-street side had fallen. A cloud of dust and smoke filled the air, making it dark as twilight, and rendering it impossible to descry objects at short distance.
>
> At 1:45 o'clock the Broadway front of the Museum fell in three different sections, one after the other. . . .
>
> Another section was left in the shape of an elongated triangle, and not unlike the steeple of a church. In a few moments this sunk slowly down, the point still remaining upright and in position until the whole section disappeared.[3]

Barnum had not been in the city at the time of the fire and had heard about it through Samuel Hurd, his daughter Helen's husband, who was now the assistant manager of the museum and who had been at his office on the second floor as it began. When the fire reached a point of no return, Hurd pulled several thousand dollars from his desk and, along with account books, added them to the "many thousand dollars" in Barnum's safe, which was recovered after the fire, its contents spared. Upon escaping the building, Hurd telegrammed Barnum, who was giving a speech to the Connecticut legislature in Hartford, apprising him that the museum was engulfed and likely to be a total loss. Barnum wrote in his 1869 autobiography what newspaper reports at the time also said, that he read the telegram calmly, folded it up on his desk, and finished his speech — "in the coolest manner possible," as even the Barnum-despising *Herald* put it. That night he returned to Bridgeport, spent the evening with his family, and waited until the next morning to go to New York. He checked in at the Astor House, which, unlike a number of other buildings in the neighborhood of the museum, had not been damaged by the fire.[4]

Barnum held court in the hotel that morning, visited by sympathetic friends while offering a brave face to members of the press. In this gathering, the *Herald* wrote, "Mr. Barnum was the most buoyant of all. Instead of alluding to or mourning over his loss, he spoke of nothing but the prospectus for his new museum. This, he asserts, will surpass anything of the sort ever attempted." Barnum vowed to move farther uptown and to construct a building that "will astonish the world." His new menagerie would be triple the size of the one whose bones and ashes smoldered just across the street, and he would build a collection of curiosities unlike any "on this continent or any other." Later that day he set up in the office of his other son-in-law, David Thompson, at 35 Chambers Street, where he issued a notice to the public promising to have a new museum in six months and to find a theater within a few days so that at least some of his performers and exhibitors could get back to work. Many of his anxious employees visited him that day; Barnum said the fire made 150 people temporarily jobless, and the *Herald* ran an item listing some sixty of them by name and job, including his longest-serving employee, the naturalist Emile Guillaudeu, who had been working for the museum and its predecessors since 1810. A theatrical benefit would soon be arranged for them at the Academy of Music — possibly Barnum's idea, since the *Herald* printed this suggestion the next day in the midst of its reporting about the showman.[5]

Barnum demonstrated admirable energy, optimism, and concern for his workers, and his surefooted handling of the public-relations aspect of the disaster is astonishing if unnervingly cool-headed. He knew to act immediately, taking control of the situation, thanking his many customers and promoting the new museum he would create, while also skillfully taking advantage of the eager interest of the press in covering a disaster and its aftermath and availing himself of the natural sympathy that would flow his way after so great a calamity.

Neither the cause of the fire nor where it started has ever been definitively proven. Barnum placed its origins in a boiler room; the *New-York Times* put it in an adjacent building's basement furnace; Samuel Hurd said it was under a staircase; the museum treasurer, H. O. Tiffany, said it originated in three different places at once, suggesting deliberate sabotage. Was the cause mechanical or arson? Southern arsonists had already attacked the museum once, and rumors that it might be attacked again would only have been fueled by the prominence of the exhibit of Jefferson Davis in petticoats. If that wax figure was the cause, it was the most expensive exhibit Barnum ever mounted.[6]

■ ■ ■ ■

As the end of the war drew near, Barnum's growing political consciousness and ever-present industriousness took him in an unlikely direction. He decided to run for political office. His distaste for his Copperhead neighbors in New York and Connecticut had grown as the war proceeded, and his now strong belief in abolition led him to agree to run as a Republican or Union candidate from the town of Fairfield for the Connecticut legislature. "I did this," he wrote in his autobiography, "because I felt that it would be an honor to be permitted to vote for the then proposed amendment to the Constitution of the United States to abolish slavery forever from the land." He was successfully elected in April 1865, and he immediately got to work.

Connecticut's General Assembly quickly and unanimously voted to ratify the Thirteenth Amendment to the U.S. Constitution, making Barnum's wish come true two days after he took office on May 2. But an amendment to the state's own constitution proposing to drop the word *white* from the qualifications to vote "was violently opposed by the Democratic members," Barnum wrote. On May 26, 1865, the freshman legislator from Fairfield rose in favor of the amendment. He spoke passionately, not holding back his partisan potshots, and ruminated on how a party calling itself *Democratic* could be so opposed to democracy. He was proud of the speech, devoting thirteen pages of his autobiography to quoting what even at that length was only a summary of it, because, as he explained in a letter three days later, "the opposition interrupted me and put me on my mettle, & I gave them an hour and a half without tiring anybody."[7]

In the speech, which was widely quoted and praised in the newspapers, Barnum energetically moved to fulfill the obligations for which so many Union troops had died. He attempted to rise above the racism of his time, asserting that in his travels through the South he had observed "that the slaves, as a body, are more intelligent than the poor whites." He left little doubt in the minds of his listeners that his commitment to enfranchise black people living in Connecticut was unflinching and unwavering. More meaningfully, the speech served its purpose in the legislature, and the amendment passed. Nonetheless, when it was put before a state referendum in the fall, it failed by about five thousand votes. Black citizens in Connecticut would get the vote only with the passage of the Fifteenth Amendment to the U.S. Constitution in 1870, and the word *white* would not be removed from the state constitution until 1876.[8]

In the General Assembly, Barnum chaired both the agriculture and the state house committees, and he led a fight against railroad interests in the state government. He worried that the New York and New Haven Railroad, which served his part of the state, would use its monopoly status and political clout to hike prices for Connecticut commuters, as had been done with other commuter lines into New York. The railroad lobby, however, was already so deeply lodged in the legislature that Barnum and his allies fought them day in and day out on many fronts. Despite his lasting reputation as a cynic, his anger over the way the railroad could buy legislators was undoubtedly genuine, as was his interest in protecting voters and extending the right to vote in the state.

Indeed, the speech he was giving when he received the terrible telegram about the museum fire was in favor of a measure regulating how the railroads could increase commuter fares; that bill "was carried almost with a 'hurrah' " by the state house. Barnum later noted with satisfaction that the measure "annually adds many dollars to the assessment roll of Connecticut," since a large number of new citizens bought land along the railroad as a result. Barnum ran for the legislature again the next spring, mainly, he asserted, because a director of the New York and New Haven Railroad had vowed that he would not be elected again. Yet he prevailed, and served a second term as a representative for Fairfield. It was less eventful than the first, but Barnum acknowledged that it "was very agreeable" to him.[9]

In 1867, for the third spring in a row, his party asked him to run for office, this time for the U.S. Congress in a district including Fairfield and Litchfield counties. His Democratic opponent turned out to be a rich industrialist and a distant cousin, William H. Barnum, who would go on to have a long career in Democratic politics, even serving as a U.S. senator from Connecticut.[10]

The battle of the Barnums was hard fought and not particularly clean. P.T. made use of his contacts in the Bridgeport and New York press to publicize an anonymous letter from a potential constituent in Litchfield alleging that William H. was planning to spend $50,000 to buy votes in the election and challenging P.T. to "fight fire with fire." Despite the letter's anonymity, and therefore the possibility that P.T. or a supporter had written it, papers published both it and P.T.'s high-minded reply, to which he primly appended the Connecticut statute forbidding the bribery of voters.

Now that he was operating on a larger stage than in his previous campaigns, he ran into objections based on his long career as a purveyor of humbugs. *The Nation,* not a Democratic organ, published a long rant in the middle of the campaign bemoaning what it saw as a postwar failure to count character as the most important trait of political leaders, and used Barnum as the current example. Although the magazine's writer praised him for his antislavery and pro-Union positions as well as his defense of "sobriety and good order" — allowing "that he has public spirit and is a good neighbor" (faint praise, that) — he wrote that none of this atoned for Barnum's "having been for twenty or thirty years a depraving and demoralizing influence." It was the old argument about Barnum, that he was a humbug and that he not only felt unashamed of his behavior, but even reveled in it and the riches it brought him. The heart of their charge against him, finally, had to do with his "vulgarity."[11]

A less somber and self-satisfied attack came on March 5 from Mark Twain, then thirty-one and recently returned from the West, imagining in the pages of a New York newspaper "Barnum's First Speech in Congress," which Twain was able to obtain, the conceit went, by "Spiritual Telegraph." The introduction to the speech predicted that Barnum "will find the House of Representatives a most excellent advertising medium" and suggested that "he can dovetail business and patriotism together to the mutual benefit of himself and the Great Republic." In the imaginary speech itself, Representative Barnum managed to go on at length about all the attractions of his museum, not failing to mention (twice) that peanuts were for sale throughout the building, and calling for the impeachment of "the dread boss monkey" — that would be President Andrew Johnson — and the restoration of "the Happy Family of the Union." Twain's effort in an evening paper in New York probably had no impact on voters in Connecticut, but the eventual outcome of the race did call into question the efficacy of the Spiritual Telegraph.[12]

On April 1, Connecticut voters went for

Democratic candidates across the state, reacting in part against issues such as the one Barnum had backed in the legislature proposing black suffrage. The state's Republican governor, Joseph Roswell Hawley, who had risen to the rank of brigadier general during the Civil War, was himself defeated that day. Hawley blamed the nomination of Phineas T. Barnum as the Connecticut Republican Party's "great blunder," but he still defended Barnum as "a better man than many out of the state suppose. He is one of those fellows who have double characters, one professional & scoundrelly, the other private, church-going, decorous, and utterly abstinent from pocket-picking. . . . But he was a burden."[13]

Barnum lost handily to his distant cousin, but worse than the loss, as he wrote, was the contest itself: "The filth and scandal, the slanders and vindictiveness, the plottings and fawnings, the fidelity, treachery, meanness, and manliness, which by turns exhibited themselves in the exciting scenes preceding the election, were novel to me." He did not have what it took to "make a lithe and oily politician" and had not chosen in the campaign "to shake hands with those whom I despised, and to kiss the dirty babies of those whose votes were courted."

Still, this would not be his last foray into elective politics.[14]

Mark Twain was able to imagine Barnum puffing his museum in Congress because, as he promised the public, Barnum had opened a second museum within weeks after the first one burned. Nine days after the fire, two shows benefiting his employees played at the Academy of Music, where everyone involved, from the performers and musicians to the carpenters and machinists, donated their time to the cause. Barnum spoke at both showings, announcing that some of his artists would be appearing very soon at the Winter Garden on Broadway at Bond Street and that he was refurbishing the site of the old Chinese Museum, up Broadway between Spring and Prince Streets, to open a new but temporary museum. As the *Herald* reported about his appearances at the Academy, "Barnum was greeted with much applause during the delivery of his remarks, which he interlarded with characteristic anecdotes and the development of a philosophy strictly of the Barnum school." For example, he told the packed houses that he believed the fire had been sent by Providence to rid his name and that of his museum of the stench of humbug.[15]

One week later, on July 28, 1865, his Winter Garden show opened, featuring an orchestra, the presentation by his mimes of a theatrical called "The Green Monster," and a family of trapeze artists performing "Astounding Aerial Flights" — all twice daily. By September 5 the new museum was ready for a preview for the press and important friends. As Barnum and Samuel Hurd took their guests through the newly arranged space, the visitors saw that it was bigger than the old museum, divided into "five roomy saloons and a theatre or a lecture room" on four floors taking up the entire block. Besides featuring a few wax figures saved from the fire, and Ned the Learned Seal ("which by the way has grown considerably since his rescue," the *Sun* observed), Barnum's New Museum offered a new and larger "Happy Family," an aquarium, model steam engines, a glass-blowing shop, a shooting gallery, new cosmorama pictures and stereoscopes, and a reported 100,000 new curiosities, stuffed fauna, and minerals. Barnum also returned with a wide array of "human curiosities," touting a Cherokee Indian with no arms, Anna Swan and other giants, a woman weighing 660 pounds, and the Circassian beauties. Most remarkable, perhaps, was that Barnum had in so short a time constructed a new Lecture Room, with a stage fifty feet wide, red velvet seats and benches to accommodate 2,500 customers, and a huge drop curtain featuring painted images of Barnum and Jenny Lind flanking a representation of the old museum and the words, "It still lives, and rises Phoenix like from the ashes." Although Barnum's architect-builder admitted that there was still much to do, the museum opened for business the next morning.[16]

Barnum's ability to sink so much money into the new museum after losing so much in the severely underinsured old one was owed partly to his longtime nemesis, James Gordon Bennett of the *Herald*. Bennett wanted to construct a new building for the newspaper on the old American Museum land and paid Barnum $200,000 for the eleven years left in his lease. Bennett then decided to buy the land itself, but somehow when his agents came up with an offer, they neglected to subtract the $200,000 for the lease, so when Bennett sealed the deal, he in effect leased the building at the same time he was buying it. Bennett tried to wriggle out of the purchase and had his lawyer send for Barnum to inform him that he wanted his lease money back. To which Barnum memorably replied, "Nonsense, I shall do nothing of the sort, I don't make child's bargains." Bennett would eventually lose a suit by the owner of the land compelling him to pay the $500,000 he had agreed in writing to spend on the property. The day after Barnum's meeting with Bennett's lawyer, an ad for his Winter Garden show failed to run as scheduled in the *Herald*. Hustling over to the newspaper's office to find out why, Barnum was told that the *Herald* would no longer accept his advertising. Even this, though, Barnum parried. He quickly called a meeting of an association of New York theater managers, with the result that they all agreed to stop advertising in the *Herald* and to stop using the newspaper's facilities for printing playbills, a lucrative add-on that Bennett had insisted upon as a condition of running their ads. For the next two years, all the principal theaters in New York headed all their ads in the other New York papers with the words, "This Establishment does not Advertise in the New York 'Herald.' " At the end of the two years, the theater managers felt they had made their point and began to advertise with Bennett again. All of them, that is, except Barnum.[17]

Soon after the new museum opened,

Barnum went into business with a lion tamer, animal trainer, and menagerie owner named Isaac Van Amburgh, who had been established in the Broadway building that Barnum had rehabbed, exhibiting his menagerie there when not touring. Thus the seal Ned was joined by an African elephant, the country's only giraffe, lions and tigers, and "every description of wild animal." Under the new arrangement, the menagerie would continue to travel in the warm months and be on exhibit in the museum in the cold months. The Barnum and Van Amburgh Museum and Menagerie Company also bought thirty acres of land in Bridgeport, suitable for breeding and training animals for exhibition. Part of the deal in creating the new company was that Barnum would now be the museum's general manager in name only and could spend more time at home or traveling, visiting the museum only once a week when he was nearby.

He soon signed on for a lecture tour in the Midwest (then called the West), giving a talk called "Success, or the Art of Money-Getting," while also continuing his long habit of lecturing on temperance. During this time, he worked on an ambitious plan to start a free national museum and managed to enlist in the effort a number of prominent men, including the president himself. Andrew Johnson signed a proclamation urging "our Ministers, Consuls, and commercial agents" to assist Barnum in acquiring throughout the world exhibits for the new project. Following up in Washington, Barnum met with both the sitting president and a future one, Ulysses S. Grant, who gave him for exhibition a hat he had worn during the war.[18]

The summer following the congressional elections in April 1867, the Barnums sold Lindencroft, their large house in Fairfield, and moved for the season into a farmhouse on the shore of Long Island Sound, where the sea breezes were thought to be better for Charity's health. All three of Barnum's daughters now lived in New York City with their husbands, so that same summer he and Charity bought an impressive town house at the corner of Fifth Avenue and Thirty-Ninth Street, "at the crowning point of Murray Hill," to be close to his family for the seven colder months of the year. He and Charity moved into the house in November. In his 1869 autobiography, he sang the praises of city life for a man his age: "One loves to find the morning papers, fresh from the press, lying upon the

415

breakfast-table; and the city is the centre of attractions in the way of operas, concerts, picture-galleries, libraries, the best music, the best preaching, the best of everything in aesthetical enjoyments." In addition to these benefits, the Barnums were close enough to Central Park to "spend hours of every fine day in that great pleasure-ground."[19]

Having a mansion in town also made it possible to express the generosity he so often showed his friends. Two of them, a Universalist minister named George Emerson, who spent two nights a week with the Barnums for several years, and Greeley, the eminent if somewhat scatterbrained newspaper editor, were given keys to the house and an open invitation, such as this one from Charity to Emerson: "Come now as often as you can and stay as long as you can; only, remember, you are *not* company." Greeley sometimes did dwell with them for weeks on end, with Barnum often offering him such domestic comforts as slippers or a robe. Many other friends also enjoyed the hospitality of the household when they were in town. The Barnum dinner table might feature Tom Thumb and his troupe on one night and the latest fashionable author on another. Always, George Emerson reminisced about Barnum, "the incorrigible humorist at the head of the table, ready to gush at any time, seemed to have no power to keep the jokes back when knife and fork were at play."[20]

The preacher also recalled one of Barnum's many acts of charity, when he gave an organ to Emerson's church. Barnum urged his friend not to publicize the fact so that others who needed something would not besiege him. But Emerson noted that Barnum was routinely besieged anyway, his meals often interrupted by a solicitation at the door, so Barnum must simply have preferred not to take credit for this *unprofitable* act of philanthropy.

Other friends included the Reverends Edwin H. Chapin and Abel C. Thomas and a literary set he would see at the Sunday evening salon of the poets Alice and Phoebe Cary. There, on Twentieth Street, Barnum and Greeley might mingle with the latter's *Tribune* protégé Whitelaw Reid, the violinist Ole Bull, or the feminists Elizabeth Cady Stanton and Susan B. Anthony. The poet John Greenleaf Whittier also attended the soirees, but he and Barnum apparently never crossed paths. Phoebe Cary especially attracted Barnum for her spontaneous wit, and the two would sometimes go for carriage rides together in Central Park.

This life of urban leisure did not last untroubled for long. On the bitter cold, snowy morning of March 3, 1868, Barnum was enjoying those fresh-pressed newspapers at his breakfast table with Charity and Louise Thomas, the wife of Reverend Thomas, when he came upon an item on a late-closing page of the *Tribune* headlined, "Barnum's Museum Burned: The Building and Menagerie Totally Destroyed." He claims to have calmly read these words aloud to the two women, his tone so matter-of-fact that both took it as a joke. Only as he continued reading them the report, which said the fire had started at 12:30 that very morning, did Mrs. Thomas look over his shoulder to see that it was indeed true.[21]

If it seems odd that the newspaper should have reached him before anyone from his company did, consider that the fire had started in the throes of a huge snowstorm, the winds of which had pushed up large drifts in the streets, making public transportation problematic. The same drifts had allowed the fire to grow beyond containment. After the first alarm, it had taken the firemen half an hour to reach the museum, because they were fighting a blaze in a toy store on Spring Street. Although they sprayed the flames in the museum and then its ruins for hours, creating a picturesque "palace of ice" in the bitter cold, the fire could not be managed until it had done its worst. Barnum related that it started with "a defective flue in a restaurant in the basement of the building," Charles Swift's oyster saloon. The Circassian beauty Zalumma Agra, who, along with several others, slept in the building, had wakened from a restless sleep and looked out her window on Broadway to see flames pouring from a window on a floor below. Her cry of "Fire!" roused Anna Swan, who was already awake, listening to the stirrings from the menagerie, where the lions and a gray wolf had been exchanging growls and then howls. The reality of the second blaze then clicked into place, and all of the humans were able to escape the conflagration.[22]

Ned the Learned Seal was not so lucky. Although he died in the fire, more animals were saved than in the first blaze, including "one young elephant," a giraffe, three kangaroos, a leopard, two camels, three llamas, and a variety of smaller animals and birds. Once again many other animals were lost, including a number of monkeys and a tiger that managed to escape the building, frightening the many spectators watching even in the middle of the night, until "an intrepid policeman with revolver . . . fired shot after shot," killing it. In describing this fire, Barnum paused in his autobiography to express regret for the fate of the animals. "The loss was a large one, and the complete frustration of our plans for the future was a serious consideration. But worse than all were the sufferings of the poor wild animals which were burned to death in their cages."[23]

Barnum's immediate public response was noticeably different from that after the first fire. A brief notice sent to the *Tribune* reported that his company would not re-build the museum on the spot of its ruins and took the opportunity to announce that "the six lots on which the Museum stood are for sale" — seventy-five feet of street front on both Broadway and Mercer, the depth of the block being two hundred feet. He sold the lots in June for $432,000, which made a nice dent in his losses. Still, he estimated that both museum fires and the one at Iranistan had cost him more than a million dollars, and he decided now that his long museum-keeping career was at an end. George Emerson reported that the liveliest evening he ever spent at Barnum's table happened the day after the showman's second Broadway museum burned to the ground. Greeley had suggested to his friend after the first museum burned that he should "take this fire as a notice to quit, and go a-fishing." Now Barnum was ready to abide by that advice.[24]

SIXTEEN:
SHOW FEVER

In the weeks after the second museum fire, Barnum did find "a way open through which I could retire to a more quiet and tranquil mode of life." But what he would soon learn about himself was that retirement, even if it represented a slowing down from what had come before, was for him life lived at a more industrious pace than most people ever achieve. Once he had separated himself from the remains of the company that he and Van Amburgh had started, he did take part of the summer off. He could be found lolling in the White Mountains of New Hampshire or in a house he had built on speculation in Bridgeport, but even then he was not fully disconnected.

He was regularly corresponding with his friend George Wood in New York, who was starting a museum and theater in the Barnum mode at Broadway and Thirtieth Street. Wood induced Barnum to sign on as a close advisor and as someone who would not compete with him, sharing in 3 percent of the receipts for his involvement and for allowing Wood to advertise as Barnum's successor. Barnum liked the freedom from responsibility this arrangement would give him and the freedom to "go when and where I chose": "My mind especially would be employed in matters with which I was familiar, [and] I should not rust out. . . . The new museum would afford me a pleasant place to drop into when I felt inclined to do so."[1]

When at the end of August 1868 all was ready for Wood's museum to admit the public, its proprietor sent Barnum a telegram saying "he could not consider his list of curiosities complete unless I would consent to be present at the opening." Not only did Barnum eagerly leave his White Mountains vacation and hustle down to New York; he even gave the inaugural address before the first matinee performance at Wood's Museum and Metropolitan Theatre. The speech, which was printed in the next day's *Tribune,* praised Wood for his "remarkable degree of Yankee go-aheadativeness and reckless expenditure" in collecting curiosities from throughout the world, making ample use of Barnum's former agents. Barnum promised that he himself would often be available at Wood's museum "to greet my old friends and the public at large."[2]

Barnum had also continued to invest in real estate in Bridgeport and in that part of Fairfield near the Bridgeport line. Working with a small group of city fathers over a period of years, he had spearheaded the creation of Seaside Park. They had persuaded landowners along Long Island Sound to give or sell enough property to create a truly impressive public space, replete with a promenade along the shore, wide boulevards for walking and driving, a covered music stand, and new shade trees to augment those preserved on the land. A horse-drawn railway spur opened to serve the park, which soon became a favorite place for residents of Bridgeport and Fairfield to enjoy the views and catch the sea breezes. Barnum had himself purchased a thirty-acre farm and donated part of it to complete the sweep of park along the shore, and he later bought and donated several more acres to the western end of the park. The city recognized his role in the park's creation by asking him to name it. In the summer of 1868, he decided to build a new residence on the remaining acres of the farm, on a rise that would catch those breezes and look down to the water. Ground was broken and the first stone in the foundation placed in October 1868, and with the help of "a regiment of faithful laborers and mechanics, and a very considerable expenditure of money," the house was completed in eight months and ready for habitation for the 1869 summer season.[3]

Once again, Barnum hoped to build a house with all the modern conveniences for comfortable living, and he included a number of rooms for guests, each with its own dressing room and bathroom. In addition to the Victorian structure, featuring a large turret, wide porches, and a bakery's worth of gingerbread, there would be two guest cottages, one of which would shelter his eldest and youngest daughters and their families during the summers. Perhaps to satisfy the ailing Charity, who continued to be prescribed as much fresh air as possible, the kitchen was semidetached in order to keep cooking smells at bay, and the stable was situated across an avenue. Lawns stretched out in three directions from the house, which featured the usual plantings of mature trees, in addition to a "large and beautiful hickory grove" Barnum had recently purchased, and gardens, flower beds, walks, and drives.

The main house was called Waldemere, a nod to that hickory grove overlooking the sea, and the cottages were called Wavewood and Petrel's Nest. All three structures shared a view, owing to Barnum's profitable philanthropy, of the happy pleasure ground of Seaside Park and the Sound beyond. His farm on the outskirts of Bridgeport, which he had owned for many years, had been the scene of a famous joke of his, putting an elephant to work plowing and replowing the same patch of ground each time a passenger train went by on a track adjacent to his fields, implying the unlikely notion that elephants made a good substitute for mules. Now this farm, minus its pachyderm, kept his "table constantly supplied with fresh fruits and vegetables, poultry, and that choicest of country luxuries, pure cream." Barnum would live at Waldemere for two decades, enlarging and prettifying it from time to time. During those years many friends passed through his rooms. Mark Twain, who would become a friendly acquaintance if not quite a friend, and his wife would visit from nearby Hartford, and Horace Greeley would stay at Waldemere so often that one of the bedrooms was named for him.[4]

As his new house was being built — and as he was lecturing on either business success or temperance, consulting with Wood's Museum, overseeing his real-estate investments, and tending to his wide circle of friends — Barnum also began rewriting and significantly expanding his autobiography. The decade and a half since *The Life of P. T. Barnum* had appeared provided him with a second lifetime's worth of new anecdotes and cracker-barrel philosophizing. His narrative of this part of his life followed the sine curve of his fall from riches to bankruptcy and back to financial success, with the three major fires and his recovery from them part of the pattern. The new book's title would reflect the cyclical nature of these years: he called it *Struggles and Triumphs.* The revision and expansion, however, did not go at the breakneck pace that had produced the first autobiography.

In late May 1868 he wrote to his friend George Emerson, "My *life* is dragging slowly so far as writing it is concerned." Almost exactly a year later he would write to Whitelaw Reid that he was hoping to finish the book during the first part of the summer and wanted his help getting the manuscript ready for publication. Would Reid come to Waldemere for at least a week in July "to see what is needful to be done & what it is worth"? A well-known Civil War reporter and author who went to work for Greeley in 1868, Reid would take over the *Tribune* after Greeley's death and run it until his own death many years later.[5]

Struggles and Triumphs or Forty Years' Reflections of P. T. Barnum appeared in the fall of 1869. At nearly eight hundred pages, and including thirty-three engravings, it was almost exactly twice as long as the earlier edition. It would be sold through subscription agents hired by his Hartford publisher J. B. Burr. The reviews included one in the *Sun,* which called the book "interesting and conceited," citing as an example of the latter quality Barnum's quoting Thackeray saying, "MR. BARNUM, I admire you more than ever!" At the other extreme was the *Bellows Falls Times* of Vermont:

> Barnum's style is racy. He knows how to "point a period," and tells a story inimitably. The lovers of fun will be delighted by the accessions which this work brings to their stock of humor; and they who care only for facts and practical good sense, will be equally grateful to Barnum for his autobiography.[6]

Perhaps because the book was not entirely new, it got far fewer reviews than the 1855 edition, and perhaps because some of the more indefensible episodes from the early part of his career had been softened, there were fewer expressions of shock that Barnum shamelessly owned up to his humbugs and the profits he made from them. The parts of the book that were entirely new were devoted more to sharing the wisdom he had acquired as a businessman and less to his pursuit of humbuggery.

In truth, he had lately been more attentive to the exposure of humbugs than to the creation of them, having written articles on the subject for the *New York Weekly Mercury* that were gathered into a book called *The Humbugs of the World: An Account of Humbugs, Delusions, Impositions, Quackeries, Deceits and Deceivers Generally, in All Ages,* which had been published in late 1865. The subjects ranged from personal anecdotes to historical sketches. A well-polished example of the former described Grizzly Adams's last days, when Barnum agreed to loan him an expensive new beaver-skin outfit he had had made, to be returned, Adams promised, when he was done with it. When Adams had himself buried in it, he took both the suit and the satisfaction of having humbugged

Barnum to the grave. Historical chapters considered such episodes as the Dutch tulip mania and the more recent Moon Hoax. Barnum took special interest in spiritual hoaxes such as spirit-photos that pretended to show the ghosts of the dead in the background of photos of the living.

Barnum had promised in his first autobiography to expose humbugs, and in a brief introduction to *The Humbugs of the World* he professed his wish to educate the rising generation so that they could not be tricked or swindled. But his chief incentive was almost certainly to prove that humbuggery existed on a scale ranging from harmless to dangerous, and that his own humbugs had been meant simply to entertain at a very modest price and had harmed nobody. In this book, he offered his own definition of humbug, "as generally understood": "putting on glittering appearances — outside show — novel expedients, by which to suddenly arrest public attention, and attract the public eye and ear." By this definition, most of the subjects he wrote about in the book were *not* humbugs, but never mind. If Barnum was to retain his self-imposed title of "Prince of Humbugs," then he must alter the definition to suit his royal self.[7]

At the same time that *Struggles and Tri-*

umphs was coming out, Barnum engaged in what could be viewed as his last great humbug, or perhaps as his final commentary on humbuggery — or even as a metahumbug. Back in 1854, in a speech titled "The Philosophy of Humbug," he had told the story of how he had once commissioned an eighteen-foot skeleton to be constructed out of old bones, with the intention of burying it and digging it up later as an archaeological find. But by the time it was completed, he had become so deeply involved with Tom Thumb that he didn't have time to carry out the hoax, so he had the skeleton sold. Later, his story goes, someone offered to sell it back to him for $20,000, not realizing that Barnum had been its originator.[8]

Now, in 1869, a very familiar-sounding scheme had entered the news via a man named George Hull. A cigar-maker from Binghamton, New York, Hull had stealthily carved in gypsum the ten-foot-tall likeness of a man, which was then "distressed" to look old and buried in a vegetable garden near Cardiff, New York. A year later he dug it back up and declared it to be a petrified giant. Public interest in the "discovery," now dubbed the Cardiff Giant, was so great that Hull was able to sell the thing for $23,000 to a group of businessmen, who then began pulling in crowds while exhibiting it in Syracuse.

The whole scheme caught Barnum's interest, and he offered the owners $50,000 for the right to show the Cardiff Giant himself in New York City, with a $5,000 bonus if they could prove its authenticity. When the men balked, Barnum felt sure he had detected a humbug. In response, in true Barnum style, he had a small model of the giant made to show George Wood, and he suggested that Wood create and display in his museum a full-size replica in plaster, which Wood eagerly did.

When the owners of the original humbug got wind of the replica, they went to court to try to enjoin Wood from exhibiting his forgery of their giant. However, the judge expressed his doubts that the original was really a petrified man — what harm is a fake of a fake, after all? — and he agreed to order an injunction only if the Cardiff Giant himself would testify. Before long, Wood was exhibiting two replicas, and Cardiff Giants were proliferating elsewhere.[9]

Mark Twain could not resist the ridiculousness of the situation, writing in a sketch he called "A Ghost Story" how, one night as he was staying in a Broadway hotel, the ghost of the Cardiff Giant came to his room, saying he had been haunting the museum across the street because he was unable to get rest until his petrified body was reburied. To which Twain told the ghost that he was haunting the fake, and the real thing was now on display in Albany. "Confound it," the Twain character says, "don't you know your own remains?" The ghost admits to feeling like an ass and begs Twain not to let anyone know of his being taken in by the hoax.[10]

Once *Struggles and Triumphs* was written, Barnum began to chafe against retirement. He wrote, "Sometimes like the truant schoolboy I found all my friends engaged, and I had no playmate. I began to fill my house with visitors, and yet frequently we spent evenings quite alone. Without really perceiving what the matter was, time hung on my hands."

A friend from England solved his problem by visiting with his older daughter, determined to see the sights in America. John Fish, a wealthy cotton-mill owner from Bury, near Manchester, attributed his success in business to having read and followed Barnum's nostrums in the first autobiography. They had met in Manchester in 1858, when Fish introduced himself after one of

Barnum's lectures, and his professed admiration for the showman had begun their friendship. Once in the years since, Barnum had asked Fish to go to Paris to investigate a (living) giant said to be eight feet tall by the straightforward method of actually measuring him. At another time, Fish and his family had played host to Tom Thumb and his entourage when they were exhibiting in his town.

Now, in 1869, Barnum found himself "just in the humor to act as guide and exhibitor." Leaving Charity at home, he set off with Fish and his daughter Jane Ann to visit Niagara Falls by railroad. As they enjoyed the passing landscape, Barnum realized, "The contagion of their enthusiasm opened my eyes to marvels in spectacles which I had long dismissed as commonplace." After returning to New York, Barnum felt the itch to roam again, and he set off with the Fishes in January 1870 to Cuba, followed by New Orleans, then up the Mississippi to Memphis and back to the East, where they visited President Grant at the White House.[11]

Barnum enjoyed the company of his English friends so much that by April 1870 he had arranged a more audacious trip for them and a few others: to California by

Pullman car, stopping in Salt Lake City. There Barnum lectured to an audience that included "a dozen or so of Brigham Young's wives and scores of his children." During a visit afterward at Young's home, the two men joked about the possibility of the showman putting the prophet on display in New York. After giving his account of this meeting, Barnum hoped "Brigham" would have a new revelation reversing his position on plural marriage.

When Barnum's party reached California, spending a week in the San Francisco area, his "show fever began to rise." Visiting Seal Rock, just off the Pacific shore of San Francisco, he had the notion of shipping ten sea lions to New York, where he could exhibit them in a pen in the East River off Manhattan's Upper East Side. He also learned of a new little person named Leopold Kahn, smaller than Charley Stratton had been when Barnum first met him and "so handsome, well-formed, and captivating that I could not resist the temptation to engage him." He immediately christened the boy Admiral Dot and had an admiral's uniform made for him so that he could be introduced in it to the local press. Admiral Dot went on exhibition for three successful weeks in California before going to Wood's

Museum in New York. The country had an absence of little show people at that time, since Barnum had helped send the members of the Tom Thumb wedding party on their three-year world tour.

On their way back east, Barnum's party spent two weeks in Yosemite, having paused to see the giant sequoias at Mariposa and send Wood a thirty-one-inch-thick chunk of sequoia bark to put on display. They also stopped in Denver, where Barnum gave more lectures and made his first visit to the newly formed intentional community that his friend Greeley had helped found as Union Colony No. 1; it would soon take Greeley's name, which it retains to this day. Planned as a farming community inspired by New England's small towns, it would also be a place where alcohol was strictly forbidden.

After Barnum's party returned to New York in June, he and the Fishes joined Charity at Waldemere, where the Carey sisters visited for several weeks, staying at the Petrel's Nest cottage. In September, Barnum, Fish, and eight other men went to Kansas to hunt buffalo. There, at Fort Hays, Lt. Col. George Armstrong Custer took a break from slaughtering Indians to support Barnum's party in slaughtering the fast-disappearing bison. Custer "received us like princes," Barnum wrote, fitting them up with horses, guns, and fifty cavalrymen for protection. Fish proved to be an incompetent horseman, while Barnum managed to kill two of the noble beasts and help kill a third. After only a couple of hours and the deaths of twenty buffalo, however, the party found the "wanton butchery" less pleasurable than they had anticipated, and called off the hunt.

Soon after leaving Kansas, Barnum would have the opportunity once again to fall back into the sort of hunting he liked best — seeking not game but talent, rustling up new acts and curiosities across the land, another step in his return to the full-blown life of a showman.

Back on the East Coast, Barnum answered a request from William C. Coup, a former employee who wanted Barnum to join him and a partner in putting on a large traveling show, a new iteration of a circus that the two men had recently begun. Born in Indiana in 1836, Coup had run off to join the circus at age fourteen, attaching himself to Barnum's Great Asiatic Caravan, Museum and Menagerie when it passed through Terre Haute featuring Tom Thumb and other signature acts. By 1870 he had become an experienced circus manager and, along with a former clown named Dan Castello, had started a circus that plied the waters of the Great Lakes, sailing their show from port to port.[12]

Now Barnum agreed to lend his name to Coup's enterprise (for 3 percent of the receipts, the same deal he had with Wood), as well as his money and his talent for acquiring acts and oddities, to help create a new and better circus by the following spring. Under the agreement, Barnum would own two-thirds of the new show, and Coup and Castello would own the other third. Barnum spent the winter getting Admiral Dot "well trained," bought from Wood the summer rights to his menagerie, and acquired other oddities, including one of the many Cardiff Giants now in circulation. Plus he felt he could profitably hire the Bunker Siamese Twins, Chang and Eng, whom he had successfully exhibited in England, along with Anna Swan and others of his old museum attractions.

Coup should come to New York himself, Barnum advised, and help in the preparations over the winter. Meanwhile the old showman sprang into action. Among many other efforts he wrote two letters to his

Boston friend Moses Kimball. One said, in its entirety, "Have you got an Egyptian mummy in your museum that you will sell? If not, can you tell me where I can buy one?" In the second, he took time to offer some explanation: "I *thought* I had finished the show business (and all other), but just for a flyer I go it once more." Then he inquired about live seals, saying he would write a Down East postmaster for suggestions if Kimball did not have any seals at his disposal.[13]

Barnum wrote in a later iteration of his autobiography that he had known Coup for years and admired his judgment and "executive ability." But when the man arrived in New York and saw the "thousands upon thousands" that Barnum was spending, Coup said he feared the costs "would ruin the richest man in America." Barnum reassured him "that I was not wholly inexperienced in the show business, and that, in any event, I was to 'foot the bill.' " He would leak to the press that he had spent $500,000 to $750,000 on the new show, but he felt confident that he could spend "money like water" because his name would be a bigger draw than traveling circuses could generally rely upon, and also because the three acres of canvas in his growing show could accommodate ten thousand people, more than enough to recoup the daily expenses for an enterprise that would require five hundred men just to get it from place to place.[14]

As usual on matters of showmanship, Barnum was right. The show opened in Brooklyn on April 10, 1871, offering, in addition to the Coup and Castello circus, "a museum, menagerie, caravan and hippodrome." For all of that spring and summer, as it traveled from New York into New England, up to three thousand people had to be turned away each day, and the press raved about what had been created.[15]

It's tempting to see this burst of energy as the beginning of Barnum's second career, the one he is more famous for today, as a circus man rather than as a showman. But these activities were continuous with those he had been pursuing for more than three decades and represented the end of one of the few efforts at which he had not fully succeeded: being retired. Barnum had not stopped being a showman, public lecturer, or real-estate investor for any part of his attempted retirement, but the slower pace that had left him with time on his hands was, he now realized, at the ripe old age of sixty, not for him. It wasn't that he was incapable of leisure, for he never stopped enjoying the pleasures of city life or of warm friendships or of clambakes by the shore during Seaside Park summers. Yet he always seemed to need a clear project to occupy him.

Still, he would no longer be the hands-on manager he had generally been during his museum years. Barnum did not go along when the new circus left Brooklyn, and he would rarely accompany his shows on the road again in the coming years. Instead he would remain on the East Coast and manage as much as he could from there.

In keeping with this new role, when the circus returned to New York in the fall of 1871, he prepared as warm a reception for it as he could. His advertisements for the "great travelling museum, menagerie, caravan, hippodrome, international zoological garden, and Dan Castello's Mammoth Circus" made the customarily understated claim that it offered "a really colossal combination of amusements having no parallel in the world's history," with an entry fee of "only 50¢, the same as charged for an ordinary small circus." He gave one of his patented off-the-cuff speeches when the show opened on November 13 at the Empire City Skating Rink, a huge structure at Third Avenue and Sixty-Third Street with a roof supported by cast-iron arches. He pledged to give people ten times their money's worth and an environment free of vulgarity. He also talked up the new offerings at the Empire Rink, including a second chunk of bark from a giant California sequoia, this one a cross-section forming a ring large enough to enclose two hundred children.[16]

The weeks-long run at the Empire Rink helped make the first year of his great show profitable. Although Barnum counted the season as a success, in February 1872 Coup and Samuel Hurd, who had now become an investor in the show, as well as its treasurer, approached him with figures intended to prove that his ambitious plans for the 1872 season, given what he intended to spend on more horses and more of everything, were likely to result in a loss of several hundred thousand dollars. The problem was the daily expense of employing so many people, upward of a thousand, when many days of the season would be wasted in transporting the show in cumbersome wagons over muddy and unreliable roads.

Barnum responded that he had already seen this challenge and planned to meet it by transporting the circus exclusively by train. By doing so, a range of twenty miles a day could be extended to one hundred miles a day, allowing them to reach larger and more profitable towns and cities in less time. He predicted that using trains would give them the equivalent hauling power of *"two thousand men and horses"* if they had continued to travel by road. In response to Coup and Hurd's concerns, Barnum wired railroads to see whether they were game, and the response came back as "generally favorable." Using railroads to transport circuses was nothing new; smaller circuses had used this method as the railroads quickly spider-webbed the growing country after the Civil War. But nothing had been attempted on this scale before, and learning to efficiently load onto trains what amounted to a small city was a remarkable feat of organization that would be achieved only by trial and error. Coup later said that the first time they loaded the sixty-five cars making up the circus train, it took his workers twelve hours — far, far too long to allow enough time for travel, unloading, and constructing that rolling city in a new location in a timely way.[17]

But after the first attempt, in New Brunswick, New Jersey, they soon got the hang of it. In 1872 they traveled down the Eastern

Seaboard as far as Virginia, then as far west as Kansas, and finally ended up in Detroit. The crowds came by the thousands each day, often traveling long distances themselves on special excursion trains put on by the railroads, but also in wagons, on horses, and by foot. Barnum wrote that when the circus would pull into a new town before dawn, they "usually found wagon loads of rural strangers — men, women and children — who had come in during the night and 'pitched camp.' " Although his expenses were $5,000 a day, or $780,000 for the season, Barnum claimed that the 1872 profits amounted to $1 million. In this first year that the circus traveled by train, he tried to join it in the big cities, where he would often also give temperance speeches. He wrote in his 1872 edition of his autobiography that his circus associates believed the free temperance speeches, which were so crowded that people had to be turned away, were drawing off potential circus customers.[18]

In October he made another trip to Colorado with John Fish and a friend from Fairfield named David Sherwood, intent on expanding his real-estate empire. He and Sherwood bought a large cattle ranch near Pueblo, and Barnum would continue to invest in the state for years to come. "I am charmed with Colorado," he confessed, "the scenery and delightful air," and especially with the "lively, thriving city of Denver." He once again gave a temperance lecture in the city and returned to the teetotaling community now called Greeley. A not insignificant part of Denver's appeal was that his daughter Helen now lived there with a new husband, a doctor she had married after divorcing Samuel Hurd in 1871. The circumstances of the divorce, which included rumors of infidelity on her part, apparently did not alienate Barnum from either party, because it was soon after Helen's breakup with Hurd that Barnum invited him to join the circus business.[19]

In August 1872 Barnum bought a building on Fourteenth Street in Manhattan called the Hippotheatron and had it fixed up to his specifications as a winter venue for parts of his circus and equestrian show and the beginnings of what was planned to be a huge museum and menagerie. It opened in the middle of November, drawing what Barnum referred to as "the better classes, for whose good opinion it has ever been my fortune to cater." Just as he had helped make theatergoing palatable to those who had prior moral objections, he now through scrupulous enforcement and an onslaught of publicity assured the public that the circus and the hippodrome were also suitable to those who had been reluctant to expose their children, and themselves, to profanity, drunkenness, brawling, and other public displays of turpitude commonly associated with the circus.

Barnum went to New Orleans in the middle of December to attend to a part of his circus sent on a southern tour, a venture combining "my humanitarian feelings with my pecuniary interests" by sending to warmer zones the exotic animals in the show that were sensitive to cold weather. He was in New Orleans breakfasting at the St. Louis Hotel on the morning of Christmas Eve when another of the dread telegrams from Samuel Hurd arrived: "About 4 A.M. fire discovered in boiler-room of circus building; everything destroyed except 2 elephants, 1 camel."[20]

As was by now a well-established habit, Barnum's first move, at least as portrayed in his memoirs, was an act of supreme sangfroid. He sent out telegrams to Europe asking for more animals and more automatons, the latter having been especially successful with audiences of late in the show's museum department. Then he telegraphed

Hurd, asking him to tell newspaper editors that he had already committed half a million dollars to rebuilding his show and would have a "new and more attractive travelling show than ever early in April." Only then did he permit himself to shudder at the thought "of the terrible sufferings of one hundred wild beasts, in their frantic, howling efforts to escape the flames." He most regretted the loss of "four beautiful giraffes," an especially delicate species, hard to keep alive in the United States in those days, which in their fear during the fire would not allow themselves to be moved to safety.

When he returned to New York a week later, he found Coup and Hurd looking glum, the latter predicting it would take at least till summer to get a show back on the road, and the former suggesting that they sit out a year and reopen in 1874. In his telling, Barnum laughed at them, and reported receiving telegrams from Europe that very day saying that both animals and automatons were being procured without a hitch. By February he could write that more curiosities and animals than he had ever owned before, including two giraffes, had arrived in New York, with even more to

come in the following month. Hurd and
Coup, he said, were now "in high feather."

SEVENTEEN:
MARRIAGE BONDS

As he had predicted, Barnum's Travelling World's Fair was back on the rails by the first week in April 1873, this time requiring more than ninety-five rail cars, compared to the sixty-five needed to start the 1872 season. The 1873 show would travel through New England and into the Midwest, then go north into Canada, drawing five million visitors in six months.

Between visits to his circus, Barnum spent much of the summer of 1873 at Waldemere, with the usual clambakes, seaside drives, and visits by friends, all the while "surrounded by my children and troops of grandchildren." But he made no mention of Charity. His wife of almost forty-four years had always had a propensity for nervousness, which early on both Barnum and their daughter Caroline would joke about and which led to her decision to not accompany Barnum on most of his many travels. After

Barnum's midcareer bankruptcy, however, her health had taken what became a permanent turn for the worse, the cause of which was never specified. At one point in the early 1860s Barnum feared for her life, but she recovered enough that their friend George Emerson could write about his time staying with the Barnums in the late 1860s, "One day she would be under doctor's treatment, and so much a sufferer as not to be able to take her place at the table; while the next day she would be equal to her favorite ride in the Park, for shopping at Stewart's, and for what she never was willing to delegate, the immediate supervision of the household." By the early 1870s, however, she had been diagnosed with heart disease and nearly died of an attack during the winter of 1872–73.[1]

In the months that followed, her health must have improved, for by the early fall of 1873, Barnum decided to "run over and see the International Exhibition at Vienna," setting sail for England on the Cunard Line steam paddle-wheeler R.M.S. *Scotia* and arriving in Liverpool. There he met his friend John Fish, who had been the last person to shake his hand when he left England fourteen years before. Barnum spent several days with Fish at his house in Southport on the coast north of Liverpool, presumably joined by Fish's daughters, Jane Ann, with whom he had done so much traveling in America, and Nancy, who had also visited America and stayed with a cousin of Charity's the year before.[2]

After traveling a bit in the English countryside with Nancy and her father, Barnum visited friends in London and then trotted around Europe, catching the World's Fair in Vienna just before it closed and visiting a number of cities in Germany, including Hamburg, where he bought "nearly a shipload of valuable wild animals and rare birds." He was preparing to leave Hamburg for a visit to Italy when, on November 20, he received the worst possible telegram from Samuel Hurd.

Charity had died the day before, Hurd said, after having become paralyzed and lying unconscious for a day. "Sudden and unexpected," Barnum called her death, and he used the word *anguish* twice in rapid succession when describing his reaction. He acknowledged that he was needed by his family to be there by her coffin, but he also emphasized how hard this death was on him, far away and in lonely isolation. He did not leave his hotel room for several days, and on the Saturday when he knew the funeral was taking place — he had been telegraphing instructions to New York related to her arrangements — "my lonely head was bowed, and my tears flowed in unison" with those of his family and friends. Charity had died at their Fifth Avenue town house, in the presence of her family and some of those friends, and after her body was transported to Bridgeport for a funeral at Waldemere, it had been placed in the receiving vault at Mountain Grove Cemetery in Bridgeport, awaiting Barnum's return. Oddly enough, he did not make immediate plans to go home so that he could console his daughters and end his own loneliness while drawing consolation from them and his friends.

Barnum matter-of-factly pointed out that Charity "had been a suffering invalid more or less for eighteen years," and she had often "prayed for death to come as an angel of mercy to take her 'home.' " He offered no explanation for why he did not return to New York. Instead he went back to London, where he could be among friends, and "spent several weeks in quiet." In letters he mentioned a concern about his own health, saying that Charity's death had set him back and that he suffered from sleeplessness.

From what was about to happen, it seems

evident that Nancy Fish was one of those who consoled him during this period and was the reason he did not return home. Born in 1850, Nancy, now twenty-three, would have been a child when Barnum first met John Fish, but Barnum had gotten to know her through letters she wrote to her father when he and her sister had started exploring America with Barnum. In fact, he would later say in an interview that the letters had been so charming he had fallen in love with her without having met her. He was careful not to mention her anywhere in his accounts of 1872 and 1873, but it seems that he was hoping to get to know her better on this trip to Europe. It's hard to guess where their relationship would have gone had Charity lived, but following her death, Nancy became Barnum's chief source of consolation. And this friendship would soon develop — if it had not already done so — into a romance.

Whatever his family and friends at home were feeling about his absence, Barnum's fellow Universalists did their best to cover for him. Rev. Abel C. Thomas traveled from Philadelphia to conduct the funeral service, offering memories of Charity and consoling words. Charity had been close friends with his wife and had pronounced him to be "what every minister ought to be." George Emerson wrote his long memoir about Charity and his experiences in the Barnum household. In it he praised Charity's easy and generous hospitality and reported that although she never initiated jokes or funny stories, she was quick with a riposte — which especially delighted Barnum when he was the object of it. He and Barnum would often look for ways to distract her from her infirmity, which would attack her nerves, "perhaps causing her to exaggerate the immediate trouble," as Emerson delicately put it.[3]

However deep his private grief was, Barnum seems to have reacted to Charity's death much as he had to the four devastating fires he had faced. He wrote, "My tongue ceased to move when I attempted to say, as surely we all ought unhesitatingly at all times to say, 'Not my will, but Thine be done.'" But his ability to absorb this greater blow went beyond religious faith or his natural optimism. Even to this tragedy he responded decisively and swiftly, and it is hard not to fault him for it.

He and Nancy fell so much in love over the coming months that, on Valentine's Day of 1874, they were secretly married in a civil ceremony in London, even giving a false address for where they were living at the time. Charity had been dead for less than three months. The impropriety of remarrying so quickly, and the blow that its exposure would give to his family and to his public reputation, sealed his lips and hers. If members of her family had been aware of the secret marriage, they never revealed it either. Was it grief or lust that drove him to do something so extreme, or was it that odd tendency of public figures to take undue risks, as if to test the power of their own celebrity if caught? After all, Barnum's face and name were almost as familiar in England as they were in America, so the risk was certainly there. But he was not caught, not for well over a century after his death, when the British marriage certificate finally came to light.[4]

Barnum at last left for home from Liverpool on April 18, again sailing on the *Scotia,* stopping first at the Fish residence in Southport, presumably to drop off his new wife. He spoke of his delight at finding his children and grandchildren in good health upon reaching New York, but he launched himself right into business matters the very afternoon of his arrival, and it was weeks of busy days in the city before he returned to the tranquility of Waldemere. In late June his fellow Bridgeporters gave him a public testimonial dinner. The timing of this alcohol-free event, attended by more than two hundred people from near and far, including representatives of all the New York papers, was presumably connected to the death of Charity and his return to an empty house. But Barnum did not say so, and only one of the speeches he reprinted or summarized in his autobiography covering 1874 even mentioned Charity. This particular speech, by a local doctor, gave her all praise for the beauty of the three houses the Barnums had built locally and for their impressive grounds and gardens, declaring that her influence had inspired many others in the city to beautify their own residences. The evening's dinner, however, was meant to be all about Barnum, and it was. As lonely as Waldemere without Charity might have seemed, he must have felt warmed by this dramatic public display of affection from the people who knew him best. His own affection for the city of Bridgeport was undoubtedly stronger than ever. He had sold the large house on Fifth Avenue since Charity's death there, so Waldemere was now his principal residence.[5]

In July Barnum, now sixty-four years old, reported that he was "in robust health with scarcely ever an ache or a pain" and that he was "blessed with a vigor and buoyancy of spirits vouchsafed to but few men of fifty or even less." He had spent "a pleasant summer at my charming Waldemere." He did not say with whom he spent that summer, but one of the newspaper articles about the late June dinner referred to Barnum's "friends from abroad." Whether or not these were the Fishes we do not know, though it seems more than likely. Barnum and Nancy were making plans for a public wedding in New York that fall.

On September 16 one of Barnum's preacher friends, the Rev. Edwin H. Chapin, married Nancy and Barnum at Chapin's Universalist Church of the Divine Paternity, on Fifth Avenue at Forty-Fifth Street. Perhaps because Nancy, now twenty-four, was in fact already married, she eschewed wedding white, wearing a "slate-colored dress," "a black velvet hat with blue feathers," and diamond earrings. Barnum, wearing black evening dress, kissed his young bride on the cheek after the vows and blessing were said. Members of both families were on hand, having been informed of the nuptials over the summer, and "a large gathering of gratified friends" were also present to witness the ceremony. The *Herald* primly reported that there "was no ostentation or nonsense about the wedding."[6]

After spending their wedding night at the Windsor Hotel, the couple went off for a honeymoon to a resort in the White Mountains, then to Saratoga Springs, and back to Waldemere in early October. A family legend, perhaps apocryphal, reports that when the couple arrived home, where wedding receptions were planned, they found Barnum's family awaiting them on the porch, still wearing mourning clothes for Charity, even now not a year dead.

EIGHTEEN:
EXCITEMENT, PEPPER,
& MUSTARD

Business did not slow down for Barnum even through the eventful year of 1873. While away in Europe, he had hatched another bold project with Coup and Hurd, leasing land in Manhattan between Twenty-Third and Twenty-Fourth Streets, the whole block east of Madison Avenue. There they constructed a Roman hippodrome track, a zoo, an aquarium, and a "museum of unsurpassable extent and magnificence." The shipload of animals and birds he had purchased just before Charity's death was intended for this venture, and when the length of Barnum's period of disengagement following her death began to concern Coup, Castello was sent to England to get the old man moving again.[1]

In early 1874 Barnum and Castello got to work seeking out all that was needed to stock the new show with curiosities both animal and mineral. The usual flurry of telegraphs to his agents, followed by large outlays of cash, had the usual effect. The hippodrome track would feature chariot races, thoroughbred races, and races of every other kind that Barnum and his partners could imagine, from ostriches to monkeys to elephants. Each show would begin with a Congress of Nations, for which Barnum bought a complete replica with costumes, pennants, gilded conveyances, and other paraphernalia of the Congress of Monarchs, which had been showing in London for several years. Advertised as "The Event of 1874," Barnum's Roman Hippodrome opened in New York on April 27, just three days before his return to the city from Liverpool.

The day of his arrival he bought an ad in the next day's papers seeking fifty donkeys for a new "Donnybrook" act at the Hippodrome. He visited the show that night, taking the first of what would be, over the years to come, many carriage rides around a hippodrome track. He acknowledged the crowd's "enthusiastic reception," an expression of their "appreciation of my greatest effort in my whole managerial career." In fairness, the New-York Tribune, even several years after the death of its editor and Barnum's friend Horace Greeley, agreed with him, making the point that Barnum had thought first of creating a grand spectacle, and only second of extracting money from his customers, although that money was indeed rolling in.[2]

The Hippodrome could accommodate ten thousand people, and Barnum wrote that for weeks thousands of would-be customers were turned away from the evening performances; his advertisements encouraged the public to attend afternoon shows to be sure of getting a seat. By June, when it was clear that the Hippodrome would continue to reward Barnum's investment of more than half a million dollars, he decided to enclose part of the Madison Avenue site with glass and install heating for the winter months; he would send the show on the road in late summer while the construction work was being done.

In May, Barnum had paid a visit to his friends the Rev. and Mrs. Abel Thomas at their country house outside Philadelphia, after which he wrote Mrs. Thomas to say that although he had enjoyed himself at their "charming retreat," country life was not really for him. "I have lived so long on excitement, pepper, & mustard that plain bread & milk don't agree with me — or rather, it is *too late* to change my tastes in that direction." Neither the sad loss of Charity nor the distraction of an energetic new young wife was going to inspire in Barnum any sort of retreat from his life as a showman.[3]

Soon after they were married in early 1870, Samuel L. Clemens and his wife, Olivia (or Livy), began an after-dinner habit of reading from Barnum's recently published *Struggles and Triumphs*. The book made an impression on Clemens, encouraging him in the years ahead as he promoted himself as a public lecturer and as the writer Mark Twain. Barnum's autobiography meant so much to him that when Clemens felt death nearing in the autumn of 1909 and "took a dying man's solace in rereading his favorite books," Barnum's autobiography was one of them, alongside Samuel Pepys's diaries and Thomas Malory's *Morte d'Arthur*. Before becoming acquainted with Barnum's book, he had written that bitingly satirical piece in which he imagined Barnum's first speech as a congressman, and at about the same time had visited Barnum's American Museum and suggested that "some philanthropist" ought to torch the place again.[4]

In 1870, emboldened by their mutual friend Joel Benton, who was visiting Barnum at Waldemere, the showman reached out to Clemens. He wanted to know whether Mark Twain would write something for him, to appear in *Barnum's Advance Courier,* an advertising newspaper Barnum had developed for his new traveling show, to be distributed in towns before the circus arrived. This innovation would contain a variety of materials promoting the circus, including testimonials by well-known writers and public figures. In his letter, Barnum offered to pay Clemens for his work, or swap it for ads or notices for his recent book, *The Innocents Abroad.* Barnum's associate John Greenwood Jr., dispatched by the showman to find items for the museum, had been part of the band of innocents who joined Clemens in some of the travels chronicled in the book, a further reason why Barnum might have felt that there could be profit in contacting Clemens. But now, despite his newfound appreciation of the showman, Clemens declined Barnum's request, as he would repeatedly do during the 1870s.

In spite of Clemens's reluctance to be used for promotional purposes by Barnum, the two men developed a kind of friendship. They had many friends in common, among them Horace Greeley, and both men had been present at a party celebrating what turned out to be Greeley's last birthday, his sixty-first, in February 1872, at a private home on West Fifty-Seventh Street.[5]

Although Clemens would not write on demand, he did find Barnum a good subject, and in 1874, when a great comet was visible in the northern hemisphere for much of July, he wrote a humorous sketch for the July 6 *Herald* called "A Curious Pleasure Excursion." In it, he informed his readers that he had teamed with Barnum to rent the comet for "an extended excursion among the heavenly bodies." The plan was to fix up a million staterooms in the tail of the comet, each room with all the amenities, ranging from hot water to a parachute. Such public amusements as a driving park and bowling alleys would also grace the comet, and a daily newspaper would be published as they flitted among the stars. The cost would be $2 per fifty million miles of travel, and the date of return would be December 14, 1991. Requests for further information were to be addressed "to my partner but not to me."[6]

Barnum wrote in response, "My dear Clemens, I owe you a thousand thanks for taking me into partnership," and invited him and his family to Bridgeport for clambakes and "jolly times." Clemens seems to have accepted, because within two weeks he was expressing his enthusiasm for a project the two men had discussed, a collection of the odd letters each of them received as public personalities. Barnum had sent him a sample, to which Clemens responded, "Again I beseech you, don't burn a single specimen, but remember that *all* are wanted & possess value in the eyes of your friend." Over the next few years, Barnum would send him the best of these letters, "bushels" of which he had been destroying before the Clemens project came along. But in the end nothing came of these plans.[7]

An easy habit developed between the Barnums and the Clemenses of visiting back and forth between Bridgeport and Hartford. Nancy liked literary people, and when Clemens sent him a stack of his books, Barnum wrote him, "My wife ardently hopes to see you place your autograph in these volumes under the roof of Waldemere. There will be a *row* if her anticipations are blasted." Six months later, Barnum wrote of a visit that he and Nancy had made to Clemens's Nook Farm home, "My wife is deranged on the subject of a *fernery* like yours, so our call on you the other day will be cheap if I get off for $1000 or $1500."[8]

Barnum persisted in sending Clemens long letters describing the latest efforts in his traveling show and requesting that Mark Twain write something about it. Often the thrust of his description was not just the variety and magnificence of what Barnum had put into the shows, but how much they had cost him to put on. Clearly Barnum seemed to feel that Clemens would be impressed by these large expenditures, and just as clearly Clemens was not. These letters don't just feel obtuse; they feel more than a little embarrassing.[9]

When Barnum asked Clemens to come down from Hartford to introduce him for a speech he would be giving to benefit the poor, he seemed to know that the answer would be no, and so he implored, "This once, & I will *never,* NEVER, NEVER ask a like favor of you." Once again, the answer from Hartford was no. Yet exactly three months later, in January 1878, Barnum began another letter, "This is a *begging letter! Awful!!*" He asked this time for only five lines above Twain's signature, to be included in a collection of "congratulatory utterances" on Barnum's career by "distinguished gentlemen," which he intended to publish in his circular for the next season. The letter ended on an imploring note, calling Clemens "My dear boy" and hoping he had not written in vain. Yet again, he had. Barnum's response to this latest rejection sounded notes of frustration and even self-pity. If Mark Twain could only have said publicly some of the complimentary things he had said in letters to Barnum, well, "it would have been *nice.*"[10]

That Clemens had a high opinion of Barnum's autobiography seems to have been something Barnum knew, and he was sure to send Clemens each year's new edition. Yet he remained overeager for approval from the famous younger man, and his eagerness always had to do with winning that approval on his own, very public terms — rather than accepting Clemens's continuing resolve not to mix art and commerce. Eventually it was obvious to the two men that this dynamic was not making either of them happy; after early 1878 the flow of letters slowed, and the relationship became more distant.

In 1875 Barnum decided to incorporate the two principal shows he had going, the Travelling World's Fair and the Roman Hippodrome, along with smaller ventures, into the Barnum Universal Exposition Company, which brought into ownership his senior managers and some of his friends. However, the larger show proved a loser for the season. Several factors began to hurt attendance, the most unlikely of which was that, because the hippodrome show did not include clowns, country people would not attend, and so it did poorly outside big cities. (Barnum admitted in the year's edition only that it had been a "tolerably successful season, notwithstanding the depressed state of finances generally.") At the end of the 1875 tour, the new company was broken up, and its assets, including its animals, were sold at auction. Barnum bought back some of these assets to try out a new centennial touring show in 1876.[11]

In the meantime, he was approached by a group of Republicans urging him to run for mayor of Bridgeport. Because the town had a Democratic majority, he said he would run only if both parties supported him. They did, but even so there was another candidate in the race, and the election came down to the wire. Barnum won a one-year term by just 141 votes out of four thousand votes cast. His opening speech in April to the Common Council, whose members also served for a year, encouraged them to act honestly, impartially, and prudently. His own special interest would be to regulate as much as possible the sale of alcohol, or at least to vigorously enforce existing liquor laws. More quixotically, he also called for stamping out prostitution and gambling.

During his year in office, Barnum did make a serious dent in the sale of liquor in saloons on Sundays. As mayor, he was also an advocate for good and efficient government, finding a company that would provide gas to the city more cheaply, and pushing without much success to get the company that supplied water to the city (in which he held stock) to do a better job. The biggest stink during his mayoralty came when a local newspaper wrote that he had referred to Jewish saloon owners who had kept their establishments open on Sundays as "miserable Jews," whereas Barnum claimed he had in fact said "miserable whiskey" and asked the newspaper to print a retraction. A committee of Jewish citizens considered the matter and cleared him on the grounds of what he had presumably meant, if not on what he had actually said. The Common Council itself was largely made up of Democrats, leading to frustrations and frequent clashes. After a year Barnum decided that one term as mayor was sufficient.[12]

While mayor, he spent parts of the summer traveling to Niagara Falls with Nancy and some of her English friends, former neighbors from Southport who had been visiting at Waldemere, and stopping in at the hippodrome show as it appeared in various cities. In the fall he gave thirty lectures titled "The World and How to Live in It," under the auspices of the Redpath Lyceum Bureau, whose clients included Mark Twain, Ralph Waldo Emerson, Julia Ward Howe, Frederick Douglass, Susan B. Anthony, and many of the country's other most sought-after lecturers. He traveled as far west as Leavenworth, Kansas, on the tour, and spoke in Kansas City, Chicago, and major cities in the East. At the end of the tour, Barnum received a letter from the Bureau saying that he had delighted audiences more than any of their "best lecturers."[13]

When Barnum's 1876 American Centennial show was up and running, it would augment his tried and true exhibits with "patriotic features that gave the people a Fourth of July celebration every day." This included an abundance of American flags, a thirteen-cannon barrage before each morning's parade, marchers dressed as Revolutionary soldiers led on white horses by figures depicting Generals Washington and Lafayette, a fife and drum corps, a chorus of several hundred people singing patriotic songs, a live eagle, and fireworks at night, along with the usual museum, menagerie, and circus features. Although Coup and Castello were no longer involved, Hurd was, as were the owners of the European Menagerie and Circus, which Barnum had bought and folded into his new show.

One of his innovations in 1876 was the creation of a specially fitted-up advertising rail car that would precede the show by at least two weeks, with press agents and poster hangers — a twelve-person "paste brigade" — to stir up interest in the city or town where the show would appear as well as in the surrounding countryside. The car itself was put on display where it stopped, with a portrait of Barnum and scenes from the upcoming circus painted on either side. Up to $100,000 a year was devoted to these publicity efforts. The Centennial show traveled as far east as Nova Scotia (where the chorus sang "God Save the Queen" rather than its usual "Star-Spangled Banner") and as far west as Illinois, but the profits from the season were, Barnum wrote, only "satisfactory."

To increase the crowds and profits for the 1877 season, the patriotism was toned down and five black stallions from Germany that could stand in unison on their hind legs were introduced. Traveling on nearly a hundred steel railcars, the spectacle was now billing itself as P. T. Barnum's New and Only Greatest Show on Earth — Barnum's first use of that famous phrase. In 1877 the show would visit Canada, go across the Midwest and as far south and west as Texas, advertising ten thousand "rare and startling curiosities" and a menagerie that included a "$25,000 Hippopotamus from the river Nile." A "Greek nobleman," Capt. George Costentenus, tattooed on every inch of his body, often topped the promotional efforts.

Barnum's partners were now grumbling about their arrangement with him, suggesting that he should spend more time visiting the show on the road and that he was soaking up profits while selling the use of his name elsewhere. Hard feelings grew on both sides, as Barnum, perhaps rightly, felt that his partners were taking for granted just how much he was doing behind the scenes to bring in new performers. At least for a time, the rift was patched up, and the partnership would last through the 1880 season before coming to an end.

Near the close of this run, one of the acts that drew the biggest crowds was "Zazel, the Beautiful Human Cannon Ball," a young Englishwoman who would walk a tightrope and then dramatically sight a large cannon before climbing down into it. The cannon contained a powerful spring that projected her as high as eighty feet, sending her into a net. A harmless charge of powder sent smoke and flame up after her as she was sprung.

Such new acts did not appear by magic, as Barnum was keen to point out. Agents would approach him, seeking the prestige of having their performers appear in a Barnum show. But much of the new talent emerged through the worldwide network of agents he had spent years developing and still worked hard to maintain. In March 1877 an English weekly society paper, *The World,* published a profile of Barnum at Waldemere for one of its "Celebrities at Home" features. Even the subject himself admitted that the piece was "too flattering," but it feels persuasive in describing him contentedly spending his mornings in his "work-shop" or study, a paneled octagonal room where he sat at "a large and much littered desk, with papers strewn ankle-deep around his chair," an assistant within calling distance in the next room.[14]

Each morning, Barnum would busily answer his mail and send out requests to his agents, asking them to procure specific animals or acts he needed to fill out a show or replace an act that wasn't drawing or an animal that had died. These letters reminded his agents that he was always on the lookout for something special and would pay top dollar to procure it. He was protective of this morning time just as, later in the day, he would protect his leisure time, telling people who had business on their mind to see him the next morning.

The article in *The World* was also glowing about Nancy, praising her for the good taste displayed inside the house and the high regard in which "the best families in Bridgeport" held her for her kindness, intelligence, and good conversation. Barnum's "full face beams with extra smiles when he is near," the reporter wrote.

Not a month later, however, sadness would envelop this happy home. On April 11, 1877, Barnum's youngest daughter, Pauline, died suddenly at the age of thirty-one, having first caught measles and then diphtheria. She left behind her husband, Nathan Seeley, a daughter, two sons, and a broken-hearted father. The family was "stricken with a heavy sorrow," Barnum wrote, adding that only his faith kept the blow from being "insupportable." In midsummer he and Nancy sailed to England for two months, where he gave lectures and visited with old friends, whose solace he had sought soon after Charity's death three and a half years before.[15]

That November, Barnum chose to step back into politics once more, now representing not Fairfield but Bridgeport in the Connecticut General Assembly. This time he was given the chairmanship of the Temperance Committee, where he worked on behalf of his favorite cause. He would be reelected the following November for a fourth term as an assemblyman, and during that year he introduced an amendment to abolish capital punishment, a Universalist cause. At age seven, he had witnessed the hanging of a black man in Danbury before a huge, carnival-like crowd. He remembered later that his mother had groaned when the man's body dropped, and his memory of it as an adult disgusted him. Now, as a legislator, he could try to do something about it.[16]

During this legislative session in Hartford he also distinguished himself by enlivening a debate over tax exemptions for religious and educational entities, proposing with mock seriousness that his own "great moral show" ought certainly be included among those exempted institutions. In January 1878 he wrote a letter marked "private" to the *Tribune*'s editor and owner Whitelaw Reid, asking for a "fair showing" should his name be put forward as a Republican candidate for the U.S. Senate from Connecticut. It wasn't, and instead, in 1880, he ran for the state senate from Bridgeport. He was beaten this time around in an unusually vituperative race, and soon after the loss he wrote in a letter that he "never had any real taste for office, & now in my 71st year I have a real dislike for it." He expressed his relief, as ever looking on the bright side, at not having to spend time in Hartford that might have been devoted to his children and grandchildren. Although there would later be some faint rumblings about his running for president on a Prohibition ticket, with this his political career came to an end.[17]

Barnum's name recognition, his speaking ability, and his strong opinions had often tempted the Republican Party to put him forward for elective office, and his own eagerness to run was surely an outgrowth of his need for respectability. Whenever he was in office, though, he did not rest on his celebrity. Barnum was genuinely civic-minded, generously contributing to his city and his church, and the voters who knew him best chose him to represent them. His five terms in office, four in the assembly, one as mayor, gave him opportunities to put his political and moral views into play, and he acquitted himself honorably as an officeholder, if not always as a candidate. Perhaps he did not change the world, but he worked hard at getting things done and lived up to the Founders' ideal of the citizen politician. The exigencies of politics drove him away more than the voters did, and for this reason it was probably for the best that his attempts at higher office never succeeded. More than anything else, his forays into politics were an expression of his restless energy and productivity, and it is hard to imagine him, Mark Twain's parody notwithstanding, mired in the halls of Congress.

After losing the election in 1880, Barnum returned his focus to his touring show. In this season, one of his most vexed, and in the end most telling relationships would erupt in public acrimony. For more than a decade, Barnum had engaged in a contentious back-and-forth with Henry W. Bergh, the wealthy son of a New York shipbuilder who had served as one of President Lincoln's envoys to Russia before returning home to found the American Society for the Prevention of Cruelty to Animals.

In Barnum's telling, and to some extent in the newspapers of his time, which referred to him as "The Great Meddler," Bergh was a comic figure, prone to act before he thought and to base his strong condemnations on an imperfect understanding of the fauna he sought to protect. Just months after his society was founded in 1866 and an anti–animal cruelty law was passed, which gave the society the responsibility of enforcing the measure, Bergh took on Barnum for publicly feeding live animals to his boa constrictor. He accused Barnum of being a "semi-barbarian" for allowing the practice, which Bergh called an "atrocity." He predicted that no animal would allow itself to starve if dead food were available, which his opponent took issue with. Barnum sent the letter in which these charges were made to famed Harvard zoologist Louis Agassiz, who agreed with Barnum that the snakes would eat only live food. Barnum kept feeding his boas live prey and saw the ordeal as an unnecessary fuss. Yet Bergh did achieve a small victory, convincing Barnum at the very least to stop making a public spectacle of the feedings, which thereafter happened only at night.

For the 1880 circus season, Barnum had imported from Germany a horse named

Salamander, which would jump "through flaming hoops of blazing fire . . . over burning gates, bars & barriers," as one dramatically colorful circus poster promised. This again sparked Bergh's concern. On the first night, one of the handlers mishandled a hoop, and Salamander's mane and tail seemed to have caught fire, which brought an immediate reaction from Bergh. He ordered Barnum to stop putting on the act.

Barnum, however, held that Bergh had got it wrong, that the horse had not been burned at all, because the hoops were not blazing with real fire but a chemical compound that only looked like fire. Ever the showman, Barnum announced to the world that he would reprise the act on a particular day, and invited Bergh and his "Berghsmen" enforcers to attend. The dispute had of course made the papers, so the circus was crowded with patrons and reporters when Barnum entered the ring and announced, "Either Mr. Bergh or I shall run this show, and I don't think it will be Mr. Bergh." Bergh himself had chosen not to be present for the challenge, but ranged around the circus ring were a number of his agents and policemen, apparently ready to arrest Barnum. In front of the crowd, Barnum ran his hand through the flames and then stepped through one of the burning hoops. Ten clowns then "performed a number of ludicrous antics through the hoops," followed by Salamander. Barnum then invited an ASPCA official to do the same thing, which he did, after which he declared that the flames were harmless and Bergh had been mistaken. As the crowd cheered wildly, the enforcement officers departed, the police captain "looking somewhat crestfallen."[18]

Although Barnum drew the maximum amount of publicity value from his victory, he wrote, "This episode did not impair my personal regard for Mr. Bergh and my admiration of his noble works." This is perhaps the most Barnumesque thing about their rivalry: the regard was real and mutual between the two. At the beginning of the same month of the Salamander dispute, Bergh had recommended Barnum for the board of the Bridgeport ASPCA, which was just forming, citing the showman's "generous and sympathetic instincts" for animals. In the inevitable speech he had given upon entering the ring for the Salamander fire demonstration, Barnum had pointed out that he had decades before been a member in England of the royal society upon which Bergh had patterned his ASPCA and that he had lobbied Bridgeport's mayor to start a local chapter. After the chapter was founded, Barnum liked to style himself the "Bergh of Bridgeport." Eventually the two men became friends, and in 1885 Barnum invited Bergh to Waldemere for the inevitable clambake, Bergh presumably accepting on the condition that the clams were indeed baked and not still alive. When Bergh died during a huge snowstorm in March 1888, a wreath from Barnum was among the few decorations near the altar for Bergh's "impressive funeral services" at St. Mark's Church in Manhattan, and Barnum marched in the processional.[19]

After fighting hard with elbows out for their own point of view, both men may be credited with a willingness to not demonize and ultimately dismiss the other but to see what was good about a man with whom they strongly disagreed. It's worth pointing out, though, that Bergh, despite the gaps in his zoological knowledge and his occasional overzealousness, would be seen by history as far more than the comic figure that Barnum and others accused him of being. What he started has done and still does a remarkable amount of good. Barnum may have known animals and their habits better than Bergh did, and had a clear economic incentive to treat them as well as the state of human knowledge about wild animals permitted, retaining naturalists and successful animal keepers to care for his menageries. But even leaving aside troubling questions in our own day about the morality of capturing, training, and displaying wild creatures, it must be recognized that Barnum's unceasing efforts to cull animals from distant places in the world had a price beyond the dollars he boasted about spending in their procurement. Capturing them was often a bloody business, and transporting them an imperfect science, as was keeping them alive once they arrived in an often inhospitable climate. The Smithsonian Institution in Washington was a frequent recipient of the remains of exotic animals that died in Barnum's care. The showman undoubtedly regretted these losses for more than their financial consequences, but the show business demanded that they be replaced, and Barnum's own credo was to always add more than had been lost.[20]

Nineteen: And Bailey

In March 1880 the first elephant conceived in America was born in Philadelphia, at the winter quarters of the Great London Circus. The glut of publicity surrounding the birth impressed Barnum, and when the baby was two months old, he telegrammed its owners, three Jameses surnamed Bailey, Cooper, and Hutchinson, offering $100,000 in cash for the mother, named Hebe, and her offspring, which would eventually be known as Little Columbia. As Barnum good-naturedly wrote, "They gleefully rejected my offer, pleasantly told me to look to my laurels, and wisely held on to their treasure." Not only that, but they began an advertising campaign under the heading "What Barnum Thinks of the Baby Elephant," reproducing his telegram with its lavish offer.[1]

Barnum was also impressed by how well the three younger men had turned the tables on him, using his own methods. "Foemen 'worthy of my steel,' " he called them. The Great London had dogged Barnum's circus in the previous season, often scheduling dates in the same towns to draw off his business. Even in Bridgeport itself they had outsold Barnum's show two to one. "Barnum finally retreated to the West," according to an 1891 article that had Bailey as its source, "and Bailey had the East to himself."[2]

The aging showman realized he had finally met his match, and he concluded it would be wiser to join them than to continue competing with them. Difficult negotiations began, as Barnum decided at the same time to extract himself from his existing partnership, but by late August he had an agreement with Bailey and Hutchinson, their partner Cooper having withdrawn. The new arrangement would combine the two circuses, at least in the first year, with Barnum responsible for half of the expenditures and receiving half the profits, and the other two men each in for a quarter of the same. None of the three would draw a salary, and the two younger men, whom Barnum called "sagacious and practical managers," would run the show with advice from Barnum, who would be encouraged but not required to be present at performances. Barnum also agreed not to sell the use of his name elsewhere, unless he decided to start another museum.

As the ink was drying on their agreement, Barnum, Bailey, and Hutchinson decided to combine their wintering operations on land Barnum owned in Bridgeport — the very same land where Barnum had years before so ostentatiously farmed by elephant for the benefit of passing railroad passengers. The site's adjacency to a railroad line — the New York, New Haven, and Hartford — was its major advantage. A huge shed more than three hundred feet long went up in the fall of 1880 to shelter eight tracks containing scores of railroad cars. Other buildings contained what the cars transported: an elephant house; another for lions, tigers, and leopards; one with a large pond for amphibians (where, Barnum said, the elephants were allowed to visit for a bath); another for other caged animals; and stables for up to seven hundred horses. A nursery tended to newborn animals, and a number of shops repaired the equipment, from gilded chariots to harnesses. All of the structures were heated by steam to an appropriate temperature.

A circus ring was set up to give performers a chance to practice in the off-season. Many of the hundreds of performers — and those who supported them, who raised the tents and handled other equipment, and who trained and cared for the animals — would make their homes in Bridgeport or thereabouts, establishing the city as an important circus town well into the next century, a boon to rival the establishment of East Bridgeport three decades earlier.[3]

In the middle of November, while all of this frenzied construction was under way, Barnum was in lower Manhattan wrapping up his affairs with his former circus partners when "he was seized by a violent pain in the abdominal region" and "with much difficulty" gotten to Samuel Hurd's house at 334 Lexington Avenue. Several doctors examined him, including his family doctor from Bridgeport, and they agreed that he had a blockage in his intestine. They gave him morphine for the pain, and for more than a week he was critically ill. By Thanksgiving Day, November 25, he was able to sit up and visit with friends at Hurd's, but he was sickened again in early December. A violent inability to keep food down dropped his weight from 215 pounds to an alarming 144. By the middle of the month, he asked that all the congregations in Bridgeport pray "for His blessings to rest upon me," and there was real fear that he would die. (Even in extremis, he or someone he knew managed to get his appeal to the churches published in the *New-York Times.*) Barnum himself later wrote that he spent "many weeks between life and death." By the spring he was well enough to travel to Florida to complete his recovery, but he did not return north until April, and so missed the grand opening of the Barnum & London Circus at his Hippodrome site, which was now known as Madison Square Garden.[4]

The arrangements by his new partners more than satisfied Barnum. Half a million people watched as the new circus snaked its way through the crowded streets on Saturday night, March 26, 1881, beginning and ending at the Garden. The parade featured twenty elephants large and small, golden chariots, car after car containing animal cages — some drawn by wild animals ranging from camels to zebras — open cages of tigers and leopards with their trainers, a dozen riders on horseback in military uniforms representing as many nations, Gen. and Mrs. Tom Thumb in their tiny carriage, four brass bands, a steam calliope, a chariot full of bagpipers, and much more, all illuminated by torchlight, fireworks, limelight, and electric lights. As the *Tribune* succinctly put it, "The procession was very long." People paid up to $10 for a spot in a window overlooking the parade route.

Two days later, when the circus opened in Madison Square Garden, admission was fifty cents, half that for children under nine. "The only drawback," a writer for the *Herald* said of the combined circus performing in three rings surrounded by a hippodrome track, "was that the spectator was compelled to receive more than his money's worth. . . . While his head was turned in one direction, he felt that he was losing something good in another." Among the attractions was the baby elephant, not yet named, that had brought the circuses together, "now one year old and still nursing," as an advertisement for the show put it. The circus paid all expenses for nearly a hundred newspapermen from outposts along the route that the show would follow to come to New York for its grand parade and opening show. Freebies for journalists were nothing new, especially in the entertainment business, but to appeal for good press coverage on this scale, and to assure it for the months the circus would be out on the road, was positively Barnumesque. As the showman himself put it, the effort and expense yielded "a magnificent return."[5]

After a short run in New York, the circus went to Washington, where Barnum met it on his return from Florida, feeling well enough to call on the newly inaugurated President James A. Garfield, to whom he had sent a congratulatory and promotional letter in March, headed *"No office wanted!"* and including an eerie expression of hope: "Do please have the kindness to *live,* and then our country will be blessed." (President Garfield would be shot a few months later and die of his wounds in September.) Barnum gathered endorsements for the show from the president, who called him "the Kris Kringle of America," and other Washington worthies. He also had time in April to sue the *Philadelphia Sun* for writing that he did not own the circus but only leased his name to it. The newspaper relented and the suit was withdrawn.[6]

As further evidence of his recovery, he, Nancy, and his grandson Clinton Hallett Seeley — Pauline's oldest son — sailed to England in May, staying for a month, after which he reported that he was now "invigorated by that finest of all tonics, a sea-voyage." In August he presented to his native village of Bethel a comically oversized Baroque bronze fountain topped by a statue of Triton. The fountain had originally been placed just beyond the fence at Waldemere, sized for its distance from the house and its backdrop of Long Island Sound. Saxon writes that Barnum tried to give the thing to Bridgeport, but when its Common Council demurred, he dropped it on Bethel instead. The day of the presentation, August 19, 1881, turned into a village holiday, with a large crowd before which Barnum gave a nostalgic homecoming speech about growing up there. Even given his warm memories of his boyhood, Barnum concluded that the present was "a more charitable and enlightened age," evidence that "the world is continually growing wiser and better."[7]

Barnum's optimism might have been enhanced by the recovery of his health but also by how well the new combined circus was doing on the road. It would travel more than twelve thousand miles in 1881, before closing for the season in Arkansas in November, having netted more than $400,000. The next year the show would clear more than $600,000, and it would be profitable every remaining year of Barnum's life.

Early in 1881 there had been some testing of the limits of authority on both sides in the new arrangement, and several of Barnum's people left when they felt preempted by the London Circus managers. Hutchinson, nicknamed Lord Hutchinson by Barnum's people, was especially irksome to them. He had worked for Barnum before, as a sales agent for *Struggles and Triumphs,* and had been head of the concessions for the Cooper and Bailey circus. Now he was the financial officer for the new circus and Bailey's second in command. When the frustration he caused induced Barnum's bookkeeper for the show to quit, Barnum replaced him with a cousin of Nancy's from England. The cousin, Benjamin Fish, who had also previously worked for a Barnum show, would discover that Bailey and Hutchinson's bookkeeping left something to be desired. But he ultimately counseled that this unscrupulousness be overlooked because of how much money the show was making. The partnership held together, but it undoubtedly reassured Barnum to have a family member watching the show's finances.

Besides employing Fish to look out for his interests on the road, Barnum had two other faithful employees in Bridgeport who helped him with his many interests. From offices on Main Street, Henry E. Bowser closely watched Barnum's other business finances, assisted with his correspondence, and generally kept things moving smoothly with or without Barnum's immediate involvement. Charles R. Brothwell, whose background was in public works, managed Barnum's real-estate empire, advising him on purchases and sales, overseeing construction projects, and handling rental properties. Barnum's holdings just in Bridgeport and East Bridgeport were estimated to be worth more than a million dollars in 1880, plus he owned a considerable amount of property in New York City, on Long Island, and in Colorado and a number of other heartland states. Barnum liked to call Bowser and Brothwell his "Busy B's," and they seem to have been as loyal and honest as they were busy.[8]

But it was another B, James Anthony Bailey, who was undoubtedly the great find of Barnum's later business life. Bailey was a showman through and through, even acquiring his surname from a circus advance man named F. H. Bailey, who hired him at the age of fourteen. Named James McGinnis when he was born in Detroit on July 4, 1847, the boy lost both his parents by the age of eight and was afterward treated as the Cinderella of his guardians' family. "I was made to work like a dog," he later said. "On the slightest provocation I was whipped. . . . I was kept working so hard that I was always late at school, so I was continually being whipped by the teacher and kept after school." He ran away from this unhappy arrangement at twelve, barefoot and wearing "a big straw hat"; his "only possession was a jackknife, with one broken blade." He worked for a farmer until he met Bailey in Pontiac, Michigan, and after that did a variety of jobs, including posting bills for the circus before working in 1865 as clerk to a sutler (a civilian who sold provisions to the army) for Sherman's army near the end of the Civil War.

After the war, back in the show line, he eventually saved enough money to buy into a circus, and by 1874 he was half owner of Cooper & Bailey's International Allied Shows. That circus went on an extended tour in 1876, sailing from San Francisco, making its way through the Pacific to Australia, Tasmania, Java, New Zealand, and from there to Peru, around Cape Horn, and eventually up to Rio de Janeiro. The circus made money on the Pacific part of the tour but lost many animals on the rough and lengthy passage to Peru, and the South American tour did not pay. When they returned to New York in December 1878, they restored themselves by buying the

Great London Circus and its menagerie with what money they had left and soon became the threat to Barnum that led to the uniting of the two major shows.[9]

Bailey and Barnum were different in striking ways, but ways that turned out to be complementary. As the lion tamer George Conklin, who worked for what became Barnum & Bailey, recalled:

> Barnum was a big, strong man; Bailey was small and thin; Barnum was seldom troubled; Bailey was always anxious. There was never a man who loved publicity more than Barnum, while Bailey disliked personal notoriety. . . . He enjoyed best being the great silent power that made the show go and grow. . . . Bailey was the first man to appear in the morning, and no detail was too small for him to consider.[10]

Bailey was extremely hardworking, not only the first man up when the circus was on the road but continuously in evidence as he kept personal tabs on every aspect of the show. Yet he was also extremely taciturn. According to Conklin, "he seldom spoke to anyone round the show except on business," but instead was often seen nervously "chewing away on an elastic band, and slowly turning his pocketknife between a thumb and forefinger." By the time he teamed up with Bailey and Hutchinson, Barnum, who had for most of his career also sweated the details, was perfectly happy to be the face of the circus, to meet with presidents, create publicity stirs, and make occasional forays to England to find new acts, while leaving the day-to-day operations to his partners. On his seventy-eighth birthday (one day after Bailey's forty-first), Barnum wrote to Bailey, "You manage [the circus] ten times better than I could do it, & I have no fault to find."[11]

That anxiety Conklin alludes to led to some serious health problems for Bailey, including one breakdown in the mid-1880s that required him to leave the circus and sell out his share. On his own seventy-fifth birthday, Barnum wrote to Mrs. Bailey, expressing his concern for her husband and assuring her that he himself had had similar problems, having "overworked my *brain.*" His diagnosis was that Bailey too was suffering from too much *"thinking"* and advised her, "Mr. Bailey need not *think* of the show for six months to come." He promised her that it was being run by good people and wouldn't suffer from Bailey's being away from it: "It will be well managed and make money." It was an extremely kind letter meant to reassure the couple, and offered the parting advice, "Keep quiet in a cool place — don't fret, but look on the bright side." In that year, 1885, the circus netted $312,000, an improvement of about $35,000 over the previous year. Bailey did return in 1887 and would continue to manage the circus until his own death fifteen years after Barnum's.[12]

Throughout the 1880s, Barnum often mentioned his age in his letters, with a combination of wonder that he had somehow grown so old and pride that he was still both enjoying life and prospering as a showman. Soon after his health crisis, he also began to focus on his mortality, in a practical but not a morbid way. In early 1882 he filed his will, a seventeen-page document he wrote out in longhand, which he continued to work on in his remaining years.

But at just this time his life offered one last act to compare with his promotions of Tom Thumb and Jenny Lind: the enormous African elephant known as Jumbo. The great beast — weighing seven tons and reaching nearly twelve feet at the highest point of his back — was said to be the largest elephant in the world and was undoubtedly the largest beast most people had ever seen.

Jumbo had been a beloved feature of the Royal Zoological Gardens in London's Regent's Park for more than sixteen years when one of the circus agents asked the superintendent of the zoo, a friend of Barnum's named A. D. Bartlett, whether the Zoological Society might sell him. To his surprise, and Barnum's shock, the society said yes. Barnum had "often looked wistfully on Jumbo, but with no hope of ever getting possession of him," because the elephant had for so long been such a great attraction, providing rides to thousands and thousands of British children, including the royal offspring of Queen Victoria. Even Barnum himself had ridden the beast years before with Tom Thumb.

What Barnum didn't know was that Jumbo had reached a time in life when male elephants can become obstreperous, owing to a hormonal condition known as musth, and according to Bartlett, Jumbo had on occasion "commenced to destroy the doors and other parts of his house, driving his tusks through the iron plates, splintering the timber in all directions." Although these "fits of temporary insanity" were few and far between, Bartlett had become so worried about them that he asked the Zoological Society for a rifle powerful enough to kill Jumbo if one of his fits endangered the public or his keeper. Given this, the society was all too willing to let the elephant go for £2,000, or $10,000, which Barnum eagerly agreed to pay, plus all expenses of getting him out of the zoo and across the Atlantic.[13]

When news of the sale hit the British papers, pandemonium broke out. The reaction was partly wounded national pride: could what had become a cherished British institution really be allowed to go to America, and at the hands of a man who had once threatened to buy and remove Shakespeare's birthplace? But even more powerful was the simple affection that so many British children and former children felt for the beast. They believed his absence would diminish the whole experience of growing up British. As Barnum put it, "The newspapers, from the London 'Times' down, daily thundered anathemas against the sale, and their columns teemed with communications from statesmen, noblemen, and persons of distinction advising that the bargain should be broken at all risk." Queen Victoria herself telegraphed Bartlett asking for the facts of the case, and the Prince of Wales demanded that Bartlett explain in person how the sale had taken place. Both royals then denounced it. The great critic John Ruskin, a fellow of the Zoological Society, also decried the sale as "disgraceful to the City of London and dishonorable to common humanity," and declared himself "not in the habit of selling my old pets or parting with my old servants" because "I find them subject occasionally . . . to fits of ill-temper."[14]

A legal challenge to the contract between Barnum and the society led to a temporary injunction preventing Jumbo's removal, but the suit was soon rebuffed in court and the injunction lifted. British schoolchildren contributed to a subscription meant to buy Jumbo back, and the *Daily Telegraph* wired Barnum from London, asking the terms necessary to change the showman's mind. Barnum's reply was that he would not undo the deal for even £100,000 — and as the paper's cable had offered for him to "answer, prepaid, unlimited," Barnum took the free opportunity to toot his horn as a showman and toss in some advertising language about his circus.[15]

At the same time, the London correspondents for American newspapers managed to rouse national pride in the United States. On both sides of the Atlantic, then, what became known as Jumbomania broke out, with a flood of Jumbo-inspired paraphernalia, poems, songs, letters, and other tributes. People flocked to Regent's Park for one last viewing, augmenting the zoo's income, Barnum claimed, by £400 per day, which he regretfully and to his own mind graciously allowed the society to keep despite his now owning the exhibit.

In February an attempt was made to walk Jumbo from the zoo to a ship, but as soon as the beast got outside the gates of the familiar zoological gardens he let out a trumpet call, lay down in the street, and refused to budge. When Barnum's agent cabled for advice, the showman replied, "Let him lay there for a week if he wants to. It is the best advertisement in the world." But the next day Jumbo was allowed to return to his enclosure in the zoo, from which he would not move for several weeks. During this time he received visits from the archbishop of Canterbury and his wife, dukes and duchesses, and the Lord Mayor of London. It was also during this time that the hysteria to keep him in London reached a high point.[16]

Eventually Barnum's agent realized that the reason for Jumbo's stubbornness was that Matthew Scott, the keeper who had attended him since the elephant had first arrived at the zoo from France at age five in 1865, was working at cross-purposes with the attempt to get Jumbo moving. Not only had Scott received a substantial amount of income from the fare for each of what he estimated to have been "hundreds of thousands" of Jumbo rides that he had overseen, but many of his countrymen let Scott know that it was his patriotic duty to discourage his charge from decamping. First, Barnum's agent offered to quintuple Scott's wages, and when that didn't work, he threatened to fire him. The very next day, March 22, Jumbo assented to leave his enclosure for a specially built box on wheels that would carry him to the ship and also serve as his new quarters throughout his journey to New York.[17]

According to Scott, "thousands of people, many of them women, tramped all the way to [St. Katharine] Docks, six long miles, to see him off." Jumbo was fed more than the usual amount of buns and other unhealthy treats along the way, including two bottles of ale. After he was finally transported by lighter to the oceangoing vessel *Assyrian Queen,* the odd ritual of a luncheon celebration, with many invited guests from the Zoological Society, took place. At the luncheon, William Newman, a Barnum employee known as "Elephant Bill," who had been sent over to England to help with the removal and transport of Jumbo, received a gold medal from the society "for his coolness and skill in managing the monster," as the *Tribune* put it. Scott and Newman took turns on the fifteen-day voyage of sitting with their charge, whose cage was little bigger than he was. Although the passage was generally rough and for the first two days Jumbo was seasick and wouldn't eat, much of the time after that was spent in eating or drinking. A typical day's nourishment on the ship included "ten or fifteen loaves of bread, two bushels of oats, three quarts of onions, a bushel of biscuit, two hundred pounds of hay," and as many treats as those onboard could feed him. "He was never stinted in his supply of liquor," the *Sun* reported, "and when he condescended to drink water, took in ten to fifteen gallons at a time."[18]

On the morning after his arrival at Quarantine, Barnum and Hutchinson went out by boat to meet Jumbo up the river near the Jersey City piers, where the *Assyrian Queen* had anchored. Its captain, John Harrison, hailed them with the shout, "Jumbo is all right; fine as silk." Barnum "clambered nimbly" on board the ship, and "his eyes sparkled with boyish eagerness" to see Jumbo again. When he was led down to the big cage, he cried out, "Dear old Jumbo," and "seemed inclined to weep." He declared that he had spent $50,000 acquiring the beast, at which point Hutchinson coughed theatrically and suggested that the real amount was more like $30,000. Barnum asked those assembled how high the elephant could reach with his trunk, hazarding a guess of forty-nine feet. His figure was again challenged when a keeper responded that the real height was a mere twenty-six feet. To which Barnum complacently replied, "If I were a showman, I would have exaggerated it, but there's nothing like the truth." Barnum objected when Jumbo was given a quart of whiskey but did not prevent him from drinking it, and soon after he himself had drunk a ginger pop, he departed.[19]

It took the rest of the day and evening to get Jumbo to Madison Square Garden, as he was lifted in his traveling box onto a barge, which was pulled by a tug to a Manhattan pier, and then a derrick set the box on a flat wagon on land. All of these operations proved difficult and time-consuming. Barnum had sent sixteen horses to pull the wagon, but even with the assistance of two ropes, each two hundred feet long and manned by hundreds of people in the crowd, the wagon would not move. Elephants were then sent for from Madison Square Garden, but eventually the wagon was pulled to more solid ground and moved onto Broadway, only there meeting the two rescue elephants. It was 1 a.m. when Jumbo finally reached the Garden, but because the box was too large to fit through the entrance, he was unceremoniously left outside, his cage covered with tarps to protect him from the cold. The next morning, Scott coaxed him out of the cage, into the Garden, and around the hippodrome track to his new, if temporary home.[20]

Barnum wrote in his edition for 1882 that it took only two weeks of exhibiting "the most famous beast alive" to earn back his investment. Although he would travel tens of thousands of miles by rail for the better part of four seasons, Jumbo's duties remained relatively few: to march in the circus parade into new towns, to give rides, to eat appalling amounts of treats, and to be on exhibit as part of the larger menagerie. Not for him the tricks and dancing of the thirty smaller performing elephants in the Greatest Show on Earth: given his extraordinary size, his dancing might well have been on a par with Barnum's. Under the showman's teetotaler management, Jumbo was no longer permitted to indulge his taste for whiskey, but he was allowed a nightly quart of ale alongside Scott, who would down his own quart.[21]

Something about his enormous size, coupled with his gentleness, opened people's hearts to Jumbo, and he became the greatest attraction the circus offered for the time he was with it, drawing many people for the single purpose of seeing him. He would bring in more than a million dollars in the four seasons he was in America, Bailey estimated. So it was a tremendous emotional loss to two nations, and a financial loss to the Barnum show, when on the evening of September 15, 1885, Jumbo was struck by the engine of a Grand Trunk freight train outside St. Thomas, Ontario. Scott had been leading both Jumbo and a relatively diminutive elephant named Tom Thumb along a main track. The circus cars were on a track on one side, and a ten-foot embankment on the other. The train, which had been unscheduled, whistled down an incline, trying unsuccessfully to stop, first striking Tom Thumb and breaking his leg and then crushing Jumbo, who was unwilling to go down the embankment and was too large to fit in the space between the tracks. After being struck from behind, Jumbo was pushed a hundred feet. A disconsolate Scott tried to soothe his groaning friend for the long minutes until he was gone. Apparently unwilling to enlist the other elephants for the morbid task, those in charge rallied more than a hundred circus workers to pry and pull Jumbo's corpse off the tracks and over the embankment, where the grieving Scott lay with it all night.[22]

News of the tragedy went out by wire to the far reaches of the earth, and Barnum heard it the next morning at his favorite hotel in New York, the Murray Hill. Whatever his true feelings about the death, he could not resist tastelessly telling a reporter that although he had planned to return Jumbo to England for a visit, "while men propose, locomotives dispose." On the one hand, Barnum let it be known that he valued Jumbo at $300,000, but on the other hand it was to his competitive advantage to somewhat underplay the blow this represented to his show, especially at a time when Bailey was on leave for his mental health and ready to sell out his share. Barnum told the press that a taxidermist was hurrying to the site to preserve Jumbo's hide and skeleton. Perhaps because so many animals died in the circus business, Barnum had had the foresight nearly two years earlier to make arrangements with Henry A. Ward, of Ward's Natural Science establishment in Rochester, to be telegraphed immediately "if we lose Jumbo (which heaven forbid!)" so that he could immediately go about his work. Ward went to the site when learning of Jumbo's demise, and Barnum wired him there, "Go ahead, save skin and skeleton. I will pay you justly and honorably." It was one of the most heroic jobs of taxidermy ever. The skin alone weighed more than 1,500 pounds, and the tons of rotting remains were consigned to a huge bonfire as the skeleton was exposed.[23]

By the next season, both the hide (somewhat overstuffed to make Jumbo seem even bigger than he had been) and the skeleton were ready to go on display with the circus, mounted on wheels so that they could be pulled in the circus parade. Meanwhile Barnum had purchased from the Royal Zoological Society an elephant named Alice, which had been presented without much evidence as Jumbo's "wife" before he had left the zoo in London and was now being called Jumbo's "widow" in the British press. As the supposedly grieving widow, she followed the mounted Jumbo specimens in the parade, and other elephants meant to be her attendants followed her, having been trained to wipe their eyes in sorrow with black cloths. Eventually the stuffed Jumbo would go to Tufts College (whose athletic teams are to this day known as the Jumbos) and the skeleton to the American Museum of Natural History in New York, in whose collection it remains.[24]

Bailey officially retired from the circus soon after Jumbo's death, with Barnum and Hutchinson buying him out and bringing in a rich circus owner from Chicago, William W. "Chilly Billy" Cole, and Bailey's former partner James E. Cooper, who ran the menagerie. Barnum wrote Bailey a friendly letter saying how much he admired him and expressing his hope that he would fully recover and eventually get back in business with him.[25]

The new arrangement did not satisfy Barnum as the old one had, in part because the new contract left him only a three-eighths owner, so for the first time he did not have majority control and had to negotiate with his three partners. He got along fine with Hutchinson and Cole, but he and Cooper tangled over what was to be done with the animals in the menagerie when they died. Cooper felt strongly that the dead animals should be sold and not given away to the Smithsonian or elsewhere, as it had been Barnum's wont to do. What might seem like a minor problem deeply irritated Barnum. Although in 1886 the circus visited 144 cities in twenty-one states and the next year the number of cities was up to 175, the profits for both years were merely satisfactory.

By the end of the 1887 season, however, Bailey was indeed recovered and Barnum reached out to him. Yes, he was ready to return to the circus, and Barnum's other partners took their share of the profits and "withdrew from the firm, with my free consent." For $150,000, Bailey bought his way back into an equal share with Barnum, and one of the most famous partnerships in entertainment history, Barnum & Bailey, was officially born.[26]

TWENTY:
LAST YEARS

Less than a month after Barnum and Bailey signed their new agreement, the fifth and last great fire of Barnum's lifetime occurred. It began on the night of November 20, 1887, in the main animal building of the Bridgeport Winter Quarters, and except for thirty of the thirty-four elephants in the show and one lion, all of his animals again perished in the flames. One of the elephants who died was the widow Alice, and another was a rare and much-publicized white elephant that Barnum had acquired from Burma in 1884. The white elephant had been led to safety, but for some reason went back into the burning building. He was "again and again" rescued, but each time went back into the fire, finally succumbing. Barnum concluded that he had "determinedly committed suicide." One escaped elephant made a beeline for Long Island Sound, but died the next day of exposure.

Even the poor lion who got loose did not live long. Having found his way into a barn, he was eating a cow and her calf when a neighbor of the barn's owner shot him dead through a window. Barnum was once again staying at the Murray Hill Hotel when the blaze happened, and when Nancy read him the telegram describing the disaster, he said to her, "I am very sorry my dear, but apparent evils are often blessings in disguise. It is all right." And with that, she recounted, he was back to sleep in three minutes.

This time it was Bailey who went quickly to work, asking agents around the world to help him replace the lost animals. Barnum said he saw Bailey eleven days after the fire, seated at his desk, which was cluttered with letters and telegrams. When Barnum asked him what he was doing, Bailey "coolly remarked, 'I am ordering a menagerie.'" Bailey said he now knew from the correspondence on his desk where to get what they needed, and added, "In six hours we shall own a much finer menagerie than the one we have lost." Whether or not this story is completely true, it makes clear that Barnum now realized, if he had not already known it, that he had found his perfect other half and needed no other. Less than eighteen months later, at the age of seventy-nine, Barnum wrote to Bailey, "I shall certainly stick to life & *to you* as long as I can. *You suit me exactly* as a partner and as a friend."[1]

In his last years, Barnum had both the time and the means to set his affairs in order. Death did not sneak up on him. In the previous decade, he had lost his wife and beloved youngest daughter, and as the 1880s began, two of his closest preacher friends, Abel Thomas and Edward Chapin, both died. At the time that Barnum had been so ill, he recounted, Chapin had from his own deathbed sent a daily messenger inquiring about his health. Minnie Warren had died in 1878, followed by Commodore Nutt in 1881, and then two years later Tom Thumb, little Charley now grown portly, died of apoplexy at home in Massachusetts at the age of forty-five. Barnum was in Montreal at the time; he wired Lavinia his sympathy and then released the text of the telegram to the newspapers. After ten thousand people had passed by Charley's coffin before a church service in Bridgeport, he was buried in Mountain Grove Cemetery, where a marble, life-size likeness of him atop the Stratton family monument to this day stares at Barnum's own monument a few feet away. Near the end of the long burial rite, Lavinia fainted into her mother's arms and had to be carried to her carriage.

Another great blow came to Barnum in 1887, when Jenny Lind Goldschmidt died in London on November 2. She and Barnum had remained on good terms, and the news stirred the warm feelings he had harbored for her when they had been touring together: "I remember the glorious voice of the Nightingale, not alone in the raptures of unrivalled singing, but low and soft, with pitying, tender words, as she sought to comfort one in trouble; or ringing out in the hearty laughter of blithe and vigorous young womanhood."[2]

Barnum had wanted to leave a male heir, and even after Charity and he had had four daughters, he hoped that Nancy would give him the chance to pass on his name. When that did not happen, he persuaded Pauline's oldest son, Clinton Seeley, whom Barnum fondly called Clinte, to change his middle name from Hallett — Charity's maiden name — to Barnum, thus becoming Clinton Barnum Seeley. The persuasion involved a gift of $25,000. Barnum did everything he could to prepare the boy to succeed him in the circus after he was gone, writing to Bailey, "It is better for you & me that my successor be named Barnum." As it turned out, though, Barnum Seeley did not much enjoy circus life, and Bailey did not think much of the boy.[3]

Late in life, Barnum started to style himself "The Children's Friend," in part because of all he had done in his lifetime as a showman to entertain families with kids. Less than a year before he died, he asked Bailey to put that moniker under his portrait in circus publicity materials, and justified the wish by explaining, "It pleases parents & children." But it also pleased Barnum himself. In his last book, *Funny Stories,* he wrote that on his final visit to London, when he and Bailey took the whole show there, the circus posters showed his picture with his name below it. But, he claims, in the United States it was no longer necessary to put his name on posters under his image, just the words "The Children's Friend." The title was no less true for being awarded to himself by himself. From his earliest days as a museum owner, he had always insisted that any enterprise in which he was involved be appropriate for every member of the family, and half-price tickets for children were almost always part of his advertising pitches. Barnum's role in the more general movement to make theatrical performances acceptable for the whole family helped open up the theater to children. In 1855 he had begun the controversial practice of sponsoring baby shows at the American Museum that, for better or worse, filled the establishment with children, their mothers eager to win cash prizes for finest or fattest baby or best twins.[4]

When in 1883 the Society for the Prevention of Cruelty to Children had taken him to court on the grounds that the performances of a cycling family called the Elliott Children were putting them at risk, Barnum set up a private showing for doctors and lawyers, including, as it happened, the three judges who would hear the case. The doctors gave the act a clean bill of health and the judges followed their lead. After the not-guilty judgment, Barnum walked up to his accuser in court, offering to pay him $200 a week to be displayed as a man who would "take the bread out of those children's mouths." In a reprise of his performance when the ASPCA had charged him, Barnum appeared in the center ring of Madison Square Garden to point out that he was a director of the society that was accusing him, and his wife Nancy was the vice president of the Connecticut chapter of the SPCC.[5]

In the 1880s a series of books and stories for young people began to appear under Barnum's name, although the question of how involved he was in their production has never been resolved. A likely answer is that the circus promotion department churned them out with Barnum's oversight and occasional participation. Arthur Saxon speculates that because Nancy had her own literary ambitions, she might have lent a hand as well. Barnum had written an adventure book in 1876 called *Lion Jack: A Story of Perilous Adventures among Wild Men and the Capturing of Wild Beasts, Showing How Menageries Are Made,* followed by a sequel called *Jack in the Jungle.* Many of the subsequent children's books and stories also had subjects related to the capturing of animals and other aspects of the showman's own career.[6]

Barnum's last years often found him surrounded by grandchildren and then great-grandchildren. Nancy had entered married life determined not to stay at home, as Charity had, while Barnum was off on his many travels, and she even wrote an article for *Ladies' Home Journal* warning, "It is an ominous state of things when husband and wife can really enjoy separate pleasures." So the two spent many happy hours together going to the theater or visiting his shows on the road, vacationing in the mountains of New Hampshire, passing the warm months at Waldemere, and making frequent trips back to England to visit her father and friends. But by the 1880s Nancy began to suffer from the same sort of nervous disorders that Charity had, and she began to spend time in posh sanitariums while Barnum was often on his own.[7]

In an 1882 letter to a grand-niece, he explained that he was on the road with the circus, waiting for Nancy to get well because "I thought I would rather be alone in these 3 cities with the show than alone in New York with nothing to do." In 1886 he wrote the daughter-in-law of his friend Abel Thomas that Nancy "has her ups & downs, the latter being twice as numerous as the former. It gives me pain & regret to see & think of, for she really suffers much." Barnum's own health was surprisingly good during these years, and when he wasn't still deeply engaged in his businesses, he spent more and more time either writing to or doting on the children in his family. One recipient of his letters was the grandson of his daughter Helen, Henry Rennell, known as Harry, born in 1882 and living with his family in Harlem. "I think about you and would like to see you every day," Barnum wrote to his great-grandson in the early spring of 1887. In midsummer, when he and Nancy were vacationing in the Adirondacks and the Rennells were staying at a house in sight of Waldemere, he again wrote Harry, "You and I must ride together and see the pigs and other nice things when I get home, and we must ride every day." By September, when Harry had returned to New York with his family, "Now I am going out *alone* in my buggy," Barnum wrote. "If you were here I should drive you awful fast. Hope I shall do it next summer."[8]

In the midsummer letter, he encouraged Harry to say so if he wanted any "new whips or brooms," because "Grandpa Barnum has got plenty of money to buy them for you." He had so much money, in truth, that he spent much of his last decade thinking of ways to give some of it away. At this point in his life, his motive could no longer be thought of as profitable philanthropy, but more along the lines of Mark 8:36: "For what shall it profit a man, if he shall gain the whole world, and lose his own soul?" He had always been generous with Bridgeport, even beyond ways in which he himself could benefit. Years before, he had been involved in establishing a cemetery on the

518

western outskirts, where Mountain Grove was laid out in the best rural-cemetery-movement style, with large trees and pleasant lanes, a place to mourn or just visit surrounded by natural beauty. During the war he had donated spaces for the Union dead, and in 1882, when he was building a crypt for Charity where he himself would be buried, he gave three thousand plots for the poor, to be scattered around Mountain Grove so as not to create a Potter's field, and added another gift of $50,000.[9]

He also helped establish the first hospital in Bridgeport, where he sponsored a free bed for a poor person and served as its president until his death. Having helped create the public library, he donated books he had purchased or culled from his own collection. He continued to sit as a director on boards for water, parks, a bank, horse-pulled streetcars, and a ferry to Port Jefferson. Seaside Park remained his special project. He paid to drain soggy ground, bought more acres and donated them to the city, and laid out new lanes to drive his great-grandchildren up and down in his buggy pulled by his horse Bucephalus. His last major gift to Bridgeport was a Romanesque building on a corner lot in the heart of the city. In 1888 he bought the land for the local medical, scientific, and historical societies and gave them $50,000 to begin construction of the building, which he insisted must be fireproof. He approved the plans for the building, to be called the Barnum Institute of Science and History, soon before his death, and the last change to his will instructed his executors to pay the remainder of the building's cost, which would amount to $35,000. It opened in 1893 and stands today as the Barnum Museum. A tornado in 2010 compromised the structure and a long-term restoration is under way.[10]

Throughout his life, Barnum was a generous supporter of the Universalist Church. For more than four decades he gave money to the Bridgeport society of that faith, making regular contributions each month in addition to paying for such things as having the interior of the meeting house painted in 1848, buying Tiffany stained-glass windows and an organ, making repairs after a fire, building a parsonage, giving the society land, and leaving it $15,000 in his will, wherein he also left thousands more to other Universalist causes. He also supported other churches in Bridgeport and those he attended in New York City. But his biggest legacy related to the church was in his support of Tufts College in Massachusetts, which was nondenominational but founded by Universalists.

He first gave $50,000 to Tufts for the construction of the Barnum Museum of Natural History in the early 1880s, and then left more in his will to have two wings added to the building, in all spending about $100,000. He eagerly supported the museum, sending its curators preserved specimens of animals — many, including Jumbo, having died in his circus — and shipping them duplicates made from collections at the Smithsonian and elsewhere. Barnum kept his intention to contribute the initial money for the building secret until it was revealed at the 1884 commencement for the college. Partly this was to stave off the constant appeals for money he received from other quarters, but it was also because he was not at first comfortable letting his family know that such a large amount would be taken from their legacy. But a few days before the announcement was to be made, he wrote to the Tufts president, "Heirs may as well know I do what I like with my own." The building, the stuffed Jumbo, and the many other specimens Barnum collected for it served the college for nearly a hundred years until, almost inevitably, fire destroyed it all in 1975. It was his sixth and his very last great fire.[11]

Early on the morning of October 12, 1889, Barnum, Nancy, and young Barnum Seeley sailed on the *Etruria* for the showman's final trip to England. The night before he had received friends and at least one reporter at the Murray Hill Hotel, where a dozen people had said their goodbyes with a tone suggesting that they were afraid they would not see him again. When the next person, a good bit younger, addressed him in the same way, Barnum couldn't take it any more. "You will have the pleasure of seeing me here in America again, *if* you are here yourself," he said with humorous emphasis. "Be sure you take care of yourself, and don't get sick and die."[12]

At seventy-nine, Barnum remained strong enough for one last extravaganza, an undertaking he had been dreaming about for years and seriously planning with Bailey for months: to take The Greatest Show on Earth to London. Now he was following forty circus agents across the Atlantic and would be followed in a few days by two ships transporting the entire circus, including England's beloved Jumbo in both his postmortem forms. Barnum offered more than one figure for how much he and Bailey had spent to realize this dream, ranging from $500,000 to $3 million, and he claimed he was prepared to lose $500,000 over the course of the three-month run in Olympia Hall in Kensington. But no such sacrifice would be necessary.[13]

More than twelve hundred performers had crossed the Atlantic with Barnum and Bailey, accompanied by a menagerie of monkeys, elephants, camels, giraffes, and nearly four hundred horses, but by this point in his nearly six-decade career, it was the showman himself who was the greatest show's greatest draw. Indeed the advertisements in the London newspapers barely mentioned Bailey at all, but promised that Barnum would be in attendance at every performance, which he almost always was, despite his years. Soon after the start of each presentation in the cavernous hall, the frenzied activity in the three circus rings paused while Barnum rode in a gilded open carriage around the hippodrome track, the vast oval encompassing the three rings. One of the lion tamers later wrote that, from time to time during this slow procession, Barnum would bid the coachman to stop the matched high-stepping carriage horses, then stand up and croak out in his flat New

England accent to the immense crowd, "I suppose you come to see Barnum, didn't you? Wa-al, I'm Mr. Barnum." Then he would "make a profound bow" and receive the acknowledgment of his patrons, the men doffing their hats and the women flapping their handkerchiefs. Was it the gilded carriage, the finely liveried coachmen, or the deliberate pace of the horses that gave the proceeding the air of a royal personage acknowledging his admiring subjects?[14]

Barnum was greeted in London as a returning hero, with glowing accounts in the newspapers and with circus posters on every corner. A dinner for 150 upper-crusters (organized by, among others, Randolph Churchill, Jenny Lind's widower Otto Goldschmidt, and Oscar Wilde) honored Barnum at the Hotel Victoria, where he was staying. The Greatest Show itself was soon entertaining twelve thousand patrons twice a day at Olympia.

Although Queen Victoria was not in London and did not see the show, as she had hoped to do, two future kings of England did attend. Barnum's widow recalled that this setting "became a rendezvous for the nobility; the favorite resort of the great middle class; and the Mecca for the poor." Barnum charged as little as a shilling for many of the seats, and children were admitted at half price. As he passed through the streets of London, Nancy recalled, he could hear people refer to him affectionately as "Good Old Barnum," which "made his heart and face glow."[15]

Not only did the royals go to the circus, some of them more than once, but so did the Lord Chief Justice of England and the Lord Mayor of London and their wives. The visitor whom Barnum felt most honored by, he told the *Pall Mall Gazette*, was William Gladstone, the liberal, longtime former and still future prime minister of Great Britain, who told Barnum he had read his autobiography. After Barnum tried to puff up his famous guest, he realized "it was no use flattering that man — he could not take any flattery. Oh, he is a truly great old man." And so was Barnum himself, judging by the attention he received during the London visit — which even included modeling for Madame Tussaud's museum, to which he donated a full suit of his clothing for his wax figure.[16]

The grand finale for each of the twice-a-day performances was a new part of the show. This was a huge "panoramic and historical" spectacle developed by the Hungarian producer Imre Kiralfy called

"Nero, or the Destruction of Rome," featuring twelve hundred players and a healthy contingent of the show's menagerie, supported by an orchestra and choir. They staged a grand procession into Rome and a whirlwind of races and games. The gladiator contests alone left the stage "strewn with enough corpses to keep all the coroners in England busy for a month." For the grand finale, Nero feasted and finally died while the city burned. The stage ran along one whole side of Olympia, "half a mile long," one newspaperman declared. In the British papers, the circus ads claimed that $75,000 had been spent on scenery for "Nero" and $250,000 on costumes; presumably the figures were given in dollars instead of pounds so the amount would seem greater.[17]

On New Year's Eve a reporter for the *Licensed Victuallers' Mirror* of London tried to capture the kaleidoscopic action in the spectacle:

Dancing girls in every colour and shade of colour — all silk, satin, and glitter; Troupes of soldiers, horse and foot, in their habits as they lived; barbarians from Gaul and Germany, ladies borne on litters, Roman citizens, gladiators, elephants, priests, musicians, negro slaves, Nero on his splendid car drawn by four horses abreast. . . .

We can compare it to nothing else, as the procession passes round, as the 300 ballet girls go through their evolutions.[18]

Barnum told the *Pall Mall Gazette* that even Gladstone, "the greatest Greek, Hebrew, and Latin scholar in the world today," had found the Roman costumes "most correct" and that he "had nothing to learn from my spectacle of 'Nero.' " If Barnum here takes credit for the spectacle, he did give Kiralfy full credit in all of his advertisements, and as the show continued and "Nero" amazed its audiences, it became ever more prominent in the ads. Bailey got a good deal less credit in the publicity while they were in England, and the circus itself was often called P. T. Barnum's Greatest Show on Earth, which does not seem to have bothered Bailey at all.[19]

Besides making his daily visits to Olympia, Barnum was preparing for publication his large collection of *Funny Stories,* which was released simultaneously in London and New York in 1890. The book contained brand-new material about this visit to London and recorded in print for the first time anecdotes upon which he had drawn for the many hundreds of speeches he had given in his lifetime, but it also contained memories that had appeared in his autobiographical writings. Some of the funny stories, Barnum candidly admitted in his preface, he had "not hesitated to insert" even when he was not "absolutely certain that they are original."[20]

After the circus closed at Olympia on February 15, two and a half million people having seen it, Bailey accompanied it back to New York. Barnum stayed on in London with Nancy, who had contracted the flu and whose health was now "almost a case of life and death" and would require her to remain in England for several more months. But Barnum, who was himself "strong and *well,*" as he wrote to Bailey, expected to be back in New York, without Nancy, in time for the opening of the new season of the circus at Madison Square Garden. He waited for her health to improve somewhat and then sailed for home in March. Nancy returned in June and wrote that when he met her, "the kindly face which smiled up at me over a big bouquet" looked pallid, but that his spirits were high, and they passed a joy-filled summer at Bridgeport, surrounded by his progeny.[21]

Two years before, they had moved into a new mansion built only a few feet to the east of Waldemere itself, which they had decided was too big and too antiquated. Built solidly of brick and stone, the new Queen Anne–style structure had electricity and modern plumbing, and although the goal had been to create a smaller and simpler house, Marina — as Nancy named it — was still substantial, containing an art gallery, a music room, a library, a number of guest rooms, and an office for Barnum built around an open fireplace. With Marina ready to be occupied in the summer of 1888, Waldemere was unceremoniously torn down, its basement filled in and trees planted on the spot. Barnum gave Nancy the deed to the new house.[22]

They spent Barnum's last birthday, his eightieth, there. Nancy recalled that he seemed "on this day unusually anxious that none should be missing, unusually tender to every one present." As the family celebration was under way, so was a special dinner he had planned for all of his employees and their families. He made his way to this other event and addressed the people who had been with him, many of them for decades, expressing his gratitude "with moist eyes, and a voice that now faltered with emotion."

In one last sign suggesting Barnum believed he would never see another birthday, he gave Nancy that favorite gift of his for many years now, a copy of his autobiography. He inscribed the date and wrote, "With love forevermore."[23]

He and Nancy spent the month of August at Paul Smith's Hotel in the Adirondacks, a primitive but elegant haunt of presidents and celebrities where Barnum had been going for many years. After passing September back at Marina, where Barnum gave a last talk about his religious beliefs to his Bridgeport church, they set off for Denver to visit his daughter Helen, stopping in Chicago and Kansas City to visit The Greatest Show on Earth for his last time. They were in Denver for two weeks in October. It was, Nancy wrote, "a month of flawless happiness . . . one unbroken round of pleasure," and everyone who met them saw a "hale, hearty, handsome old man, the incarnation of vigor and hilarity, who received every stranger as an old friend." They had considered going on to Mexico or California, as the intention for the trip had been for Barnum to introduce Nancy to the West. There was even talk of going on from San Francisco to Japan. But instead they returned to Bridgeport.[24]

On November 6, soon after they got home, Barnum came down with what was at first thought to be a bad cold. A small stroke likely accompanied it, since he felt "drowsy and listless" that afternoon. Then, after a few days, came a serious stroke — Nancy called it "acute congestion of the brain" — but thanks to "great care, and his good constitution," he seemed to be on the mend by the beginning of December. His heart, however, which had been a concern for some years, had been weakened, and one of his doctors told Nancy, "The end may not be near, but this is his last sickness." The doctor warned her to keep the diagnosis from Barnum so that depression did not hurry death along, but Barnum knew just the same, and depression was simply not in his nature.

He "was always cheerful," Nancy recalled, "often merry. His room was the one bright spot in a sad house, and his hearty laugh was always heard." He dressed each day, and would sit in the bay window of his room and look out at his gardens, at the park that had been one of his grandest creations, at Long Island Sound, and on clear days at Long Island itself on the horizon. The schooner *P. T. Barnum,* built in Bridgeport, was launched on December 10; it was supposed to sail out of the harbor in front of Seaside Park, where its namesake and part owner could salute her. But the ship became ignominiously grounded, stuck to the muddy bottom, and Barnum did not see her until the next day, when she was towed past his house. During the next few months, he did not suffer from his illness and was able to keep up with his business affairs, even, as Nancy wrote, "carrying out transactions involving hundreds of thousands of dollars." Doctors and nurses were always about, as was his lawyer, his Busy B's, Bridgeport friends, and his family. He did not seem to Nancy like a dying man; still, she wrote, "there came into his eyes a great wistfulness whenever he looked on a loved face."[25]

He continued to work with Bailey on finding new acts for the 1891 season of The Greatest Show on Earth. On March 15 a letter from Barnum appeared as a paid advertisement in the *Tribune,* promoting the new show, which would open on March 26 in a rebuilt Madison Square Garden. It promised that Barnum & Bailey would continue "for all time, and as far as possible this has been provided for." The *Newtown* (Connecticut) *Bee* reported on March 20 that Barnum's doctors had agreed to let him attend the opening, and the New York papers too said that his health was improved and he would be in the city, though this was likely just part of the hype. Although he did not attend the show, when a reporter from the *Bee* rang the electric bell on the front door of Marina on April 3 and was admitted to speak with "the king of the amusement world," he found said king reading in a New York newspaper about the show's opening. Barnum told the reporter, in the last great understatement of his life, that he "was always glad to meet a newspaper man." Soon he was offering up to the writer his plans for his own funeral, lamenting that he could not be cremated because there was no facility nearby. He followed up with a joke about a man spreading his first wife's preserved ashes on his icy front steps so that his second wife would not slip.[26]

Two days after this interview, he asked Nancy to stay with him "every moment of the little time that is left," and at midnight on the following day his heartbeat grew irregular. Those in the family not already present were wired that his hours left on earth were few. During that same night, he told Nancy that his last thoughts were of her. He roused the next morning to hear some election news, to speak comforting words to Nancy, and to whisper greetings to the family members who were gathered around him. Soon his heart began to beat faster and faster and then slower and slower until, just after 6:30 p.m. on April 7, he died.[27]

In the next few days before his funeral, as Barnum's body lay cooling on ice in Marina, a wreath of roses went up on its carved-oak front door. The flag on the house's lawn flew at half mast, as did flags across the city and on boats in the harbor. All the public buildings and many of the private ones in Bridgeport were draped in black and white, as were the buildings for Barnum & Bailey's Winter Quarters. Photos of Bridgeport's most famous and generous resident, draped in black, also appeared in the windows of many residences in the city. Local children boldly knocked on the front door of Marina to ask if they might have one of the roses from the wreath as a keepsake. Such was the sorrowful intimacy they felt for the showman who had given them so much pleasure.

The newspapers that had been his lifeblood did not desert Barnum upon his death. The *New-York Times* weighed in with a six-thousand-word obituary, and the *Times* of London called him "an almost classical figure." Hundreds of newspapers across the American continent shared the sad news with the millions of their readers who had visited the American Museum in their youth or more recently attended a Barnum & Bailey extravaganza in their city or town.[28]

On Friday, April 10, the day of his funeral and burial, the Bridgeport Public Schools were closed, as were the factories and most of the businesses in town. The Greatest Show on Earth itself went dark, as forty-three of its representatives, led by James Bailey and including Imre Kiralfy, made their way to Bridgeport to pay their respects. A late-morning prayer service at Marina for the family and close friends was followed at 2 p.m. by a public funeral at the South Congregational Church, where a suffocatingly dense crowd still left thousands out in the street. Although Barnum had asked to be buried in a plain pine box, his coffin was of cedar with silver trim. The text for the service was from Luke, a favorite expression of Barnum's: "Not my will, but Thine be done, O Lord." His preacher from New York, Robert Collyer, who had begun his working life in England as a blacksmith, gave the funeral address, stressing his friend Barnum's truthfulness and generosity and suggesting that the words on his tomb might read, "Here rests one who never rested." The hymns sung included "I Long for Household Voices Gone," the text by John Greenleaf Whittier, and "O Love Divine, That Stooped to Share," with a text by Oliver Wendell Holmes. At the end of the service, the hundreds in the church wept as they sang "Auld Lang Syne."[29]

But by the afternoon of the next day, as Barnum himself would surely have wanted, the spectacle in Madison Square Garden resumed. Rome would be destroyed twice, at 2 p.m. and 8 p.m., courtesy of Kiralfy. One hundred circus performers — clowns, aerialists, trick horseback riders — and one hundred "amazing acts," from magicians to snake handlers, would fill the three rings, and the hippodrome track would offer zebra, elephant, and other wild animal races. "Mystifying illusions" would accompany "an entire world of startling features." "Children in ecstasies," the ad in the *Tribune* that day proclaimed, "adults astounded." Barnum rested at last in Mountain Grove Cemetery, but the spectacle he had created would, decade after decade, continue to bear his name and delight the millions who would see it.[30]

ACKNOWLEDGMENTS

When I met the Barnum scholar A. H. Saxon in Bridgeport, Connecticut, in March 2016, I was distracted enough by the tour he gave me of Barnum points of interest in that city — the large seated statue of the man gazing out at Long Island Sound from Seaside Park; Barnum's grave site in Mountain Grove Cemetery; Saxon's own collection of Barnum-related art, posters, and memorabilia — that I barely noticed two self-published, spiral-bound notebooks he handed to me. Titled *Barnumiana,* these books by Saxon are modestly described as "a select, annotated bibliography of works by or relating to P. T. Barnum." Once I got home and was able to focus on them, I realized what a valuable gift he had offered me, a painstaking work of scholarship enlivened by his strong, witty opinions, and a perfect guide for someone still trying to wrap his arms around the literature by and about Barnum. Saxon's tour and his bibliography were the first of many acts of generosity that Arthur, as I have come to know him, extended to me as I worked on this book, from telling me where the bodies were buried (and where one particular body was not) to scanning images, thoughtfully reading and annotating a late draft of the book, and always being available, encouraging, and amusing. He did this as he was completing his own final book about Barnum to go with his fine biography and his selected letters of the great showman. The debt I owe him, however, in no way implicates him in any of my book's shortcomings.

Another formidable Barnum scholar, Neil Harris, whose 1973 book, *Humbug,* is both a biography and a social and cultural history, suggested as I was contemplating this book that "each generation seems to need its own" new take on Barnum, and offered his encouragement.

Others who encouraged me early on include David Barber, Ann Beattie, Ernest B. Furgurson, George Gibson, Adam Goodheart, David Grogan, Robert Gross, Edward Hoagland, William Howarth, Ann Hulbert, Malcolm Jones, Kitty Kelley, Ralph Keyes, Donald Lamm, Anne Matthews, Richard Moe, Anton Mueller, Cullen

Murphy, Richard Nicholls, Richard Snow, and Charles Trueheart.

Later in the process, people who helped with a kind word, a reference, or in some other way include David Brown, Lincoln Caplan, Carol Johnson, Steve Lagerfeld, Kathy Lawrence, Walter Nicklin, Eric Nye, Lincoln Perry, Henry Sloss, Wendy Smith, and Todd Thompson. Brenda Wineapple has, as is her way, propped me up throughout with her gracious encouragement and interest.

Those who offered support from institutions include Kathleen Maher, Adrienne Saint-Pierre, and Tova Clayman from the Barnum Museum; Elizabeth Van Tuyl and Mary Witkowski (retired) from the Bridgeport History Center of the Bridgeport Public Library; Carolle Morini and Mary Warnement of the Boston Athenaeum; Michelle A. Krowl of the Library of Congress; Emily Bell at the Widener Library, Harvard University; Kerry Schauber and Lu Harper of the Memorial Art Gallery, University of Rochester; Pamela S. M. Hopkins of the Tisch Library, Tufts University; Nancy Stula of the William Benton Museum of Art at the University of Connecticut; Francis P. O'Neill of the Maryland Historical Society; and Kimberly Reynolds of the Boston

Public Library. My special thanks among these goes to Adrienne Saint-Pierre, who was friendly, helpful, and encouraging over a period of years.

I was lucky to be able to access the online resources of the Sheridan Library at Johns Hopkins University for much of the time I was researching this book. I'm grateful to my friends David Everett and Ed Perlman for making this access possible, and to Elise Levine, Sharon D. Morris, and Feraz Ashraf for their help in extending my eligibility for using this valuable resource. The Library of Congress's Chronicling America website gave me easy access to nineteenth-century newspapers and the Internet Archive to nineteenth-century books.

John Churchill and Frederick Lawrence, colleagues at the Phi Beta Kappa Society, also offered support and good cheer over the years. Coworkers at *The American Scholar* — Steve Anderson, Sally Atwater, Stephanie Bastek, Sudip Bose, Sandra Costich, Taylor Curry, Katie Daniels, Bruce Falconer, Margaret Foster, Allen Freeman, and David Herbick — patiently listened to more P. T. Barnum lore than they might ever have thought possible. Thank you for your forbearance and your friendship. My profound thanks go to Sudip Bose for reading a late version of the book closely and offering his wise comments. Noelani Kirschner, a former intern and continuing contributor to the *Scholar,* helped me immeasurably with fact-checking and photo research. Thank you for your good work, Noelani.

I have many people to thank at Simon & Schuster. First, Jonathan Karp, who acquired the book and offered his enthusiasm throughout. Next, Jonathan Cox, who edited the manuscript with immense energy and care, and did much to improve and focus it. Thanks, too, to Emily Simonson, who has worked with Jon Cox on the final stages of getting the book into print. Mark LaFlaur, a production editor who is himself a writer, made me grateful for his good judgment and conscientiousness, and I thank him and Judith Hoover for their fine copy editing. My gratitude also goes to Will Staehle for the exceptional cover design, to Lewelin Polanco for the handsome interior design, and to the art director, Jackie Seow. I look forward to working with Madeleine Schmitz and Nicole Hines on the publicity and marketing of the book.

Sarah Chalfant of The Wylie Agency has represented me for nearly two decades. Having her standing so ably beside me has been tremendously reassuring, and she and Rebecca Nagel have done so much to make this book happen. Thank you both for your determination, intelligence, and efficiency.

Many of those mentioned above are my friends, but a few friends who have lived this book with me day in and day out include Steve Goodwin, Russ Powell, and Jon Wist. Jon is also creating a website for the book. Melanie and Bill Hinzman offered frequent dips in their pool and other forms of liquid refreshment to look forward to. My thanks to all of them. Two friends for much of my life as a grown-up died as I was at work on this book. For nearly four decades, Cheryl Merser was always there on the phone or through email. Mario Pellicciaro, whom I have known since I was an undergraduate, was wise, modest, faithful, and full of good cheer, the best possible friend. This book is dedicated in part to his memory.

Thanks to my sister, Laurie Kelly, and my sisters-in-law, Charlotte Gatto and Susan Barritt. My sons, Matt, Cole, and Sam Wilson, remain a source of tremendous joy and pride. The latter two have enriched our lives by marrying well, to Shannon Welch and Sameen Ahmadnia, respectively, and now each of these wonderful women has produced an adorable child. I also dedicate this book to those two infants, Leyli and Lars, and to their grandmother, Martha, with whom I would eagerly share another lifetime.

BIBLIOGRAPHY

Adams, Bluford. *E Pluribus Barnum: The Great Showman and the Making of U. S. Popular Culture.* Minneapolis: University of Minnesota Press, 1997.

Bailey, James Montgomery. *History of Danbury, Conn., 1684–1896.* New York: Burr Printing, 1896.

Barnum, P. T. *Funny Stories Told by Phineas T. Barnum.* New York: George Routledge and Sons, 1890.

———. *The Humbugs of the World: An Account of Humbugs, Delusions, Impositions, Quackeries, Deceits and Deceivers Generally, in All Ages.* New York: Carleton, 1866.

———. *The Life of P. T. Barnum, Written by Himself.* New York: Redfield, 1855.

———. *Struggles and Triumphs, or, The Life of P. T. Barnum, Written by Himself.* Ed. George S. Bryan. 2 vols. New York: Alfred A. Knopf, 1927. This edition is based on editions of Barnum's autobiography published in 1855, 1869, and 1889, and includes Nancy Barnum's "The Last Chapter," plus excerpts from annual appendices Barnum wrote in his later years. The many different editions of the autobiography featuring these appendices are accessible in digital archives.

Bartlett, A. D. *Wild Animals in Captivity.* London: Chapman and Hall, 1899.

Bondeson, Jan. *The Feejee Mermaid and Other Essays in Natural and Unnatural History.* Ithaca, NY: Cornell University Press, 1999.

Bulman, Joan. *Jenny Lind: A Biography.* London: James Barrie, 1956.

Burrows, Edwin G., and Mike Wallace. *Gotham: A History of New York City to 1898.* Oxford: Oxford University Press, 1999.

Clemens, Samuel L. *Mark Twain's Sketches, New and Old.* Hartford, CT: American, 1875.

Conklin, George. *The Ways of the Circus; Being the Memories and Adventures of George Conklin, Tamer of Lions.* New York: Harper, 1921.

Cook, James W. *The Arts of Deception: Playing with Fraud in the Age of Barnum.* Cambridge, MA: Harvard University Press, 2001.

———, ed. *The Colossal P. T. Barnum Reader.* Urbana: University of Illinois Press, 2005.

Coup, W. C. *Sawdust & Spangles: Stories & Secrets of the Circus.* Chicago: Stone & Co., 1901.

Dennett, Andrea Stulman. *Weird and Wonderful: The Dime Museum in America.* New York: New York University Press, 1997.

Dickens, Charles. *American Notes for General Circulation.* London: Chapman and Hall, 1842.

Doesticks, J. K., and P. B. Philander. *Doesticks: What He Says.* New York: Edward Livermore, 1955.

Donley, Carol C., and Sheryl Buckley. *The Tyranny of the Normal.* Kent, Ohio: Kent State University Press, 1996.

Emerson, George H. "The Barnums." *The Repository,* 51–52 (1874), pp. 215–20.

Field, Maunsell B. *Memories of Many Men and Some Women.* New York: Harper & Bros., 1874.

Fitzsimons, Raymund. *Barnum in London.* New York: St. Martin's Press, 1970.

Foster, George C. *New York by Gas-Light.* New York: Dewitt & Davenport, 1850.

Freedley, Edwin T. *A Practical Treatise on Business: Or How to Get, Save, Spend, Give, Lend, and Bequeath Money.* Philadelphia: Lippincott, Grambo, 1855.

Goodman, Matthew. *The Sun and the Moon: The Remarkable True Account of Hoaxers, Showmen, Dueling Journalists, and Lunar Man-Bats in Nineteenth-Century New York.* New York: Basic Books, 2008.

Harris, Neil. *Humbug: The Art of P. T. Barnum.* Boston: Little, Brown, 1973.

Holland, H. S., and W. S. Rockstro. *Memoir of Madame Jenny Lind-Goldschmidt: Her Early Art-Life and Dramatic Career, 1820–1851.* 2 vols. London: John Murray, 1891.

Hone, Philip. *The Diary of Philip Hone, 1828–1851.* Ed. Allan Nevins. New York: Dodd, Mead, 1936.

Howe, Daniel Walker. *What Hath God Wrought: The Transformation of America, 1815–1848.* New York: Oxford University Press, 2007.

Irving, Washington. *Washington Irving's Sketch-Book.* New York: Longmans, Green, 1905.

Kunhardt, Philip B., Jr., Philip B. Kunhardt III, and Peter W. Kunhardt. *P. T. Barnum: America's Greatest Showman.* New York: Alfred A. Knopf, 1995.

Leech, Margaret. *Reveille in Washington, 1860–1865.* New York: Harper & Row, 1941.

Lehman, Eric D. *Becoming Tom Thumb: Charles Stratton, P. T. Barnum, and the Dawn of American Celebrity.* Middletown, CT: Wesleyan University Press, 2013.

Leland, Charles Godfrey. *Memoirs.* 2 vols. London: William Heinemann, 1893.

Lewis, John Delaware. *Across the Atlantic.* London: George Earle, 1851.

Ludlow, Noah M. *Dramatic Life as I Found It: A Record of Personal Experience.* St. Louis, MO: G. I. Jones, 1880.

McGlinchee, Claire. *The First Decade of the Boston Museum.* Boston: Bruce Humphries, 1940.

Nichols, Thomas L. *Forty Years of American Life.* 2 vols. London: John Maxwell, 1864.

Northall, William Night. *Before and Behind the Curtain: Or, Fifteen Years' Observations Among the Theatres of New York.* New York: W. F. Burgess, 1851.

Orosz, Joel J. *Curators and Culture: The Museum Movement in America, 1740–1870.* Tuscaloosa: University of Alabama Press, 1990.

Reiss, Benjamin. *The Showman and the Slave: Race, Death, and Memory in Bar-*

num's America. Cambridge, MA: Harvard University Press, 2001.

Reynolds, David S. *Waking Giant: America in the Age of Jackson.* New York: Harper, 2008.

———. *Walt Whitman's America: A Cultural Biography.* New York: Alfred A. Knopf, 1995.

Rosenberg, Charles G. *Jenny Lind in America.* New York: Stringer & Townsend, 1851.

Ruskin, John. *The Works of John Ruskin.* Vol. 34. Ed. E. T. Cook and Alexander Wedderburn. London: George Allen, 1908.

Ryan, Kate. *Old Boston Museum Days.* Boston: Little, Brown, 1915.

Saxon, A. H. *Barnumiana: A Select, Annotated Bibliography of Works by or Relating to P. T. Barnum.* Fairfield, CT: Jumbo's Press, 1995. First supplement in 2000.

———. *P. T. Barnum: The Legend and the Man.* New York: Columbia University Press, 1989.

———, ed. *Selected Letters of P. T. Barnum.* New York: Columbia University Press, 1983.

Shultz, Gladys Denny. *Jenny Lind: The Swedish Nightingale.* Philadelphia: J. B. Lippincott, 1962.

Smith, Albert. "A Go-Ahead Day with Barnum." In Gottfried August Bürger, ed., *Wild Oats and Dead Leaves*. London: Chapman and Hall, 1860.

Smith, Sol. *The Theatrical Journey-Work and Anecdotal Recollections of Sol Smith*. Philadelphia: T. B. Peterson, 1854.

Stratton, Charles S. *Sketch of the Life, Personal Appearance, Character and Manners of Charles S. Stratton, the Man in Miniature, Known as General Tom Thumb*. New York: Wynkoop & Hallenbeck, 1863.

Strong, George Templeton. *The Diary of George Templeton Strong*. Ed. Allan Nevins and Milton Halsey Thomas. 4 vols. New York: Macmillan, 1952.

Thompson, C. J. S. *The Mystery and Lore of Monsters*. London: Williams & Norgate, 1930.

Twain, Mark. *Collected Tales, Sketches, Speeches, and Essays, 1852–1890*. New York: Library of America, 1992.

Wallace, Irving. *The Fabulous Showman: The Life and Times of P. T. Barnum*. New York: Alfred A. Knopf, 1959.

Wilentz, Sean. *Chants Democratic: New York and the Rise of the American Working Class, 1788–1850*. New York: Oxford University Press, 1984.

Williams, Robert C. *Horace Greeley: Champion of American Freedom.* New York: New York University Press, 2006.

Willis, N. Parker. *Memoranda of the Life of Jenny Lind.* Philadelphia: Robert E. Peterson, 1851.

Wright, Richardson. *Hawkers and Walkers in Early America.* New York: Frederick Ungar, 1927.

NOTES

Abbreviations Used in Notes

Kunhardts: Kunhardt, Philip B., Jr., Philip B. Kunhardt III, and Peter W. Kunhardt. *P. T. Barnum: America's Greatest Showman.* New York: Alfred A. Knopf, 1995.

Life of PTB: Barnum, P. T. *The Life of P. T. Barnum, Written by Himself.* New York: Redfield, 1855.

PTB: Saxon, A. H. *P. T. Barnum: The Legend and the Man.* New York: Columbia University Press, 1989.

SL: Saxon, A. H., ed. *Selected Letters of P. T. Barnum.* New York: Columbia University Press, 1983.

S&T: Barnum, P. T. *Struggles and Triumphs, or, The Life of P. T. Barnum, Written by Himself.* Ed. George S. Bryan, 2 vols. New York: Alfred A. Knopf, 1927.

Introduction: "Do You Know Barnum?"

1. Barnum tells the mermaid story well in his autobiography, *Life of PTB,* pp. 231–42.
2. Barnum, *Funny Stories,* p. 361.
3. Barnum, *The Humbugs of the World,* pp. 20, 24.
4. *SL,* p. 103, letter to Messrs. R. Griffin & Co., Jan. 27, 1860.
5. The publisher's note to Barnum's *The Humbugs of the World* quotes the New York *Sun:* "In his breadth of views, his profound knowledge of mankind, his courage under reverses, his indomitable perseverance, his ready eloquence, and his admirable business tact, we recognize the elements that are conducive to success. . . . More than almost any other living man, Barnum may be said to be a representative type of the American mind" (p. iv).

One: The Richest Child in Town

1. *Life of PTB,* p. 105.
2. Ibid., p. 10.
3. Ibid., p. 13.
4. Ibid., p. 11.
5. *S&T,* p. 749.
6. Bailey, *History of Danbury,* pp. 540–46;

Life of PTB, p. 13.

7. S&T, p. 4.

8. Life of PTB, p. 20.

9. Ibid., pp. 4–10.

10. Ibid., p. 28.

11. Ibid., pp. 28, 39.

12. S&T, pp. 13–19.

13. PTB, p. 48. From a speech Barnum gave in 1886 at a Universalist convention in Bridgeport, Connecticut, published in the Christian Leader, Sept. 23, 1886, referenced by Saxon.

14. Life of PTB, pp. 91–92.

15. S&T, pp. 52–56.

16. Life of PTB, p. 99.

17. Bailey, History of Danbury, pp. 541–46.

18. S&T, pp. 66–68.

19. Life of PTB, pp. 108–9; S&T, p. 68.

20. Ibid., pp. 69–71; PTB, 350n37.

21. S&T, pp. 56–57; Life of PTB, pp. 98, 108.

22. S&T, pp. 77, 85–86.

23. Ibid., p. 87; Kunhardts, p. 16; PTB, pp. 40–41.

24. S&T, pp. 84–85.

25. Ibid., pp. 88–89. Saxon notes that Barnum's apparent religious and political differences with Uncle Alanson could not have helped their business partnership at the Yellow Store (PTB, p. 41).

26. Howe, What Hath God Wrought, p. 228:

"It did not require much capital to publish one of the small papers typical of the day. Even a limited circulation made the enterprise viable, and papers often catered to a specific audience."

27. The letter was to Gideon Welles, editor of the *Hartford (CT) Times,* who would later serve as secretary of the navy under Lincoln. *SL,* p. 2, PTB to Gideon Welles, Oct. 7, 1832; *PTB,* pp. 42, 351n49; *S&T,* p. 90.

28. *SL,* p. 2, PTB to Gideon Welles, Oct. 7, 1832; *PTB,* pp. 42, 351n49; *S&T,* p. 90. Seelye married a Taylor; one of his sons became the president of Amherst College and a U.S. congressman, and another became the first president of Smith College.

29. On the day of his release, the *Herald of Freedom* contained a note saying in part, "We embrace the first opportunity to tender our warmest thanks to Mr. Crofut, (the Jailer), and his family, for their untiring exertions to render our stay with them as agreeable as the circumstances would permit." Song lyrics: "Notated Music: Image 2 of Strike the Cymbal!," Library of Congress, 1821, https://www.loc.gov/resource/sm1821.360050.0/?sp=2. *S&T,* p. 92; *PTB,* p. 44.

30. *Herald of Freedom,* Dec. 5, 1832.

Two: The Nursemaid

1. *PTB,* p. 45; *Life of PTB,* pp. 141–42.
2. *S&T,* pp. 97, 99.
3. Ibid., pp. 102–3.
4. Ibid., pp. 103–4; J. David Hacker, "Decennial Tables for the White Population of the United States, 1790–1900," *Historical Methods* 43, no. 2 (2010): 45–79.
5. Thompson, *The Mystery and Lore of Monsters,* p. 17. Thompson begins his study, "From the earliest period of the world's history abnormal creatures or monstrosities, both human and animal, have existed from time to time and excited the wonder of mankind."
6. Leslie A. Fiedler, "From *Freaks,*" in Donley and Buckley, *The Tyranny of the Normal,* pp. 11–25. *S&T,* pp. 104–5.
7. Ibid., pp. 105–6; *SL,* p. 8, letter to "Mr. Baker," c. Mar. 1853; *PTB,* pp. 68–69. Saxon identifies William P. Saunders, whose name appears on the written agreement between Barnum and Lindsay but is then scratched out, as the likely source of the borrowed $500.
8. *S&T,* pp. 107–8.
9. *New York Evening Star,* Aug. 7, 1835; *S&T,*

pp. 108–9.

10. "The Joice Heth Hoax," *New York Herald,* Sept. 24, 1836.

11. Kunhardts, p. 20.

12. *S&T,* p. 112.

13. Ibid., p. 111. Reiss, *The Showman and the Slave,* pp. 30–43 discusses the freak show and racist qualities of the exhibition and reception of Joice Heth. The entire book focuses on the Heth affair, providing a great deal of context for it. Still, his harsh judgment of Barnum comes at least in part from his own reluctance to see Barnum in the context of his times, and Reiss tends to read Barnum's fictional or satirical writings as pure fact.

14. Reiss, *The Showman and the Slave,* pp. 90–91; *S&T,* p. 113.

15. Edgar Allan Poe, "Maelzel's Chess-Player," American Studies at the University of Virginia, http://xroads.virginia.edu/~hyper/poe/maelzel.html; Goodman, *The Sun and the Moon,* pp. 248–51.

16. *S&T,* p. 114; Reiss, *The Showman and the Slave,* p. 116. The gist of the story is true, but it may not have happened in Boston, and not for several more months. According to Reiss, "numerous details about the humbug are either misremem-

bered or fabricated," and once the automaton story did come out, Barnum was no longer touring with Heth, who was being shepherded by Lyman. But Reiss's evidence proves only that the automaton allegation happened elsewhere, not that it didn't happen in Boston as well.

17. *Life of PTB,* p. 171.

18. Reiss, *The Showman and the Slave,* pp. 135–36.

19. Richard Adams Locke was well known for an infamous hoax from the previous year. The *Sun*'s "Moon Hoax" claimed that John Herschel, the famous British astronomer, had built a telescope powerful enough to see creatures on the Moon, including bat-people and unicorns. Goodman's *The Sun and the Moon* covers the hoax comprehensively.

20. The bet was for $350. *Sun* (New York), Mar. 1, 1836.

21. *Life of PTB,* p. 176.

22. Saxon, who has lived not far from Bethel for decades, continues to this day to search for any record of her burial or sign of her gravesite, without luck. Personal communication with author.

Three: On Broadway

1. *Life of PTB,* pp. 160, 171.
2. Ibid., p. 207.
3. Ibid., p. 193.
4. Ibid., pp. 187–88.
5. Ibid., pp. 208–9.
6. Ibid., p. 209.
7. Burrows and Wallace, *Gotham,* p. 640.
8. Nichols, *Forty Years of American Life,* pp. 231–32; *Life of PTB,* p. 211.
9. Ludlow, *Dramatic Life as I Found It,* p. 533, cited in *PTB,* p. 81.
10. *Life of PTB,* p. 215.
11. Saxon calls *Adventures of an Adventurer* "almost" a rehearsal for the autobiography (*PTB,* p. 88). That some contemporary scholars have read the work largely as a confession shows just how ambiguous a work it is and perhaps also says something about our eagerness to misread historical figures who embody times whose values do not live up to our own.
12. *Life of PTB,* pp. 215–16; Burrows and Wallace, *Gotham,* pp. 316, 320.
13. Loyd Haberly, "The American Museum from Baker to Barnum," *New-York Historical Society Quarterly* 43, no. 3 (July 1959): 272–87, http://nyheritage.nnyln.net/cdm/pageflip/collection/NYHSR01/id/12552/

type/compoundobject/show/12443/cpdty
pe/monograph/pftype/image#page/4/
mode/2up; Orosz, *Curators and Culture,*
pp. 132–33.

14. Haberly, "The American Museum from Baker to Barnum," p. 287.

15. *Life of PTB,* p. 216.

16. Ibid., pp. 216–22.

17. At the end of the decade, the journalist George C. Foster said the light sent "a livid, ghastly glare for a mile up the street, and pushing the shadows of the omnibuses well nigh to Niblo's. . . . That untiring chromatic wheel goes ever round and round, twining and untwining its blue, red and yellow wreaths of light in unvarying variety" (*New York by Gas-Light,* p. 71).

18. Dickens, *American Notes for General Circulation,* p. 216.

19. *PTB,* p. 93.

20. Doesticks and Philander, *Doesticks,* p. 47.

21. *Life of PTB,* p. 225. Barnum removed this passage from *Struggles and Triumphs,* the 1869 version of his autobiography, where he is more defensive, justifying his more extreme efforts to publicize his public entertainments by saying such things were generally done, even if he did them with "more energy, far more ingenu-

ity, and a better foundation for such promises" (*S&T,* p. 198).

22. *Life of PTB,* p. 223.

Four: The Mermaid

1. *New York Herald,* June 24, 1841, and Sept. 25, 1841.
2. *Life of PTB,* pp. 234–36.
3. Ibid., p. 231.
4. Bondeson, *The Feejee Mermaid,* pp. 36–48. William Clift no longer felt bound by his agreement to be silent about his findings when Captain Eades falsely advertised that he had vouched for the mermaid's authenticity.
5. *Life of PTB,* p. 232.
6. Ibid., pp. 238–41.
7. Ibid., pp. 238–39. "The public appeared to be satisfied, but as some persons always *will* take things literally, and make no allowance for poetic license even in mermaids, an occasional visitor . . . would be slightly surprised."
8. As late as 1845, Lyman asked Kimball if he could resume the role of Dr. Griffin and take the Fejee Mermaid on tour, so he didn't rush off to Nauvoo. *PTB,* p. 123.
9. *S&T,* pp. 207–12.
10. Letter from PTB to MK, Feb. 5, 1843,

Boston Athenaeum.

11. Ibid.

12. Harris, *Humbug.* Harris describes the controversy in Charleston in detail (pp. 64–67). Letters quoted are cited by Harris from *Charleston Mercury,* Jan. 21, 1843, and Feb. 5, 1843.

13. Letters from PTB to MK, Feb. 10 and 13, 1843, Boston Athenaeum.

14. Ibid., Feb. 21, Mar. 3 and 20, Apr. 4 and 8, 1843.

15. Ibid., Jan. 30, Feb. 10, Mar. 8, 1843.

16. Ibid., Oct. 4, 1843.

17. Ibid., Mar. 8, 1843.

18. Ibid., Mar. 22 and 29, Apr. 4, 1843.

Five: The General

1. Lehman, *Becoming Tom Thumb,* pp. 10–15.

2. *Life of PTB,* p. 243.

3. Ibid., p. 244.

4. *The History of Tom Thumb,* published in 1621, was the first fairy tale to appear in print in English; Henry Fielding wrote a play called *The Life and Death of Tom Thumb the Great,* published in 1731.

5. *The Diaries of Julia Lawrence Hasbrouck,* "December 8, 1842 — 'Thanksgiving Day,' " https://frommypenandpower

.wordpress.com/2014/12/08/december-8 -1842-thanksgiving-day/.

6. Cook, *The Colossal P. T. Barnum Reader,* p. 119. If it was indeed a Thanksgiving Day turkey, Webb does not say so.

7. Kunhardts, p. 48; Lehman, *Becoming Tom Thumb,* p. 23; Wallace, *The Fabulous Showman,* p. 74; *Life of PTB,* p. 244.

8. *New York Herald,* Dec. 9, 1842. Napoleon has been unfairly characterized as short. He was five-foot-seven, which would not have been considered short in his time.

9. *Omaha Bee,* Feb. 6, 1883, cited in Lehman, *Becoming Tom Thumb,* p. 24; Lehman, *Becoming Tom Thumb,* p. 23.

10. *Life of PTB,* p. 245.

11. *SL,* pp. 13–14, PTB to MK, Jan. 30, 1843.

12. *Life of PTB,* p. 393; *PTB,* p. 125. Saxon found information about Hitchcock in Universalist Church archives, including records showing that he returned to preaching for the last two decades of his life, after working on and off for Barnum for more than twenty years. Saxon notes that Hitchcock's church obituary in 1883 says of this long connection with the showman only that the reverend, "for a number of years, was engaged in secular life."

13. All from Boston Athenaeum.

14. *New York Herald,* Dec. 1, 1843.

15. Daily ads in Jan. 1844 in the *New York Herald, Tribune,* and *Commercial Advertiser. Commercial Advertiser,* Jan. 18, 1844; (Washington) *National Intelligencer,* Jan. 22 and 30, 1844.

16. *New York Herald,* Jan. 19, 1844; Kunhardts, p. 53.

17. *National Intelligencer,* Jan. 22, 1844.

18. *Life of PTB,* pp. 246–47; *New York Atlas,* Mar. 17, 1844, cited in Cook, *The Colossal P. T. Barnum Reader,* p. 60.

19. *New York Atlas,* Mar. 17, 1844, cited in Cook, *The Colossal P. T. Barnum Reader,* p. 60; *S&T,* pp. 242–43.

20. In the 1855 autobiography he changes the order to "regret and joy," and in the 1869 version he does not characterize the tears at all.

Six: The Queen

1. *Life of PTB,* pp. 249–50.

2. Ibid., pp. 252–53.

3. Fitzsimons, *Barnum in London,* pp. 72–73.

4. Ibid., p. 73; James Stonehouse, *New and Complete Hand Book for the Stranger in*

Liverpool (Liverpool: Henry Lacey, 1844), p. 184.

5. Fitzsimons, *Barnum in London,* pp. 74, 78–79; *Illustrated London News,* Feb. 24, 1844.

6. Robert D. Richardson Jr., *Emerson: The Mind on Fire* (Berkeley: University of California Press, 1995), p. 13.

7. *Life of PTB,* pp. 255–56. In a letter to the *New York Atlas* (Mar. 31, 1844) cited in Cook, *The Colossal P. T. Barnum Reader,* p. 61, Barnum writes that the purse contained twenty gold sovereigns, worth twenty pounds sterling.

8. *New York Atlas,* Apr. 24, 1844; Fitzsimons, *Barnum in London,* pp. 87–88; *Catalogue of Catlin's Indian Gallery* (New York, 1837), p. 35; *A Descriptive Catalogue of Catlin's Indian Gallery* (New York, 1845), p. 3. Catlin catalogues from Smithsonian Institution Archives of American Art.

9. George Catlin, *Adventures of the Ojibbeway and Ioway Indians in England, France, and Belgium* (London: Self-published, 1852); PTB to MK, July 29–Aug. 1, 1844, Boston Athenaeum.

10. *Life of PTB,* p. 56.

11. Lehman, *Becoming Tom Thumb,* p. 3.

12. The offending dog was likely not a

poodle but one of the queen's collies, named Sharp, which was well known for its bad temperament. Helen Rappaport, *Queen Victoria: A Biographical Companion* (Santa Barbara, CA: ABC-CLIO, 2003), p. 36.

13. Barnum's anecdote about the first visit to Buckingham Palace: *New York Atlas,* June 9, 1844. *Life of PTB,* pp. 256–59; *S&T,* pp. 250–53.

14. *PTB,* p. 132; *SL,* pp. 24–25, PTB to Edward Everett, Mar. 23, 1844.

15. *Times* (London), Apr. 7, 1844.

16. *Life of PTB,* p. 263.

Seven: The Continent

1. Morna Daniels, "Paris National and International Exhibitions from 1798 to 1900: A Finding-List of British Library Holdings," 2013, Electronic British Library Journal, http://www.bl.uk/eblj/2013articles/article6.html. Barnum writes in the later version of his autobiography that during this visit he also often watched Robert-Houdin perform his magic act at the Palais Royal, but those performances did not begin until the following year, so Barnum must have seen him on a subsequent visit to Paris (*S&T,* p. 260). Jean-

Eugène Robert-Houdin, *Memoirs* (London: Chapman and Hall, 1860), pp. 148–50, 173, 184.

2. *New York Atlas,* Aug. 18, 1844; Hector Berlioz Website, "Berlioz in Paris," http://www.hberlioz.com/Paris/BPOlympique.html.

3. *Life of PTB,* p. 264; *S&T,* p. 291.

4. Smith, "A Go-Ahead Day with Barnum," pp. 86–101.

5. Irving, *Washington Irving's Sketch-Book,* p. 273.

6. Smith, "A Go-Ahead Day with Barnum," pp. 91–92.

7. *S&T,* p. 294.

8. *New York Atlas,* June 16, 1844.

9. *PTB,* pp. 137–38; *New York Atlas,* Dec. 29, 1844.

10. *New York Atlas,* Nov. 24, 1844; *PTB,* pp. 37–38.

11. *New York Atlas,* Jan. 5, 1845, in Cook, *The Colossal P.T. Barnum Reader,* p. 76. "Codfish aristocracy" has its origins as a description of people in Massachusetts who got rich quick from commercial fishing. A more general meaning refers to anyone with recently acquired wealth.

12. Ibid., July 21, 1844; Feb. 16, 1845; Apr. 20, 1845.

13. *PTB,* p. 223.

14. *Illustrated London News,* Apr. 26, 1845, p. 258. The report mistakenly says that Queen Victoria had given Tom the watch.

15. *S&T,* pp. 262–64.

16. Ibid., p. 264.

17. *Illustrated London News,* May 24, 1845, p. 334.

18. PTB to "Friend Risley," Aug. 8, 1845, "Document: P. T. Barnum Letter Copybook, 1845–1846," Barnum Museum, http://collections.ctdigitalarchive.org/islandora/object/60002%3A185#page/1/mode/2u; *S&T,* pp. 268–69; *PTB,* p. 148.

19. PTB to "Friend Stratton," Aug. 6, 1845, Barnum Museum; *SL,* pp. 32, 34, PTB to Moses Kimball, Apr. 30 and Aug. 26, 1845; *New York Atlas,* Jan. 18, 1846, cited in *PTB,* p. 147.

20. Hone, *The Diary of Philip Hone,* vol. 2, p. 795; *S&T,* pp. 303, 307; Lehman, *Becoming Tom Thumb,* p. 154.

21. PTB to MK, Jan. 4, 1847, Boston Athenaeum.

Eight: At Home

1. PTB to "Mrs. B," Aug. 13, 1845, Barnum Museum.

2. *Brooklyn Daily Eagle,* May 25, 1846; Reynolds, *Walt Whitman's America,* p. 114.

3. Lehman, *Becoming Tom Thumb,* p. 64; *PTB,* p. 148.

4. *SL,* p. 35, PTB to MK, Aug. 18, 1846.

5. *PTB,* p. 150; *SL,* pp. 35–37, PTB to MK, Aug. 18, 1846, and Mar. 30, 1847. The *Great Western,* the steamship on which he had returned to New York in April, was one he would often take to cross the Atlantic, in spite of having bad relations with its captain, who at one point threatened to place Barnum in irons for too strenuously arguing about who should be conducting Sunday services on the ship.

6. PTB to MK, Jan. 4, 1847, Boston Athenaeum.

7. *PTB,* p. 150; Lehman, *Becoming Tom Thumb,* p. 71; PTB to MK, Jan. 4, 1847, Boston Athenaeum.

8. Hone, *The Diary of Philip Hone,* p. 795, cited in Lehman, *Becoming Tom Thumb,* p. 73.

9. *Brooklyn Daily Eagle,* Jan. 29, 1849.

10. *SL,* pp. 37–38, PTB to MK, Mar. 30, 1847.

11. *PTB,* p. 372n4; *Life of PTB,* pp. 401–3.

12. *Boston Daily Atlas,* Nov. 2, 1846; *S&T,* p. 309.

13. *PTB,* p. 372n7; *Brooklyn Daily Eagle,* Aug. 31, 1848.

14. *S&T,* p. 311.

15. Caroline Barnum, "Diary, July 5–Aug. 11, 1848," Bridgeport Public Library, cited in *PTB,* pp. 153–54 and Lehman, *Becoming Tom Thumb,* pp. 79–80.

16. A. H. Saxon, ed., *Tom Thumb Performs in Danbury (Extracts from the Oak Cottage Diary of James White Nichols)* (Fairfield, CT: Jumbo's Press, 2010), pp. xxiv–xxviii.

17. *Life of PTB,* pp. 366–78.

18. *S&T,* p. 313. A newspaper story at the time reported that Barnum and Kimball spent only $3,500 for the museum and that "both of them had long been in treaty for it, and but for a compromise between them, it would probably have brought from 30 to $40,000" (*Boston Courier,* Dec. 3, 1849).

19. *Life of PTB,* pp. 109, 359–62.

20. *Sun* (New York), Jan. 13, 1884, cited in P. T. Barnum, *Struggles and Triumphs; or, Fifty Years' Recollections of P. T. Barnum, Written by Himself,* author's edition (Buffalo, NY: Courier, 1884), Hathi Trust Digital Library, https://babel.hathitrust .org/cgi/pt?id=mdp.39015005687804; view=1up;seq=411.

21. Ibid.

22. *Life of PTB,* pp. 349–51.

23. *Daily National Whig* (Washington), Mar. 26, 1849, reprinting an item from the

Newark, N. J., Advertiser. A good brief description of the expedition is in Tom Chaffin, *Pathfinder: John Charles Frémont and the Course of American Empire* (New York: Hill & Wang, 2002), pp. 396–404. Chaffin writes that Kit Carson said of the guide who led the relief detail, "In starving times no man who knew him ever walked in front of Bill Williams" (p. 402).

24. *New York Herald,* Apr. 18, 1849.

Nine: The Voice

1. Shultz, *Jenny Lind,* pp. 117–18; "Jenny Lind," *Encyclopaedia Britannica,* https://archive.org/stream/encyclopaediabri16ch isrich#page/716/mode/2up/search/Lind; *Times* (London), May 5, 1847.
2. Bulman, *Jenny Lind,* pp. 158, 164.
3. *New York Herald,* July 25, 1847.
4. *S&T,* pp. 215–16.
5. Bulman, *Jenny Lind,* p. 20.
6. *Life of PTB,* pp. 296–97.
7. *Times* (London), May 11, 1849.
8. Bulman, *Jenny Lind,* pp. 195–219; Shultz, *Jenny Lind,* pp. 131–44.
9. Bulman, *Jenny Lind,* pp. 220–21, 225.
10. Shultz, *Jenny Lind,* pp. 147–48.
11. Ibid., pp. 152–55; Leech, *Reveille in Washington,* pp. 290–91.

12. *Life of PTB*, pp. 298–304.

13. Shultz, *Jenny Lind*, p. 154.

14. *Life of PTB*, pp. 302–6.

15. *Boston Daily Atlas*, Feb. 21, 1850; *S&T*, p. 327.

16. *North Star* (Rochester, NY), Feb. 22, 1850.

17. *New York Express*, cited in *Milwaukee Sentinel and Gazette*, Aug. 20, 1850; *Life of PTB*, p. 309.

18. *Life of PTB*, p. 306; Shultz, *Jenny Lind*, p. 161; *Times* (London), Aug. 21, 1850.

19. Holland and Rockstro, *Memoir of Madame Jenny Lind-Goldschmidt*, vol. 2, p. 411.

20. *Life of PTB*, p. 307.

21. *New-York Daily Tribune*, Sept. 2, 1850.

22. *Life of PTB*, pp. 307–8.

23. The kingdoms of Sweden and Norway were united under the Swedish crown for much of the nineteenth century, and the kingdoms had a united flag as well as individual flags. The *Herald* reported that in this instance the united flag of Sweden and Norway was flown.

24. *New York Herald*, Sept. 2, 1850.

Ten: Temples of Entertainment

1. *New York Herald,* June 16, 1850.
2. The availability of ice water and good ventilation mattered on summer days in New York. Barnum and the owners of other theaters promoted in their ads both fresh air and ease of escape in case of fire. See the Bowery Theatre ad in *New York Herald,* July 4, 1850.
3. *Barnum's American Museum Illustrated* (New York: William Van Norden & Frank Leslie, 1850), p. 2.
4. *The Nation,* Aug. 10, 1865, cited in *PTB,* pp. 107, 362n52; *PTB,* p. 105.
5. Speculation has it that a Boston Unitarian minister, Rev. John Pierpont, wrote the original story but remained anonymous because of the low reputation of theater (Uncle Tom's Cabin & American Culture: A Multi-Media Archive, "The Drunkard," http://utc.iath.virginia.edu/sentimnt/drunkardhp.html); *SL,* p. 39, PTB to MK, Feb. 2, 1848; *SL,* p. 42, circular letter, June 1850. Adams, *E Pluribus Barnum,* p. 119, points out that the play also appeared at the National and Bowery theaters at the same time.
6. *New-York Daily Tribune,* June 19, 1850.
7. J. B. Pond, *Eccentricities of Genius:*

Memories of Famous Men and Women of the Platform and Stage (London: Chatto & Windus, 1901), pp. 350–51, cited in *PTB,* p. 334.

8. National Park Service, "Castle Clinton," https://www.nps.gov/cacl/learn/history culture/index.htm; National Park Service, Manhattan Historic Sites Archive, "Castle Clinton National Monument," http://www .mhsarchive.org/castle-clinton.aspx ?dir=cacl.

9. *New-York Daily Tribune,* Sept. 12, 1850.

10. *New York Herald,* Sept. 12, 1850; Shultz, *Jenny Lind,* pp. 194–95.

11. *S&T,* p. 341; *PTB,* pp. 174–75; Adams, *E Pluribus Barnum,* pp. 43–44; Shultz, *Jenny Lind,* p. 202. Shultz writes that the proprietor of the New York Hotel claimed to have paid Barnum $1,000 a day if Lind stayed there, and that Barnum repeated this sort of arrangement throughout her tour.

12. *New-York Daily Tribune,* Sept. 23, 1850; Bulman, *Jenny Lind,* p. 254.

13. As Saxon points out, it is odd that this second friend did not see the publicity value in bidding for the first ticket. He was the patent-medicine purveyor Benjamin Brandreth, a household name for decades in the nineteenth century, famous

from the mass advertising of his products, and as one of the pioneers of mass advertising, an early model for Barnum (*PTB*, pp. 76, 169). Rosenberg, *Jenny Lind in America,* pp. 44–45, says that Colonel Ross did attend each of the Lind concerts in Havana the next spring. Lind's comment: Field, *Memories of Many Men,* p. 220.

14. Rosenberg, *Jenny Lind in America,* pp. 44–49.
15. *New York Herald,* Oct. 14, 1850.
16. Ibid.; Rosenberg, *Jenny Lind in America,* pp. 57–64.

Eleven: Before the Fall

1. Letter from Lind to Judge Henric Munthe, Oct. 2, 1850, in Holland and Rockstro, *Memoir of Madame Jenny Lind-Goldschmidt,* vol. 2, p. 420; *New York Herald,* Oct. 15, 1850.
2. *Life of PTB,* p. 319; Shultz, *Jenny Lind,* p. 223.
3. Letter from Lind to Amalia Wichmann, Dec. 5, 1850, in Holland and Rockstro, *Memoir of Madame Jenny Lind-Goldschmidt,* p. 423.
4. Field, *Memories of Many Men,* pp. 216–19.

5. *SL,* pp. 50–51, PTB to Joshua Bates, Oct. 23, 1850.

6. Smith, *The Theatrical Journey-Work,* p. 7; *S&T,* pp. 378–79.

7. Barnum had hoped to present Lind to America in what would have been called Jenny Lind Hall, which at a cost of $100,000 was being built and decorated on Broadway at the foot of Bond Street. The hall, which Barnum expected to seat 5,600, would be one of the largest theaters in New York, but it was not ready until October, by which time Lind had left the city on her nationwide tour. So it was instead named Tripler Hall for the two Tripler brothers who had built it. Barnum implied in advertisements that the hall was his project, and it's possible he invested in it, but the Tripler brothers were at least temporarily its owners. Lind did appear there in late October. By her final performance in the hall in 1852, and her penultimate one in America, it was under new management, as was Lind herself. *New York Herald,* Oct. 15 and Oct. 25, 1850.

8. *The Republic* (Washington), Dec. 18, 1850.

9. *Daily Union* (Washington), Dec. 18, 1850; Field, *Memories of Many Men,* p. 220.

10. *S&T,* pp. 356–57.

11. *Life of PTB,* pp. 327–28.
12. Field, *Memories of Many Men,* p. 219. He writes of Belletti, "The barytone of the troupe which accompanied her . . . was madly in love with her, and he used to lie in bed all day, weeping and howling over his unrequited affection." Kunhardts, p. 91; *Life of PTB,* p. 326.
13. *SL,* p. 56, PTB to Moses S. and Alfred Ely Beach, Feb. 10, 1851.
14. *Life of PTB,* pp. 342–43.
15. Ibid., p. 341.

Twelve: Putting Out Fires

1. *Life of PTB,* p. 348; William L. Slout, *Olympians of the Sawdust Circle: A Biographical Dictionary of the Nineteenth Century American Circus* (Rockville, MD: Wildside Press, 1998), p. 136.
2. *Life of PTB,* pp. 348–49; advertisement in *Hartford (CT) Weekly Times,* May 24, 1851, reproduced in *S&T* after p. 390.
3. *S&T,* pp. 410–12.
4. *New York Herald,* Dec. 19, 1851; *New-York Daily Tribune,* Dec. 19, 1851; *Southern Press* (Washington, D.C.), Dec. 20, 1851; George P. Little, *The Fireman's Own Book: Containing Accounts of Fires throughout the United States as Well as Other*

Countries (New York: Self-published, 1860), p. 283.

5. *S&T,* pp. 415, 417.

6. *SL,* pp. 61–62, PTB to William Makepeace Thackeray, Nov. 29, 1852; pp. 63–64, PTB to Edward Everett, Feb. 7, 1852.

7. *S&T,* pp. 412–13; Leland, *Memoirs,* pp. 200–211.

8. *S&T,* pp. 412–14.

9. *SL,* p. 80, PTB to MK, Sept. 4, 1854.

10. *SL,* p. 81, PTB to MK, Sept. 6, 1854. Redfield apparently rushed it out for the holiday gift season, and this version of the book is generally described as the 1855 edition.

11. *PTB,* p. 19.

12. *SL,* p. 83, two letters to various editors, copies of which were written both in his hand and by others. See, for example, *The Jeffersonian,* Oct. 26, 1854, which published an anecdote about one of his brothers, "From the Autobiography of P. T. Barnum."

13. If there had been hard feelings between Barnum and Redfield that fall, they might have been attributed to Barnum's having sold European rights to the book without letting Redfield know. *Evening Star* (Washington), Nov. 13, 1854.

14. *PTB,* p. 9. See also Saxon, *Barnumiana*

(1995), p. 15.

15. *New-York Times,* Dec. 12 and Dec. 16, 1854; *New York Herald,* Dec. 12, 1854; *PTB,* p. 12.

16. *Trumpet and Universalist Magazine,* Mar. 10, 1855; "Revelations of a Showman," *Blackwood's Edinburgh Magazine,* Feb. 1855, pp. 187–201; *Punch,* Sept. 1, 1855, p. 89, all cited in Harris, *Humbug,* p. 228. In fact there was a minor push to offer Barnum as a candidate for U.S. president in 1888, but nothing came of it.

17. *Trumpet and Universalist Magazine,* Mar. 24, 1855, cited in *PTB,* p. 14.

Thirteen: A Ruined Man

1. *Life of PTB,* pp. 383–85; *PTB,* pp. 192–93. Timothy Dwight IV was a former president of Yale College; quoted from his *Travels in New-England and New-York* (London: William Baynes and Son, 1828). *S&T,* p. 421. William Noble would go on to form the first regiment of Connecticut Volunteers during the Civil War. He was seriously wounded at Chancellorsville and spent a month in Bridgeport recuperating sufficiently to lead what was left of his regiment into Gettysburg after the Confederates had been driven out. Still later

in the war he was captured and sent to the infamous Andersonville prison in Georgia, as a colonel the highest-ranking Union officer sent there, and after four months was released in a prisoner exchange. Bridgeport History Center, Lehman, Eric D., "General William Henry Noble." https://bportlibrary.org/hc/barnum-and-related-items/general-william-henry-noble/.

2. *Life of PTB,* p. 385.
3. *S&T,* pp. 423–26; Chauncey Jerome, *History of the American Clock Business for the Past Sixty Years* (New Haven, CT: F. C. Dayton Jr., 1860), pp. 106–16.
4. *S&T,* p. 426.
5. Ibid., p. 441.
6. *PTB,* p. 198; *SL,* p. 91, PTB to "My dear Doctor," Feb. 2, 1856.
7. *New York Post,* Feb. 14, 1856; *S&T,* p. 440.
8. *S&T,* pp. 427; *SL,* pp. 91, 93, PTB to unidentified correspondent, Feb. 2, 1856 and to William H. Noble, Apr. 24, 1856.
9. *SL,* p. 92; *S&T,* pp. 445–47.
10. Ralph L. Rusk, ed., *The Letters of Ralph Waldo Emerson* (New York: Columbia University Press, 1939), vol. 4, p. 541, letter to Lidian Emerson, Dec. 30, 1855; Kunhardts, p. 123; *Daily Dispatch* (Rich-

mond, VA), Feb. 19, 1856.

11. *S&T,* pp. 434–37.
12. *S&T,* p. 429; *New-York Daily Tribune,* June 4, 1856; *New York Herald,* June 5, 1856.
13. *S&T,* p. 431; *New-York Daily Tribune,* June 4, 1856.
14. Lewis, *Across the Atlantic,* pp. 24–25.
15. *SL,* pp. 95–96, PTB to Benjamin Webster, Dec. 20, 1856; *S&T,* p. 450.
16. *S&T,* pp. 458, 454–57; *SL,* p. 97, PTB to Rev. Abel C. Thomas, Mar. 9, 1857.
17. *S&T,* pp. 460–65, 469–70.
18. Ibid., pp. 474–75.
19. Ibid., pp. 475–76; *Grantham Journal,* Oct. 29, 1859.
20. *S&T,* pp. 477–79; Freedley, *A Practical Treatise on Business,* pp. 306–12.
21. *S&T,* pp. 831–36.
22. Ibid., p. 478.
23. *Times* (London), Dec. 30, 1858. A recent example of a historian repeating the squeaky voice myth is Edwin G. Burrows in his 2017 book, *The Finest Building in America* (New York: Oxford University Press), p. 147.
24. *S&T,* p. 479.
25. Saxon says that about sixty of these one hundred speeches were given outside of London (*PTB,* p. 202). *Birmingham (U.K.)*

Daily Post, Jan. 27, 1859; *Cambridge (U.K.) Independent Press,* Feb. 26, 1859.

26. *S&T,* pp. 481–83.
27. *SL,* p. 102, PTB to MK, June 25, 1859.
28. *New York Herald,* Oct. 11, 1859. Numerous ads appear in newspapers in New York, Baltimore, Washington, and elsewhere in late 1859 and 1860. *SL,* p. 104, PTB to Sol Smith, Apr., 4, 1860; *S&T,* p. 493.
29. *S&T,* pp. 494–99.
30. *New York Herald,* Mar. 27, 1860.
31. *S&T,* pp. 519, 669–70; *PTB,* p. 214.

Fourteen: The War and a Wedding

1. *New-York Tribune,* Mar. 27, 1860.
2. Strong, *Diary,* vol. 3, p. 12, Mar. 2, 1860, cited in *PTB,* p. 99; Kunhardts, p. 149.
3. *New York Clipper,* cited in Adams, *E Pluribus Barnum,* p. 158; *New-York Tribune,* Mar. 1 and Mar. 30, 1860; Cook, *The Colossal P. T. Barnum Reader,* p. 135; *SL,* p. 35, PTB to MK, Aug. 18, 1846.
4. *PTB,* p. 98; *Times* (London), Aug. 29, 1846; *Life of PTB,* p. 346.
5. *PTB,* p. 99; Robert Bogdan, *Freak Show: Presenting Human Oddities for Amusement and Profit* (Chicago: University of Chicago Press, 1990), p. 141. Bogdan, a sociolo-

gist, claims, "No scientist or [mental health] professional of the nineteenth century is on record as calling any freak show distasteful."

6. The *New-York Times* ran more than two hundred stories about the prince's visit to North America. For his visit to New York, the *Times, Herald, Tribune,* and *Harper's Weekly,* Nov. 3, 1860.

7. *S&T,* pp. 514–15.

8. *New-York Times,* Oct. 14, 1860; *S&T,* p. 516.

9. *S&T,* p. 517.

10. *New-York Daily Tribune,* Feb. 27, 1860; Library of Congress Prints and Photographs Division.

11. *New York Herald,* Feb. 21, 1861.

12. *S&T,* p. 566.

13. Ibid., pp. 567–69. Barnum quotes at length from W. A. Croffut and John M. Morris, *The Military and Civil History of Connecticut During the War of 1861–65* (New York: Ledyard Bill, 1868), pp. 107–9; *New-York Daily Tribune,* Aug. 25, 1861.

14. *SL,* p. 113, PTB to Abraham Lincoln, Aug. 30, 1861.

15. *SL,* pp. 86–87, PTB to Rev. Thomas Wentworth Higginson, c. Apr. 1855.

16. *PTB,* p. 217.

17. *S&T,* p. 570.

18. Ibid., pp. 531–32. See, for example, *New York Herald,* Jan. 21, 1862.

19. *S&T,* p. 534; Leech, *Reveille in Washington,* p. 222.

20. *Evening Star* (Washington), Oct. 21, 1862; *S&T,* pp. 535–36.

21. Robert Wilson, *Mathew Brady: Portraits of a Nation* (New York: Bloomsbury, 2013), p. 137.

22. *S&T,* pp. 541, 543; *New-York Tribune,* Jan. 13, 1863.

23. Stratton, *Sketch of the Life,* p. 9; *S&T,* pp. 541–57; *New-York Tribune,* Jan. 5 and Jan. 13, 1863.

24. *S&T,* pp. 557–62; *New-York Times,* Feb. 11, 1863.

25. *Evening Star* (Washington), Feb. 12, 13, and 14, 1863; Grace Greenwood, from *Abraham Lincoln: Tributes from His Associates* (New York: Clarke Sales Co., 1895), p. 111; *Frank Leslie's Illustrated Newspaper,* Mar. 7, 1863.

26. *PTB,* p. 209; Lehman, *Becoming Tom Thumb,* pp. 154–57.

Fifteen: Fire!

1. *New York Herald,* Nov. 27, 1864; Burrows and Wallace, *Gotham,* p. 903; *Evening Star*

(Washington), Nov. 26, 1864; *National Intelligencer,* Dec. 1, 1864.

2. "On This Day," *New-York Times,* May 27, 2001.

3. *New-York Times,* July 14, 1865.

4. *S&T,* pp. 589–91; *New York Herald,* July 15, 1865. As it happened, Union general Joseph Hooker had watched the fire from the Astor House, where he had been staying.

5. *New York Herald,* July 16, 1865.

6. Kunhardts, p. 190; *New-York Times,* July 14, 1865.

7. *S&T,* pp. 575–88; *SL,* p. 133, PTB to Theodore Tilton, May 29, 1865.

8. *Hartford (CT) Courant,* May 4, 2015.

9. *S&T,* pp. 607–8.

10. William H. Barnum would become most famous, or infamous, for his long tenure as the chairman of the Democratic National Committee, during which in the 1880 presidential election he distributed a letter he knew to be fraudulent in which Republican candidate James A. Garfield purportedly wrote that he was in favor of Chinese immigration, an unpopular stance. The letter was a major "October surprise" that, although false, nearly cost Garfield the election. Cousin Barnum in 1876 earned the sobriquet "Seven Mule"

for having used those words as a code in a telegram instructing its recipient to take $7,000 from a secret presidential campaign fund. For his actions in both of these presidential elections he was widely mocked as the worst kind of unprincipled political hack. Stan M. Haynes, *President-Making in the Gilded Age: The Nominating Conventions of 1876–1900* (Jefferson, NC: McFarland, 2016), p. 106.

11. "The Two Hundred Thousand and First Curiosity in Congress," *The Nation,* Mar. 7, 1867, pp. 190–92.

12. *New York Evening Express,* Mar. 5, 1867, reprinted in Twain, *Collected Tales, Sketches, Speeches, and Essays,* pp. 210–13. As it happens, in November 1880, Twain would give a speech and dedicate a satirical poem making fun of "Bill [i.e., William H.] Barnum" (Twain Quotes, "Mark Twain Takes a Swipe at 'Seven Mule' Barnum," November 6, 1880, http://www.twainquotes.com/BillBarnum .html).

13. Hawley was breveted as a major general after the war before returning to civilian life. Letter from Joseph Roswell Hawley to Richard Henry Dana Jr., Apr. 2, 1867, cited in *PTB,* pp. 223–24.

14. *S&T,* pp. 609–10.

15. *New York Herald,* July 22, 1865.

16. *Sun* (New York), Sept. 6, 1865. The official opening did not come until November 13. Once the tours were given, Barnum had the curtain raised, exposing tables of food and drink on the stage. The showman invited his guests up, asking them to be actors in "a very clever gastronomical performance," as the *Sun* reporter put it.

17. *S&T,* pp. 615–24.

18. Ibid., pp. 638–39, 643–45.

19. Ibid., p. 673.

20. Emerson, "The Barnums."

21. *S&T,* p. 645.

22. Ibid., p. 647; *New-York Tribune,* March 3, 1868.

23. *S&T,* p. 646.

24. *New York Herald,* Mar. 3, 1868; *S&T,* p. 646; *New-York Tribune,* Mar. 4, 1868; Emerson, "The Barnums."

Sixteen: Show Fever

1. *S&T,* p. 651.

2. *New York Herald,* Aug. 31, 1868; *New-York Tribune,* Sept. 1, 1868.

3. *S&T,* chapters 45 and 46, pp. 660–74, are titled "Sea-side Park" and "Waldemere";

the quote beginning "a regiment" is on p. 671.

4. Ibid., p. 672.

5. PTB to George H. Emerson, May 23, 1868, and to Whitelaw Reid, May 20, 1869, cited in *PTB,* p. 19. Whitelaw Reid would also serve as U.S. ambassador to France and to the Court of St. James's, and in 1892 would run unsuccessfully for vice president of the United States on the ticket of incumbent president Benjamin Harrison. Reid was still settling in at the *Trib* at the time Barnum approached him for advice and was having the usual news-paperman's doubts about whether he should be doing something else: "I am sometimes haunted by my old feeling," he wrote to his friend the future president James A. Garfield, "that I might better be at magazine or book work, if I could afford it." The work with Barnum, then, would have been a short respite during which he could scratch that itch. Royal Cortissoz, *The Life of Whitelaw Reid, Vol. 1* (London: Thornton, 1921), p. 146.

6. *Sun* (New York), Sept. 24, 1869; *Bellows Falls (VT) Times,* Nov. 19, 1869.

7. Barnum, *The Humbugs of the World,* p. 20.

8. *PTB,* p. 160.

9. Barnum, *Funny Stories,* pp. 332–35.

10. Clemens, *Mark Twain's Sketches,* pp. 215–21.

11. *S&T,* pp. 484–87, 676–79; *PTB,* p. 227.

12. *PTB,* p. 232. Castello's last name was often spelled Costello.

13. Coup, *Sawdust & Spangles,* foreword; *SL,* pp. 162, 163, 165, PTB to W. C. Coup, Oct. 8, 1870, and to Moses Kimball, Nov. 22, 1870, and Feb. 18, 1871.

14. *S&T* (1872 ed.), pp. 856–57.

15. *S&T,* p. 681.

16. *S&T,* p. 682; *S&T* (1872 ed.), pp. 861–64; *Sun* (New York), Nov. 11, 1871.

17. *S&T,* pp. 683–84; *S&T* (1873 ed.), pp. 762–63; *PTB,* p. 239.

18. *S&T* (1873 ed.), p. 766.

19. *S&T,* p. 685; *PTB,* pp. 228–29.

20. *S&T,* pp. 686–87; *S&T* (1873 ed.), pp. 769–74.

Seventeen: Marriage Bonds

1. Emerson, "The Barnums," p. 219.

2. *S&T* (1873 ed.), pp. 841–43; *PTB,* pp. 228, 249, 393n10; *SL,* pp. 178–79, PTB to John Greenwood Jr. (?), Dec. 19, 1873, and to George H. Emerson, Feb. 21, 1874.

3. Emerson, "The Barnums," pp. 215–20; quote beginning "perhaps causing her to

exaggerate" is on p. 219.

4. Kunhardts, pp. 238–39. The Kunhardts say that Mary K. Witkowski, then of the Bridgeport Public Library, told them of a conversation she had with a cousin of Nancy's that led them to discover the marriage certificate in London (348n).

5. *S&T* (1875 ed.), pp. 850–64. In 1870 parts of Fairfield, including Mountain Grove Cemetery, much of Seaside Park, and the properties where Barnum's mansions were, had been, or would be, were annexed by the city of Bridgeport.

6. Ibid., pp. 851, 863, 867; *New York Herald,* Sept. 17, 1874; *PTB,* p. 253; *New-York Tribune,* Sept. 17, 1874.

Eighteen: Excitement, Pepper, & Mustard

1. *S&T,* pp. 697–98; *S&T* (1875 ed.), pp. 849–50.

2. *New York Herald,* April 26, 1874; *New-York Tribune,* May 30, 1874.

3. *SL,* p. 180, PTB to Mrs. Abel C. Thomas, May 22, 1874.

4. Andrew Hoffman, *Inventing Mark Twain* (New York: William Morrow, 1997), p. 496.

5. *New-York Tribune,* Feb. 5, 1872.

6. Twain, *Collected Tales, Sketches,*

Speeches, & Essays, pp. 573–77.

7. *SL,* pp. 182–83, PTB to Samuel L. Clemens, July 16, 1874, and July 31, 1874.

8. Ibid., pp. 193 and 195, PTB to Samuel L. Clemens, Mar. 24, 1875, and Oct. 2, 1875.

9. See, for example, *SL,* pp. 188–91, 196–98, PTB to Samuel L. Clemens, Jan. 19, 1875, and Mar. 20, 1876.

10. *SL,* pp. 202, 204, 205, PTB to Samuel L. Clemens, Oct. 10, 1877, Jan. 10, 1878, and Jan. 14, 1878.

11. *PTB,* p. 251.

12. *S&T,* pp. 710–23; *PTB,* pp. 263–65.

13. *S&T,* p. 720.

14. Ibid., pp. 727–30.

15. Ibid., pp. 725–26.

16. *PTB,* p. 32.

17. *S&T,* pp. 731–34; *PTB,* pp. 270–73; *SL,* pp. 203, 214–15, PTB to Whitelaw Reid, Jan. 10, 1878, and to Joseph Roswell Hawley, Nov. 9, [1880].

18. *S&T,* pp. 736–40; *PTB,* pp. 235–37; Edward O'Reilly, "Henry Bergh: Angel in Top Hat or the Great Meddler?," *From the Stacks* (blog), New-York Historical Society, Mar. 21, 2012, http://blog.ny history.org/henry-bergh-angel-in-top-hat -or-the-great-meddler/.

19. *S&T,* p. 737; *PTB,* p. 238; *New-York*

Times, Mar. 17, 1888.

20. The Kunhardts, p. 269, quote Bergh as saying, "Whether . . . it is humane and praiseworthy to rescue . . . rare animals from the . . . jungle . . . and drag them through Christian lands to have peanuts and tobacco thrown at them by gaping crowds and then perish as they mostly do . . . drowned, shot, or burned — is at least open to question."

Nineteen: And Bailey

1. *S&T,* p. 741n2.
2. *New-York Times,* Apr. 19, 1891.
3. *S&T,* pp. 742–43; *PTB,* pp. 285–86.
4. *New-York Tribune,* Nov. 24, 1880; *New-York Times,* Dec. 14, 1880; *PTB,* p. 273; *S&T,* pp. 743–44.
5. *New-York Tribune,* Mar. 27 and 29, 1881; *New York Herald,* Mar. 29, 1881; *S&T,* p. 745.
6. *SL,* p. 217, PTB to James A. Garfield, Mar. 12, 1881; *S&T,* pp. 747–48.
7. *S&T,* pp. 748, 753; *PTB,* p. 275.
8. *PTB,* pp. 276, 285.
9. Conklin, *The Ways of the Circus,* pp. 295–97; Richard E. Conover, *The Affairs of James A. Bailey: New Revelations on the Career of the World's Most Successful*

Showman, pamphlet (Xenia, OH: Self-published, 1957), pp. 1–3, 17.

10. Conklin, *The Ways of the Circus,* p. 299.

11. *SL,* pp. 297–98, PTB to James A. Bailey, July 5, 1888.

12. *SL,* p. 264, PTB to Mrs. James A. Bailey, July 5, 1885. Bailey married Ruth Louisa McCaddon of Zanesville, Ohio, in 1868.

13. Bartlett, *Wild Animals in Captivity,* pp. 45–49; *S&T,* pp. 756–57; *PTB,* pp. 291–92. In an article that appeared shortly after Barnum's death, Bailey, or perhaps a circus publicity agent speaking for him, took credit for having found and purchased Jumbo. A publicity effort was made after Barnum's death to downplay his role in Barnum & Bailey (*New-York Times,* Apr. 19, 1891).

14. Ruskin, *The Works of John Ruskin,* vol. 34, p. 561.

15. *S&T,* pp. 757–58; *New-York Tribune,* Mar. 11, 1882.

16. *S&T,* p. 759.

17. *Sun* (New York), Apr. 10, 1882.

18. Ibid. The distance between the park and the docks is just over four miles.

19. *New-York Tribune,* Apr. 10, 1882.

20. *New-York Tribune,* Apr. 9, 10, and 11, 1882.

21. *S&T,* p. 760, and image of an ad between pp. 758 and 759.

22. *New-York Times,* Apr. 19, 1891; *Evening Star* (Washington, D.C.), Sept. 19, 1885; *S&T,* pp. 785–86.

23. *New-York Tribune,* Sept. 17, 1885; *SL,* pp. 241, 265, letter and telegram to Henry A. Ward, Oct. 9, 1883, and Sept. 17, 1885.

24. Kunhardts, p. 301. A team led by David Attenborough for a BBC documentary studied the skeleton and concluded that Jumbo had been only 10.5 feet tall and that his bones showed the ill effects of carrying so many children on his back — often eight or nine at a time (*Sun* [U.K.], Dec. 10, 2017).

25. *SL,* p. 271, PTB to James A. Bailey, Oct. 12, 1885.

26. *S&T,* pp. 787–90; *PTB,* p. 312.

Twenty: Last Years

1. *S&T,* pp. 799–801; *SL,* p. 311, PTB to James A. Bailey, Apr. 14, 1889.

2. *S&T,* pp. 744, 764, 790; *New-York Tribune,* July 20, 1883; *Sun* (New York), July 23, 1883; Lehman, *Becoming Tom Thumb,* pp. 208–9.

3. *SL,* p. 311, PTB to James A. Bailey, Apr.

14, 1889.

4. *SL,* p. 328, PTB to James A. Bailey, Aug. 24, 1890; *PTB,* p. 115; Barnum, *Funny Stories,* p. 359.

5. *PTB,* pp. 281–82.

6. Ibid., pp. 289–90.

7. Ibid., 254–55.

8. *SL,* pp. 225, 279, 284, 288, 292, PTB to Carrie Bailey, Apr. 24, 1882; Lucy A. Thomas, July 10, 1886; Henry Rennell, Mar. 1, July 27, and Sept. 12, 1887.

9. *PTB,* pp. 316–17.

10. Ibid., pp. 279–80, 325.

11. Barnum also gave much smaller amounts to St. Lawrence University in upstate New York and Lombard College in Ohio. *PTB,* pp. 53–54, 57–58; *SL,* pp. 251–52, PTB to Rev. E. H. Capen, June 12, 1884.

12. *Sun* (New York), cited in *Indianapolis Journal,* Oct. 14, 1889.

13. Barnum, *Funny Stories,* p. 359.

14. Conklin, *The Ways of the Circus,* p. 253.

15. Nancy Barnum, *S&T,* p. 817.

16. Barnum, *Funny Stories,* pp. 366–67.

17. *Sporting Times* (London), Dec. 14, 1889.

18. *Licensed Victuallers' Mirror* (London), Dec. 31, 1889.

19. Barnum, *Funny Stories,* p. 367.

20. Ibid., p. v.
21. *New-York Tribune,* Mar. 15, 1891; *SL,* pp. 319–21, PTB to James A. Bailey, Feb. 22 and 26, 1890; *S&T,* pp. 817–18. At Barnum's request, Nancy wrote "Last Chapter" for his autobiography after his death.
22. *S&T,* pp. 811–12; Kunhardts, p. 328.
23. *S&T,* p. 818.
24. Ibid., pp. 818–19.
25. Ibid., pp. 819, 821; *PTB,* pp. 325–26.
26. *New-York Tribune,* Mar. 15, 1891; *Newtown (CT) Bee,* Apr. 10, 1891.
27. *S&T,* pp. 821–22.
28. *New-York Times,* Apr. 8, 1891; *Times (London),* Apr. 8, 1891.
29. *Newtown (CT) Bee,* Apr. 10, 1891; *Sun (New York),* Apr. 10 and 11, 1891.
30. *New-York Tribune,* Apr. 11, 1891.

ILLUSTRATION CREDITS

Frontispiece: P. T. Barnum in 1851. TCS 1.1296. Courtesy of Houghton Library, Harvard University. https://images.hollis.harvard.edu/primo-explore/fulldisplay?docid=HVD_VIAolvwork606439&context=L&vid=HVD_IMAGES&search_scope=default_scope&tab=default_tab&lang=en_US

1. P. T. Barnum in London in 1844. From portrait by Charles Baugniet. Courtesy of Barnum Museum, Bridgeport, Connecticut.
2. Charity Hallett Barnum in an 1847 oil portrait by Frederick R. Spencer. Courtesy of Barnum Museum.
3. Advertisement for an exhibition of Joice Heth. Courtesy of Bridgeport History Center, Bridgeport Public Library, Bridgeport, Connecticut.
4. Moses Kimball. From *The New England*

Historical and Genealogical Register, 1902. Courtesy of Boston Athenaeum.

5. "Fejee Mermaid." From *The Life of P. T. Barnum, Written by Himself.*

6. Three mermaids. From *The Life of P. T. Barnum, Written by Himself.*

7. Charles Stratton with his father, Sherwood Stratton. Courtesy of Bridgeport History Center, Bridgeport Public Library.

8. Tom Thumb as Napoleon Bonaparte. Courtesy of Bridgeport History Center, Bridgeport Public Library.

9. P. T. Barnum and Tom Thumb. Courtesy of Bridgeport History Center, Bridgeport Public Library.

10. The American Museum on lower Broadway in 1842. Courtesy of Barnum Museum.

11. 1855 lithograph titled "Sleighing in New York." Courtesy of Library of Congress. http://www.loc.gov/pictures/resource/cph.3g02722/

12. Three Barnum daughters, painted by Frederick R. Spencer. Courtesy of Barnum Museum.

13. Iranistan, in Fairfield, Connecticut, courtesy of Library of Congress. http://www.loc.gov/pictures/resource/cph.3g02470/

14. The singer Jenny Lind. Courtesy of Bridgeport History Center, Bridgeport Public Library.
15. P. T. Barnum and Commodore Nutt. Courtesy of Bridgeport History Center, Bridgeport Public Library.
16. The 1863 "fairy wedding" of Tom Thumb and Lavinia Warren. Courtesy of Bridgeport History Center, Bridgeport Public Library.
17. Christopher Pearse Cranch (1813–1892), *The Burning of Barnum's Museum* (1865), oil on canvas, 30 x 48 inches. Private collection.
18. Horace Greeley, editor of the *New-York Tribune.* Courtesy of Library of Congress. http://www.loc.gov/pictures/resource/pga.08505/
19. P. T. Barnum in the 1860s. Courtesy of Library of Congress. http://www.loc.gov/pictures/resource/cwpbh.02176/
20. Charity Hallett Barnum. Courtesy of Barnum Museum.
21. Nancy Fish. Courtesy of Paul Smith's College, Joan Weill Adirondack Library Archives. https://cdm16694.contentdm.oclc.org/digital/collection/paulsmiths/id/10539/
22. P. T. Barnum with Nancy and his children and grandchildren. Courtesy of

Barnum Museum.

23. Barnum & Bailey Circus poster. Courtesy of Library of Congress. http://www.loc.gov/pictures/resource/cph.3b52428/

24. Jumbo the elephant. Courtesy of Digital Collections and Archives, Tufts University.

25. Jumbo's death, 1880. Courtesy of Digital Collections and Archives, Tufts University.

26. A poster for "Great Jumbo's Skeleton" in Barnum's first Greatest Show on Earth. Courtesy of Library of Congress. http://www.loc.gov/pictures/resource/ppmsca.32620/

27. P. T. Barnum in the 1870s. Courtesy of Barnum Museum.

28. A postcard of Barnum & Bailey's Winter Quarters in Bridgeport, Connecticut. Courtesy of Bridgeport History Center, Bridgeport Public Library.

29. Barnum's Marina, to the right of Waldemere, which would be torn down. Courtesy of Bridgeport History Center, Bridgeport Public Library.

30. Poster for The Greatest Show on Earth. Courtesy of Bridgeport History Center, Bridgeport Public Library.

31. Pamphlet cover for "Nero, or the Destruction of Rome." Courtesy of Bridgeport History Center, Bridgeport Public

Library.
32. Barnum and his beloved great-grandson, Henry Rennell. Courtesy of Barnum Museum.

ABOUT THE AUTHOR

Robert Wilson is the author of *Mathew Brady: Portraits of a Nation* and *The Explorer King,* a biography of Clarence King. He is the editor of *The American Scholar,* a former editor of *Preservation,* and the founding literary editor of *Civilization* (all three of which won National Magazine Awards during his tenure), a former book editor and columnist for *USA Today,* and a former editor at *The Washington Post Book World.* His essays, reviews, and fiction have appeared in numerous publications, including *The American Scholar, American Short Fiction, The Atlantic Monthly, The New Republic, Smithsonian, The Washington Post Magazine,* and *The Wilson Quarterly* and on the op-ed, opinion, and book review pages of *The Boston Globe, The New York Times, USA Today,* and *The Washington Post.* He lives in Manassas, Virginia.

The employees of Thorndike Press hope you have enjoyed this Large Print book. All our Thorndike, Wheeler, and Kennebec Large Print titles are designed for easy reading, and all our books are made to last. Other Thorndike Press Large Print books are available at your library, through selected bookstores, or directly from us.

For information about titles, please call:
   (800) 223-1244

or visit our Web site at:
   http://gale.cengage.com/thorndike

To share your comments, please write:
   Publisher
   Thorndike Press
   10 Water St., Suite 310
   Waterville, ME 04901